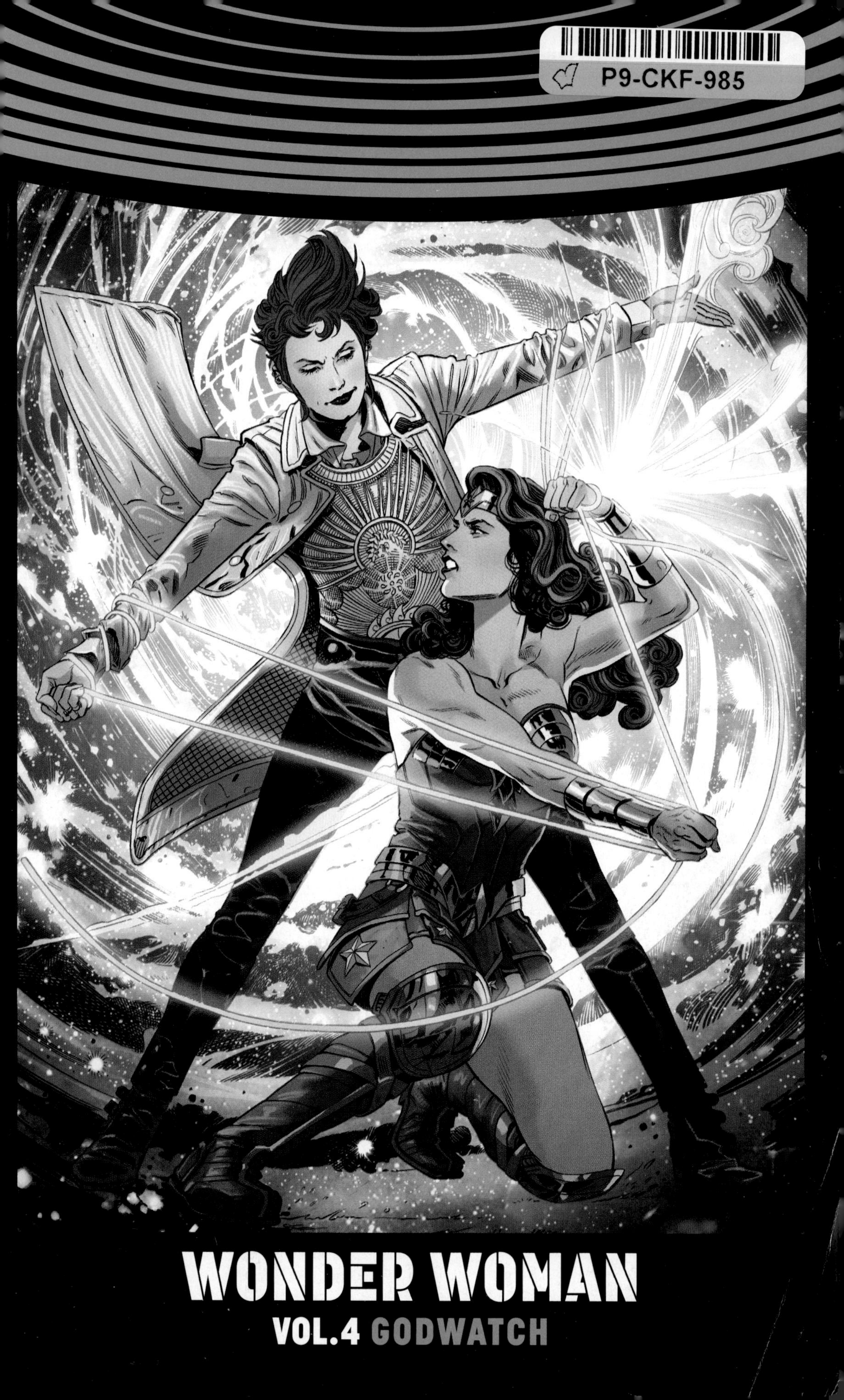

WONDER WOMAN

VOL.4 GODWATCH

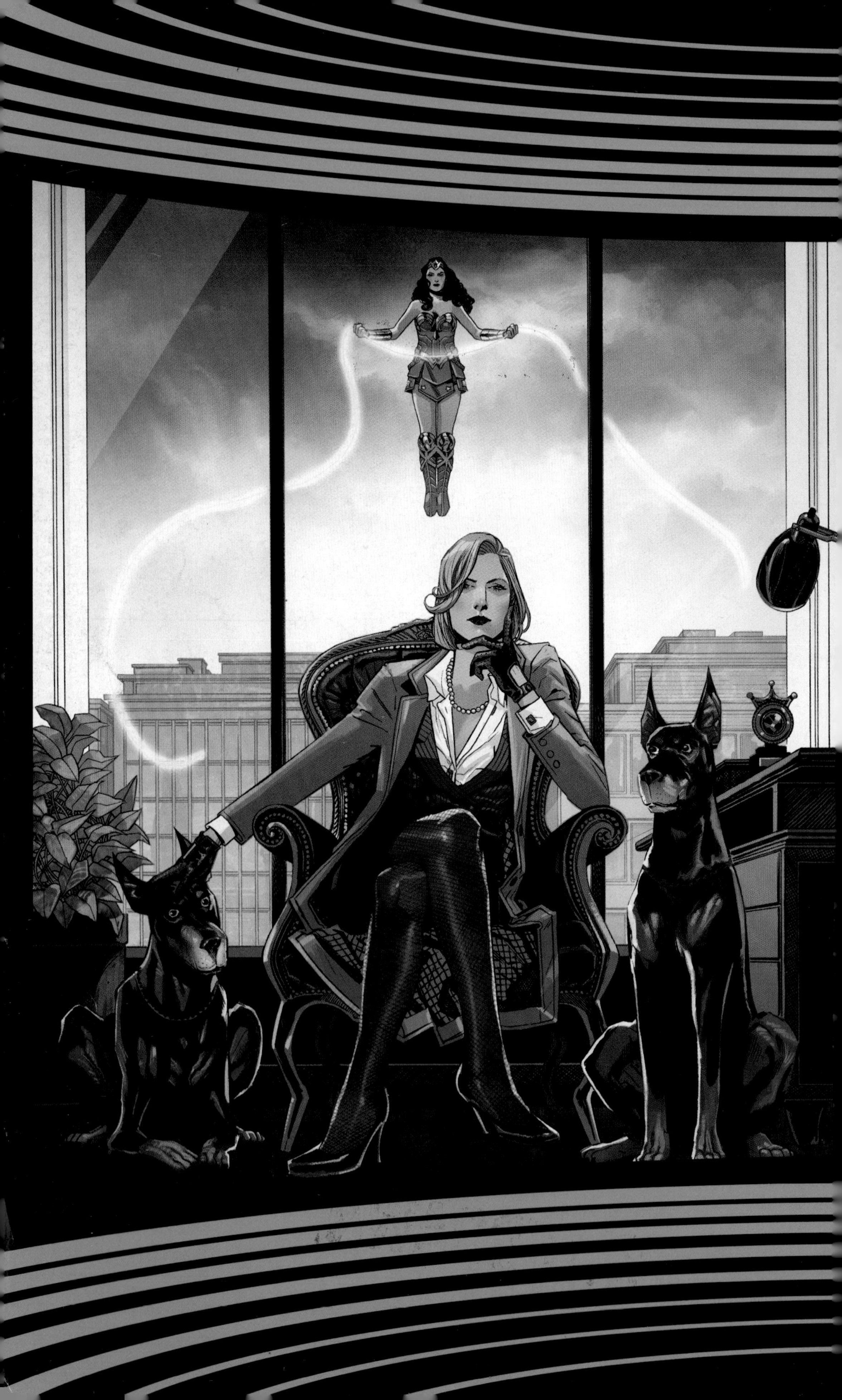

WONDER WOMAN
VOL.4 GODWATCH

GREG RUCKA
writer

BILQUIS EVELY
MIRKA ANDOLFO * NICOLA SCOTT * SCOTT HANNA
MARK MORALES * ANDREW HENNESSY * RAUL FERNANDEZ
artists

ROMULO FAJARDO JR.
colorist

JODI WYNNE
letterer

BILQUIS EVELY & ROMULO FAJARDO JR.
collection cover artists

WONDER WOMAN created by WILLIAM MOULTON MARSTON
SUPERMAN created by JERRY SIEGEL and JOE SHUSTER
By special arrangement with the Jerry Siegel family

MARK DOYLE CHRIS CONROY Editors - Original Series
REBECCA TAYLOR Associate Editor - Original Series * **DAVE WIELGOSZ** Assistant Editor - Original Series
JEB WOODARD Group Editor - Collected Editions * **ROBIN WILDMAN** Editor - Collected Edition
STEVE COOK Design Director - Books * **MONIQUE NARBONETA** Publication Design

BOB HARRAS Senior VP - Editor-in-Chief, DC Comics
PAT McCALLUM Executive Editor, DC Comics

DIANE NELSON President * **DAN DiDIO** Publisher * **JIM LEE** Publisher * **GEOFF JOHNS** President & Chief Creative Officer
AMIT DESAI Executive VP - Business & Marketing Strategy, Direct to Consumer & Global Franchise Management
SAM ADES Senior VP & General Manager, Digital Services * **BOBBIE CHASE** VP & Executive Editor, Young Reader & Talent Development
MARK CHIARELLO Senior VP - Art, Design & Collected Editions * **JOHN CUNNINGHAM** Senior VP - Sales & Trade Marketing
ANNE DePIES Senior VP - Business Strategy, Finance & Administration * **DON FALLETTI** VP - Manufacturing Operations
LAWRENCE GANEM VP - Editorial Administration & Talent Relations * **ALISON GILL** Senior VP - Manufacturing & Operations
HANK KANALZ Senior VP - Editorial Strategy & Administration * **JAY KOGAN** VP - Legal Affairs * **JACK MAHAN** VP - Business Affairs
NICK J. NAPOLITANO VP - Manufacturing Administration * **EDDIE SCANNELL** VP - Consumer Marketing
COURTNEY SIMMONS Senior VP - Publicity & Communications * **JIM (SKI) SOKOLOWSKI** VP - Comic Book Specialty Sales & Trade Marketing
NANCY SPEARS VP - Mass, Book, Digital Sales & Trade Marketing * **MICHELE R. WELLS** VP - Content Strategy

WONDER WOMAN VOLUME 4: GODWATCH

DC Comics, 2900 West Alameda Ave., Burbank, CA 91505.
Printed by Vanguard Graphics, LLC, Ithica, NY, USA. 10/13/17. First Printing.
ISBN: 978-1-4012-7460-3

Library of Congress Cataloging-in-Publication Data is available.

MIX
Paper from responsible sources
FSC® C016956

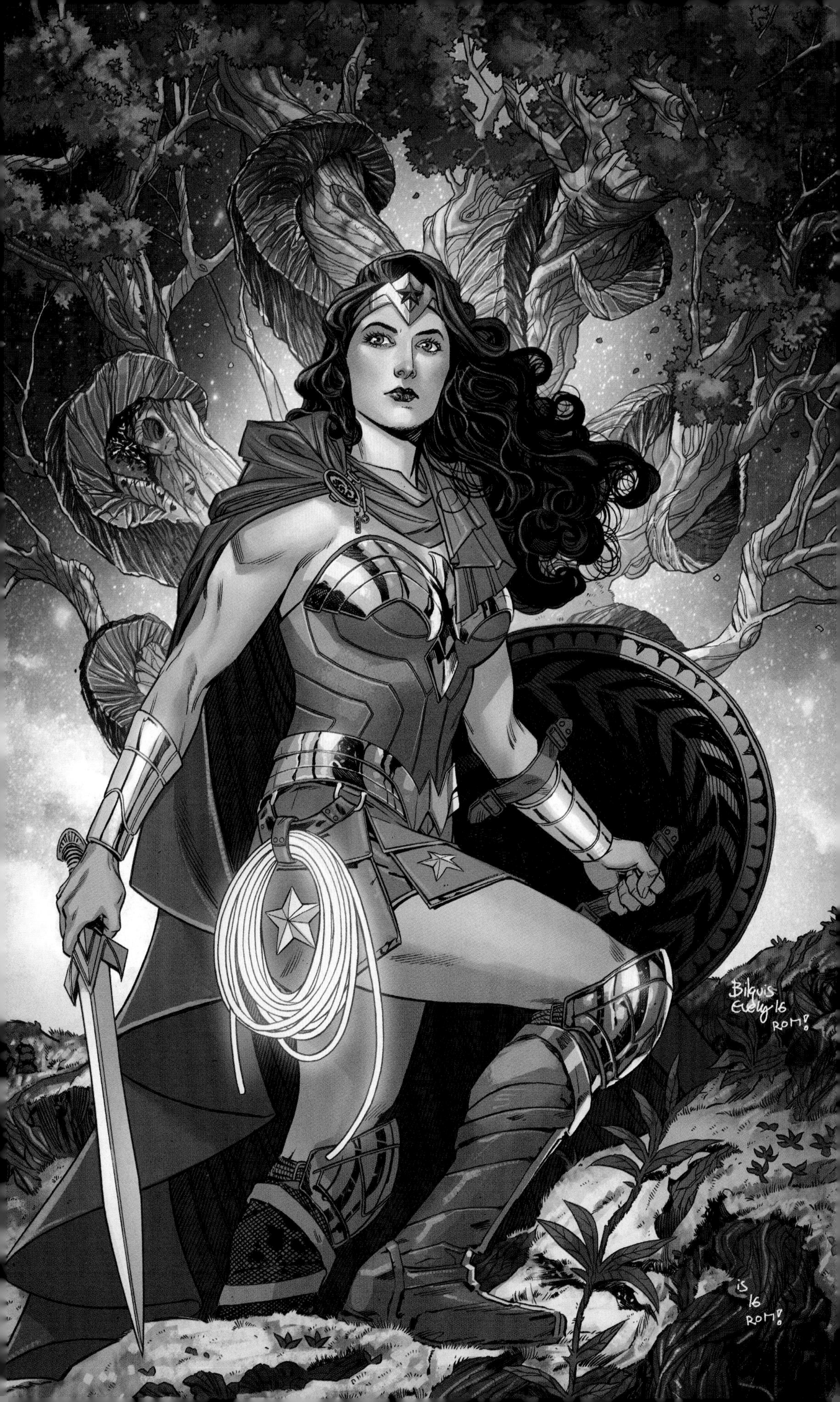
Bilquis
Evely 16
ROM!

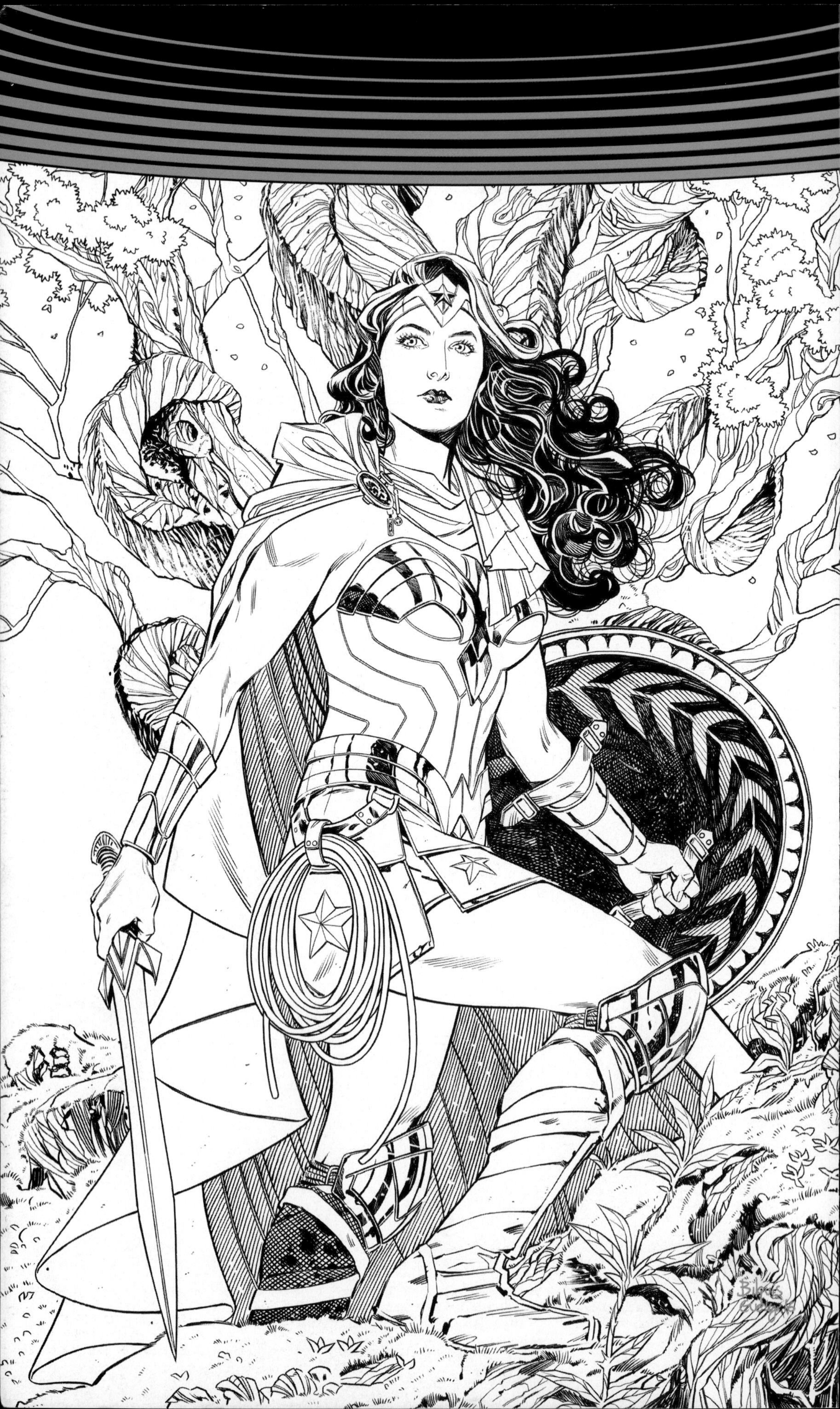

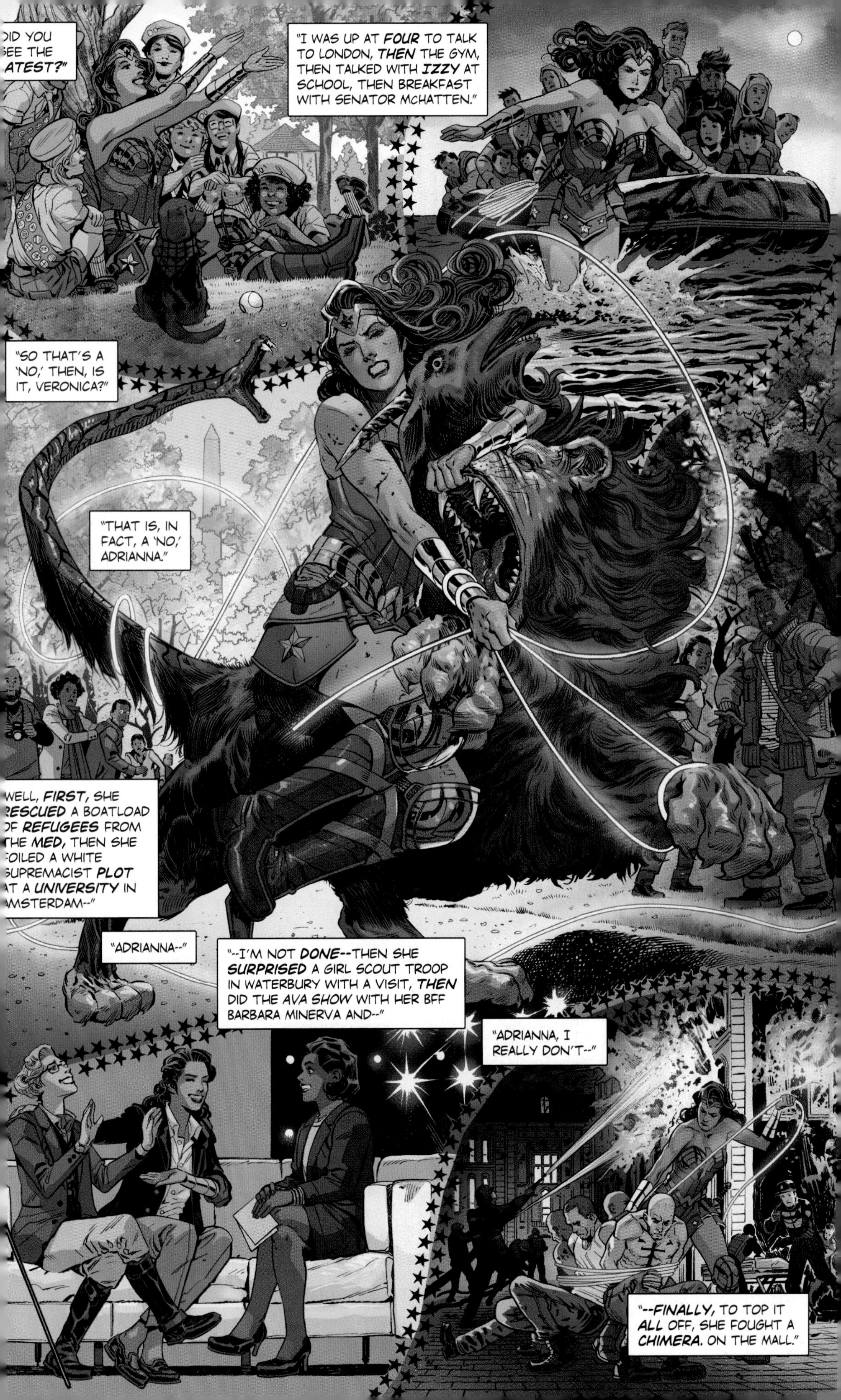
"DID YOU SEE THE LATEST?"
"I WAS UP AT FOUR TO TALK TO LONDON, THEN THE GYM, THEN TALKED WITH IZZY AT SCHOOL, THEN BREAKFAST WITH SENATOR McHATTEN."
"SO THAT'S A 'NO,' THEN, IS IT, VERONICA?"
"THAT IS, IN FACT, A 'NO,' ADRIANNA."
"WELL, FIRST, SHE RESCUED A BOATLOAD OF REFUGEES FROM THE MED, THEN SHE FOILED A WHITE SUPREMACIST PLOT AT A UNIVERSITY IN AMSTERDAM--"
"ADRIANNA--"
"--I'M NOT DONE--THEN SHE SURPRISED A GIRL SCOUT TROOP IN WATERBURY WITH A VISIT, THEN DID THE AVA SHOW WITH HER BFF BARBARA MINERVA AND--"
"ADRIANNA, I REALLY DON'T--"
"--FINALLY, TO TOP IT ALL OFF, SHE FOUGHT A CHIMERA. ON THE MALL."

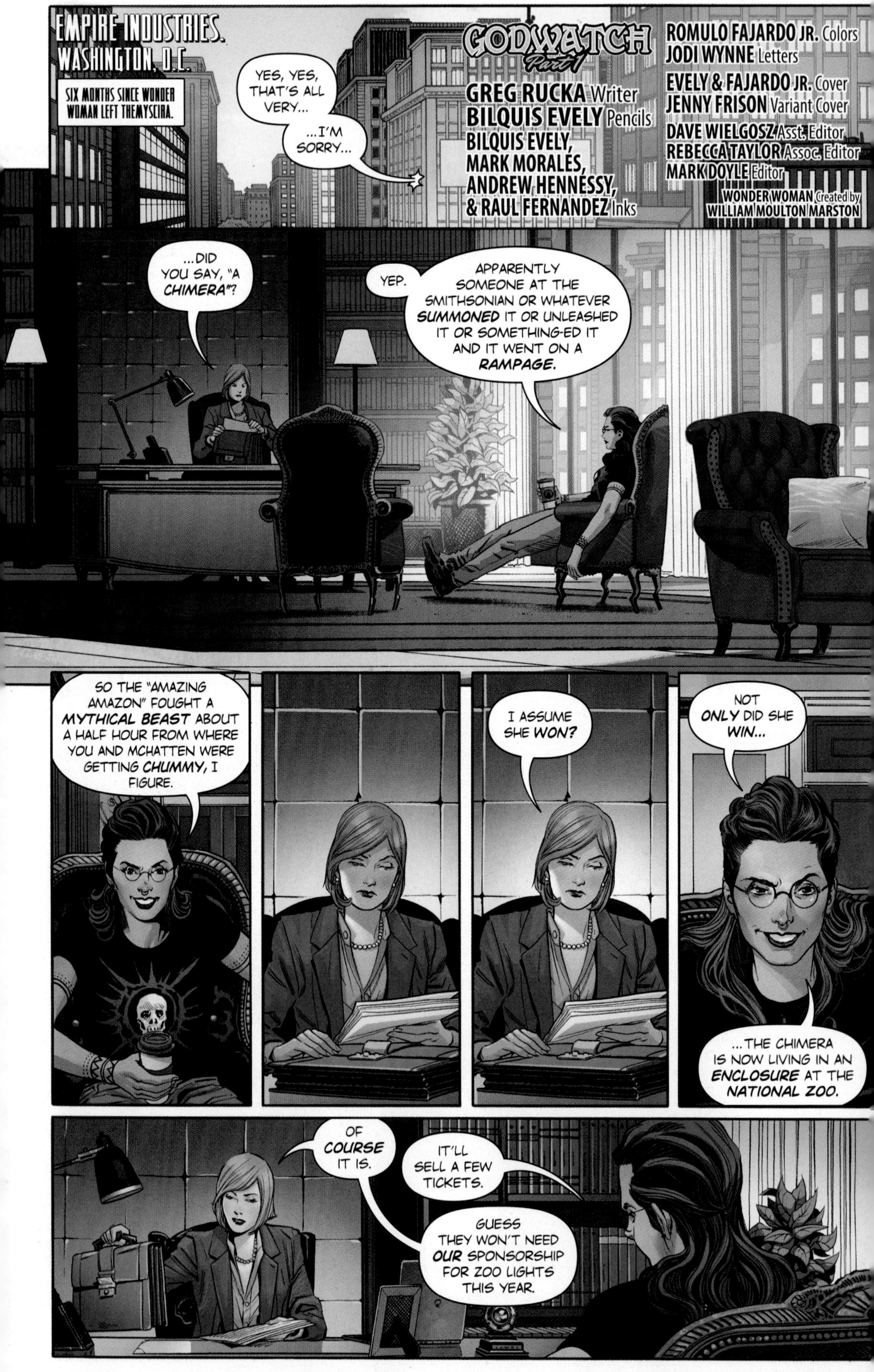

EMPIRE INDUSTRIES. WASHINGTON, D.C.
SIX MONTHS SINCE WONDER WOMAN LEFT THEMYSCIRA.
GODWATCH Part 1
GREG RUCKA Writer
BILQUIS EVELY Pencils
BILQUIS EVELY, MARK MORALES, ANDREW HENNESSY, & RAUL FERNANDEZ Inks
ROMULO FAJARDO JR. Colors
JODI WYNNE Letters
EVELY & FAJARDO JR. Cover
JENNY FRISON Variant Cover
DAVE WIELGOSZ Asst. Editor
REBECCA TAYLOR Assoc. Editor
MARK DOYLE Editor
WONDER WOMAN Created by WILLIAM MOULTON MARSTON
YES, YES, THAT'S ALL VERY...
...I'M SORRY...
...DID YOU SAY, "A CHIMERA"?
YEP.
APPARENTLY SOMEONE AT THE SMITHSONIAN OR WHATEVER SUMMONED IT OR UNLEASHED IT OR SOMETHING-ED IT AND IT WENT ON A RAMPAGE.
SO THE "AMAZING AMAZON" FOUGHT A MYTHICAL BEAST ABOUT A HALF HOUR FROM WHERE YOU AND MCHATTEN WERE GETTING CHUMMY, I FIGURE.
I ASSUME SHE WON?
NOT ONLY DID SHE WIN...
...THE CHIMERA IS NOW LIVING IN AN ENCLOSURE AT THE NATIONAL ZOO.
OF COURSE IT IS.
IT'LL SELL A FEW TICKETS.
GUESS THEY WON'T NEED OUR SPONSORSHIP FOR ZOO LIGHTS THIS YEAR.

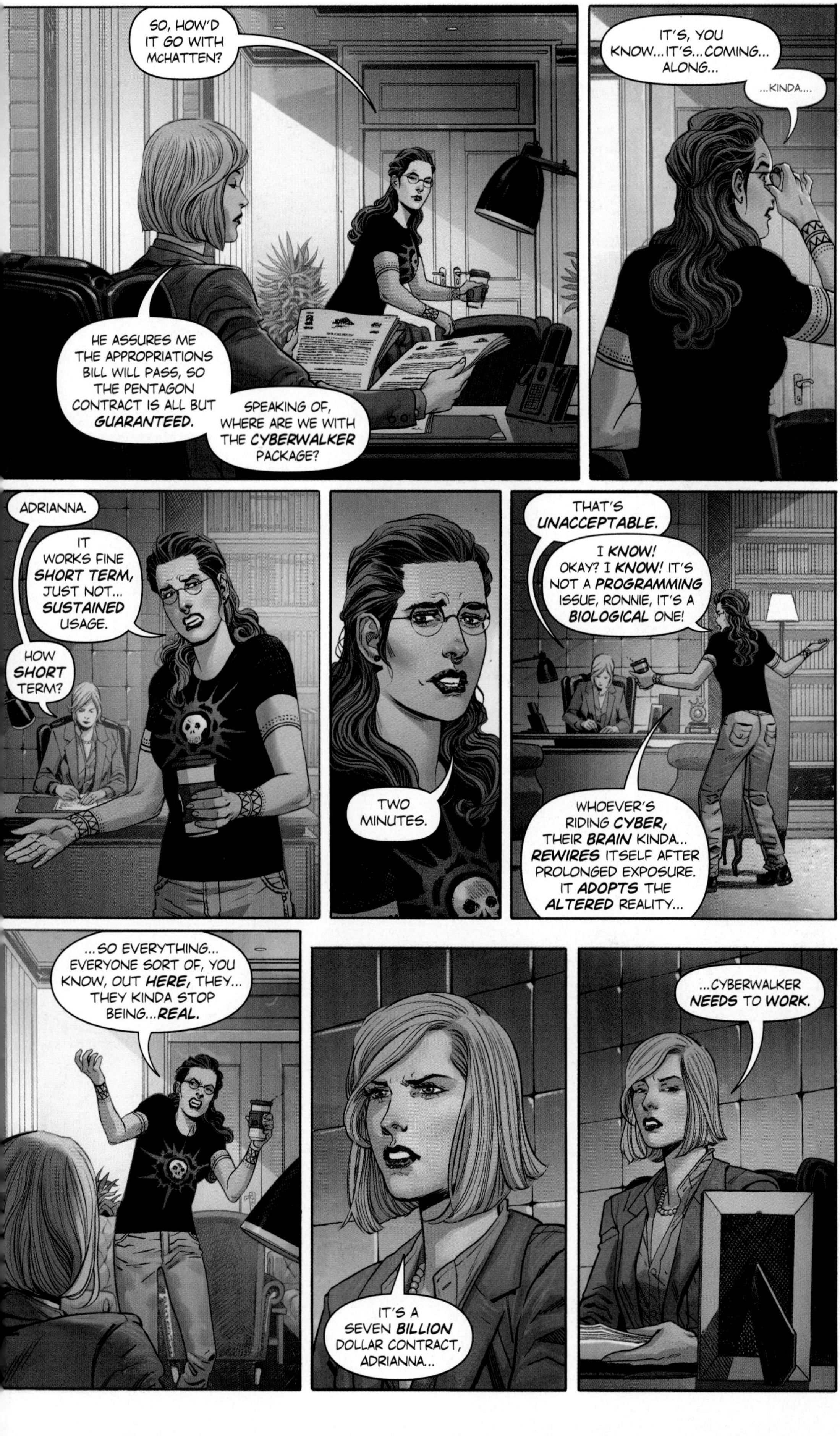

SO, HOW'D IT GO WITH MCHATTEN?
HE ASSURES ME THE APPROPRIATIONS BILL WILL PASS, SO THE PENTAGON CONTRACT IS ALL BUT GUARANTEED.
SPEAKING OF, WHERE ARE WE WITH THE CYBERWALKER PACKAGE?
IT'S, YOU KNOW...IT'S...COMING... ALONG...
...KINDA...
ADRIANNA.
IT WORKS FINE SHORT TERM, JUST NOT... SUSTAINED USAGE.
HOW SHORT TERM?
TWO MINUTES.
THAT'S UNACCEPTABLE.
I KNOW! OKAY? I KNOW! IT'S NOT A PROGRAMMING ISSUE, RONNIE, IT'S A BIOLOGICAL ONE!
WHOEVER'S RIDING CYBER, THEIR BRAIN KINDA... REWIRES ITSELF AFTER PROLONGED EXPOSURE. IT ADOPTS THE ALTERED REALITY...
...SO EVERYTHING... EVERYONE SORT OF, YOU KNOW, OUT HERE, THEY... THEY KINDA STOP BEING...REAL.
IT'S A SEVEN BILLION DOLLAR CONTRACT, ADRIANNA...
...CYBERWALKER NEEDS TO WORK.

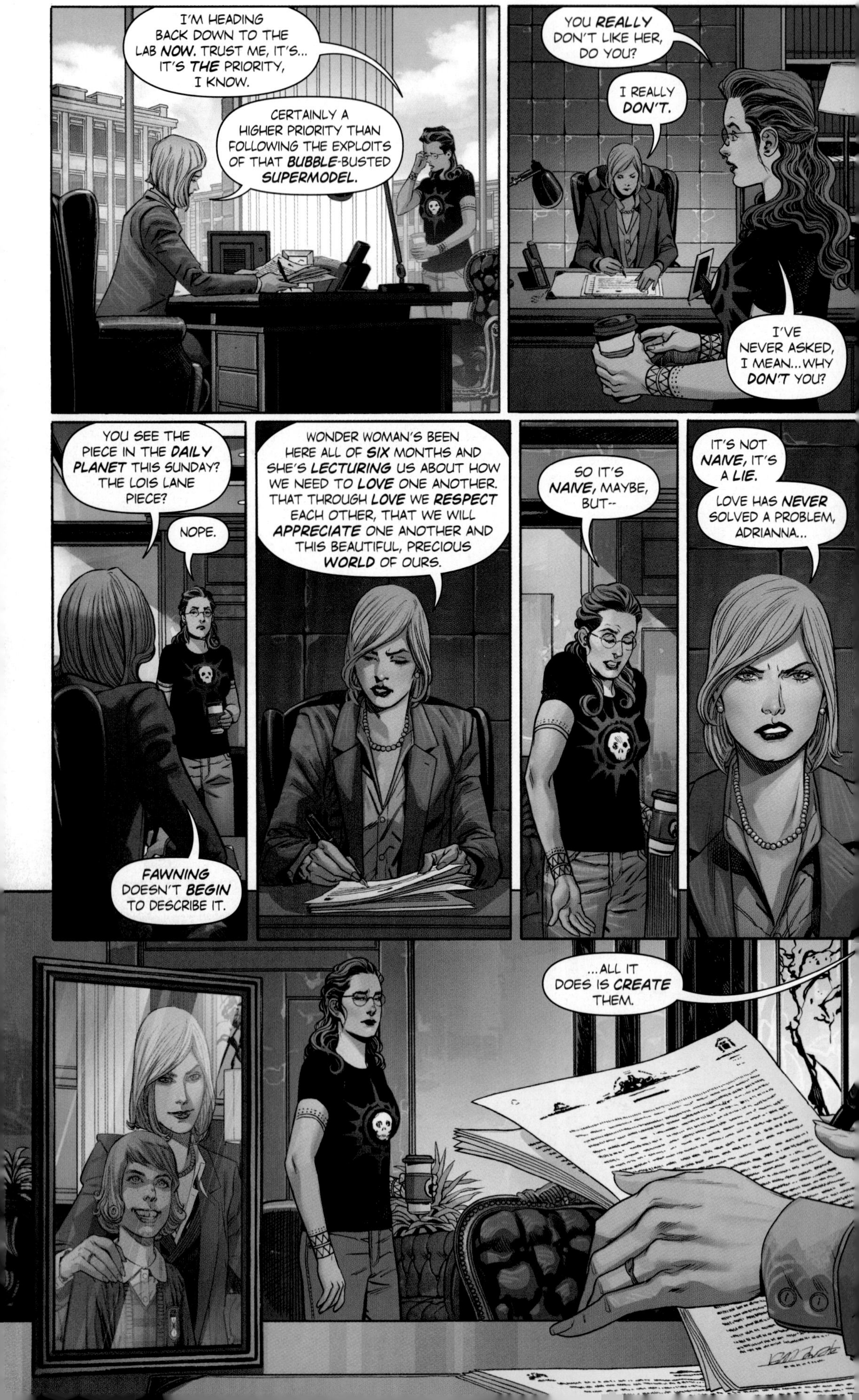
I'M HEADING BACK DOWN TO THE LAB NOW. TRUST ME, IT'S... IT'S THE PRIORITY, I KNOW.
CERTAINLY A HIGHER PRIORITY THAN FOLLOWING THE EXPLOITS OF THAT BUBBLE-BUSTED SUPERMODEL.
YOU REALLY DON'T LIKE HER, DO YOU?
I REALLY DON'T.
I'VE NEVER ASKED, I MEAN...WHY DON'T YOU?
YOU SEE THE PIECE IN THE DAILY PLANET THIS SUNDAY? THE LOIS LANE PIECE?
NOPE.
FAWNING DOESN'T BEGIN TO DESCRIBE IT.
WONDER WOMAN'S BEEN HERE ALL OF SIX MONTHS AND SHE'S LECTURING US ABOUT HOW WE NEED TO LOVE ONE ANOTHER. THAT THROUGH LOVE WE RESPECT EACH OTHER, THAT WE WILL APPRECIATE ONE ANOTHER AND THIS BEAUTIFUL, PRECIOUS WORLD OF OURS.
SO IT'S NAIVE, MAYBE, BUT--
IT'S NOT NAIVE, IT'S A LIE.
LOVE HAS NEVER SOLVED A PROBLEM, ADRIANNA...
...ALL IT DOES IS CREATE THEM.

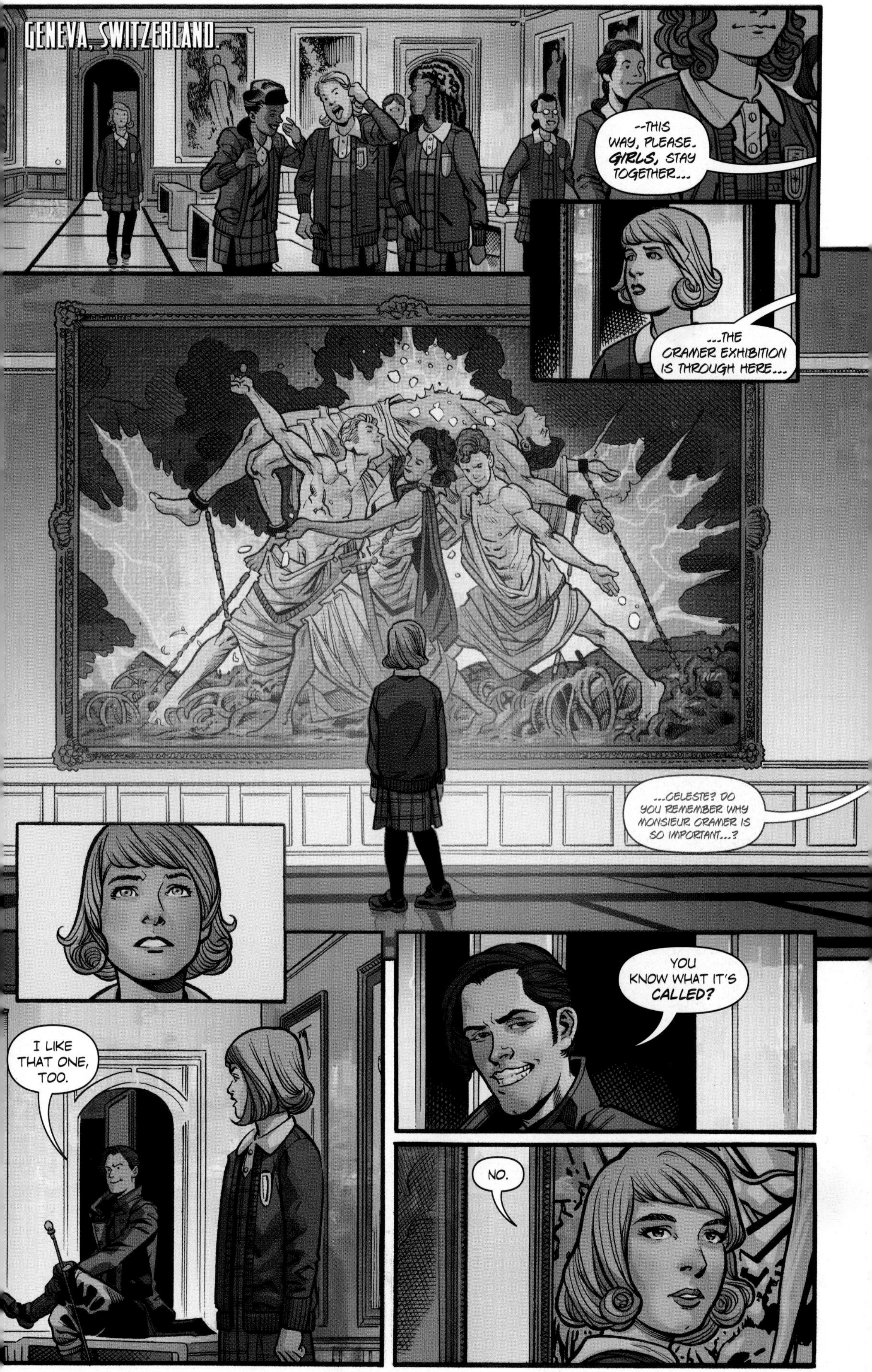
GENEVA, SWITZERLAND.
--THIS WAY, PLEASE. GIRLS, STAY TOGETHER...
...THE CRAMER EXHIBITION IS THROUGH HERE...
...CELESTE? DO YOU REMEMBER WHY MONSIEUR CRAMER IS SO IMPORTANT...?
I LIKE THAT ONE, TOO.
YOU KNOW WHAT IT'S CALLED?
NO.

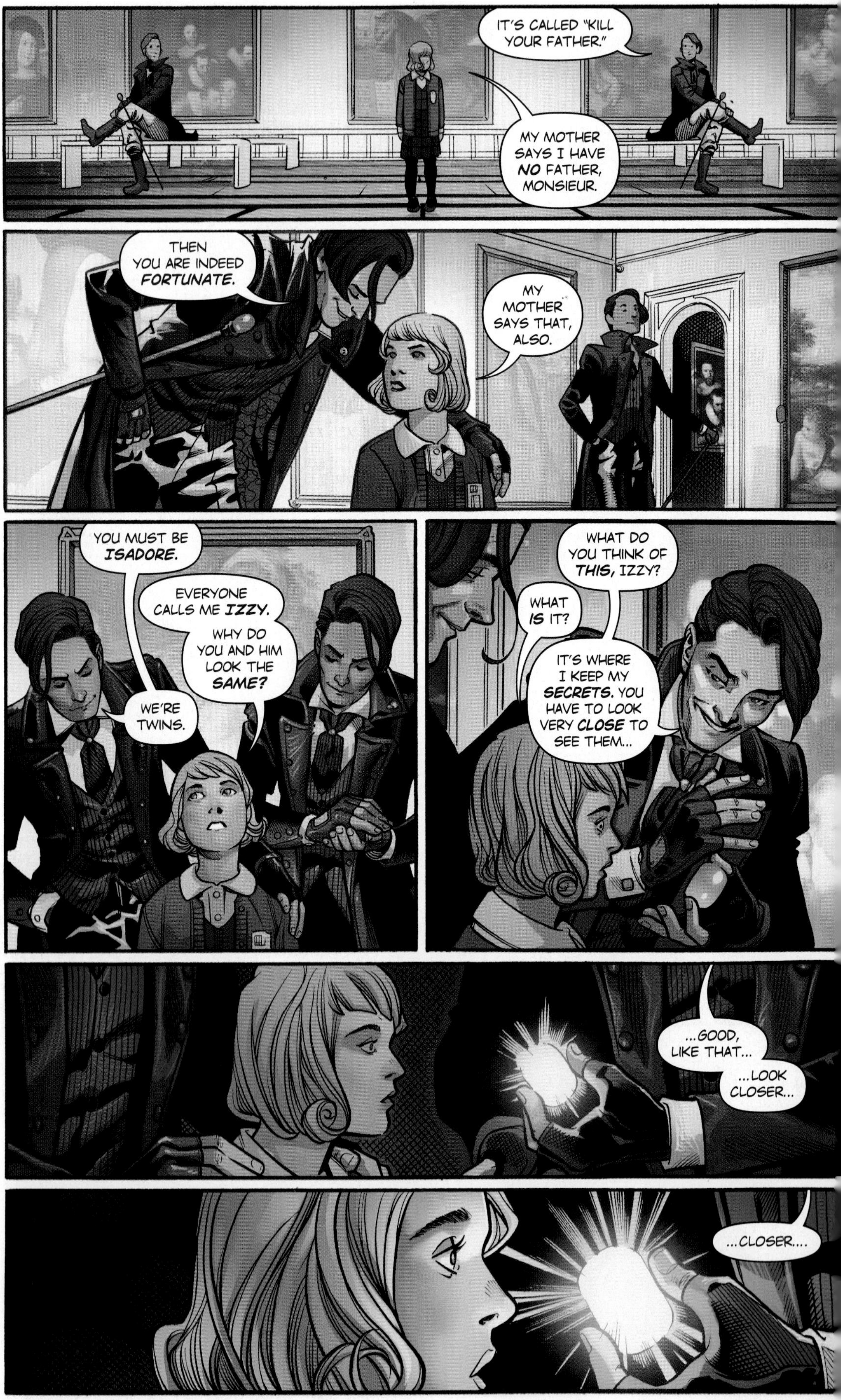

IT'S CALLED "KILL YOUR FATHER."
MY MOTHER SAYS I HAVE ***NO*** FATHER, MONSIEUR.
THEN YOU ARE INDEED ***FORTUNATE.***
MY MOTHER SAYS THAT, ALSO.
YOU MUST BE ***ISADORE.***
EVERYONE CALLS ME ***IZZY.***
WHY DO YOU AND HIM LOOK THE ***SAME?***
WE'RE TWINS.
WHAT DO YOU THINK OF ***THIS,*** IZZY?
WHAT ***IS*** IT?
IT'S WHERE I KEEP MY ***SECRETS.*** YOU HAVE TO LOOK VERY ***CLOSE*** TO SEE THEM...
...GOOD, LIKE THAT...
...LOOK CLOSER...
...CLOSER....

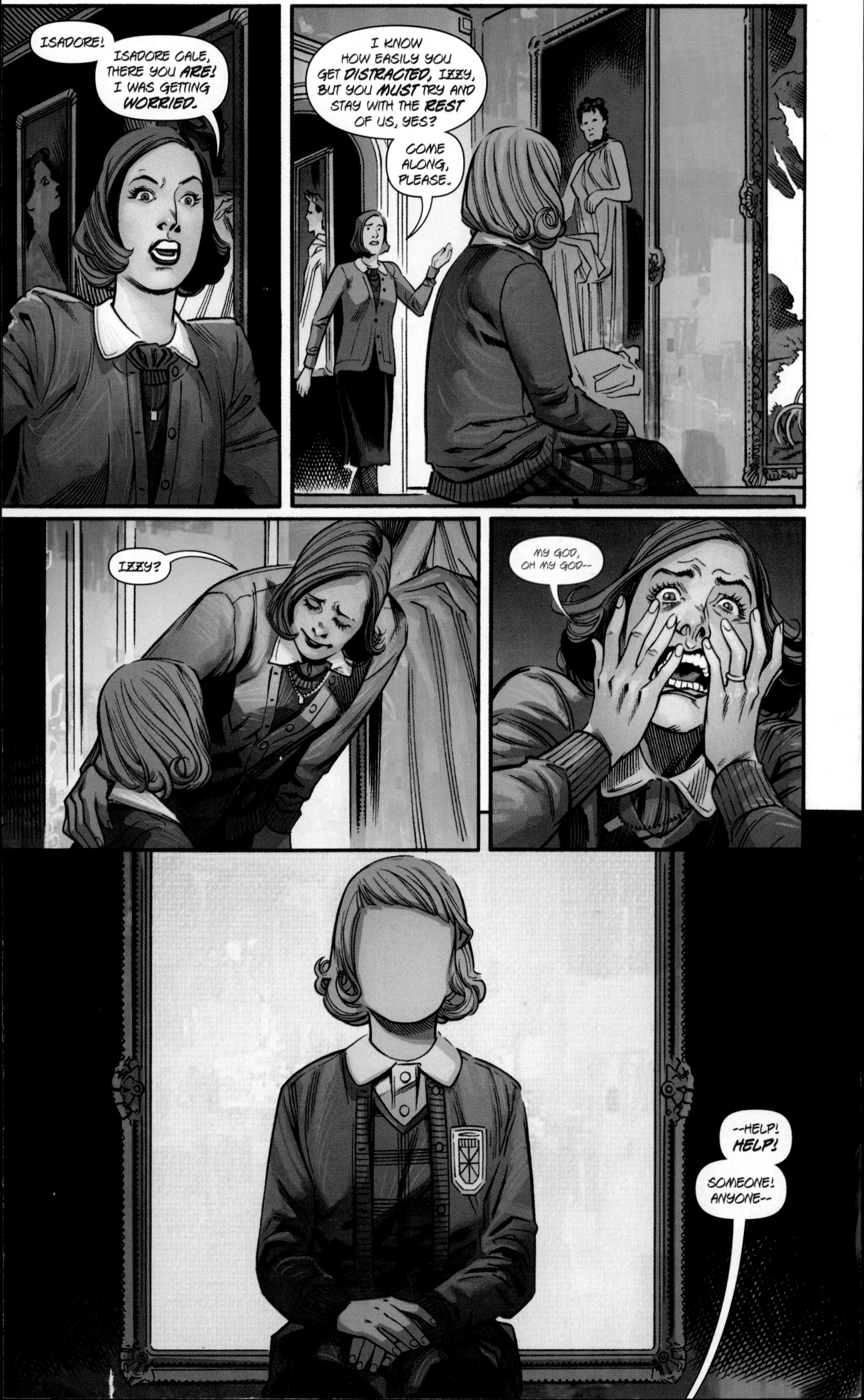
ISADORE!
ISADORE CALE, THERE YOU ARE! I WAS GETTING WORRIED.
I KNOW HOW EASILY YOU GET DISTRACTED, IZZY, BUT YOU MUST TRY AND STAY WITH THE REST OF US, YES?
COME ALONG, PLEASE.
IZZY?
MY GOD, OH MY GOD--
--HELP! HELP!
SOMEONE! ANYONE--

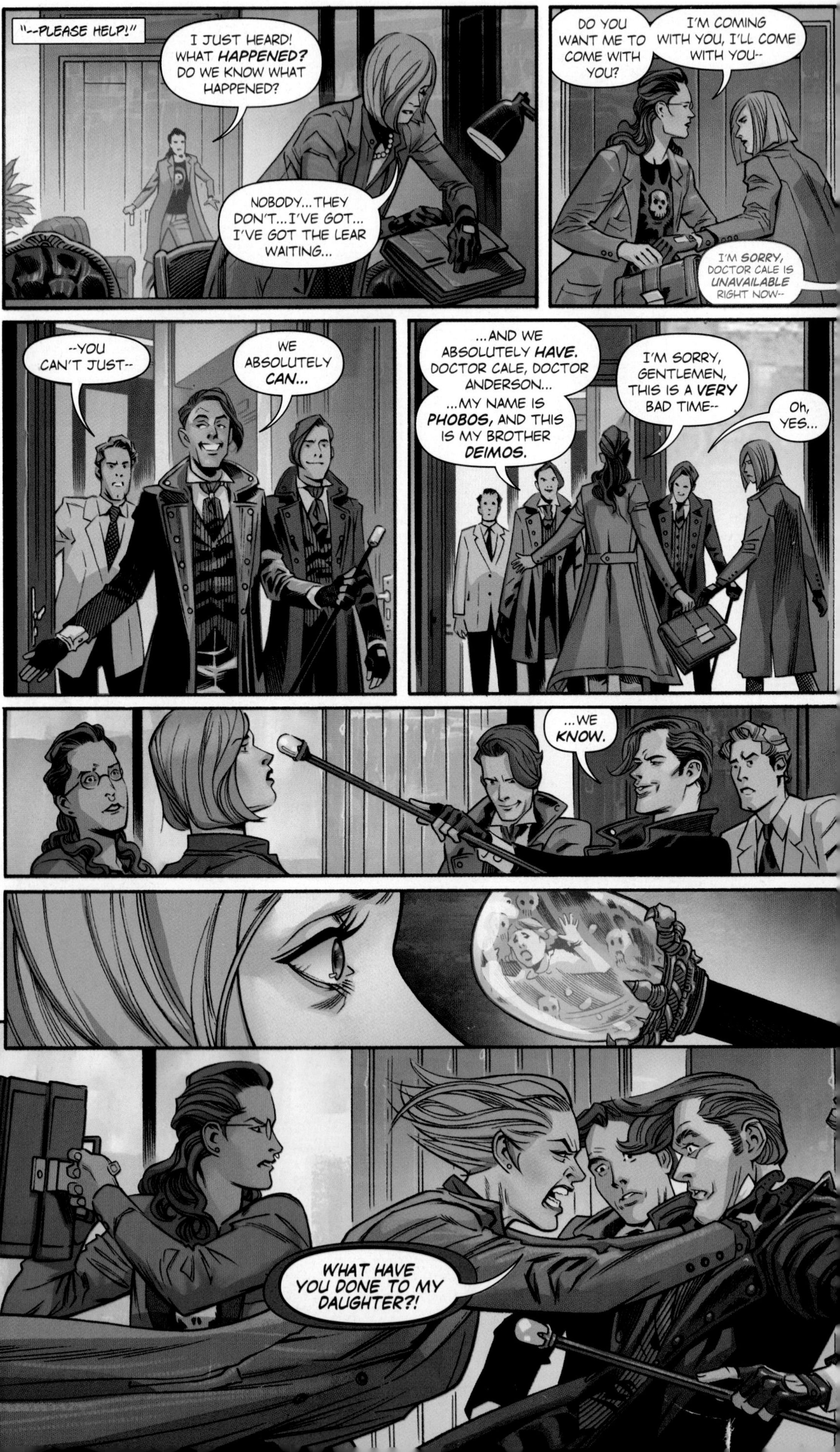
"--PLEASE HELP!"
I JUST HEARD! WHAT HAPPENED? DO WE KNOW WHAT HAPPENED?
NOBODY... THEY DON'T... I'VE GOT... I'VE GOT THE LEAR WAITING...
DO YOU WANT ME TO COME WITH YOU?
I'M COMING WITH YOU, I'LL COME WITH YOU--
I'M SORRY, DOCTOR CALE IS UNAVAILABLE RIGHT NOW--
--YOU CAN'T JUST--
WE ABSOLUTELY CAN...
...AND WE ABSOLUTELY HAVE. DOCTOR CALE, DOCTOR ANDERSON...
...MY NAME IS PHOBOS, AND THIS IS MY BROTHER DEIMOS.
I'M SORRY, GENTLEMEN, THIS IS A VERY BAD TIME--
Oh, YES...
...WE KNOW.
WHAT HAVE YOU DONE TO MY DAUGHTER?!

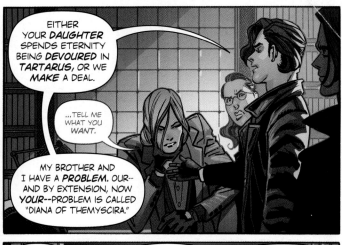

EITHER YOUR **DAUGHTER** SPENDS ETERNITY BEING **DEVOURED** IN **TARTARUS**, OR WE **MAKE** A DEAL.

...TELL ME WHAT YOU **WANT**.

MY BROTHER AND I HAVE A **PROBLEM.** OUR-- AND BY EXTENSION, NOW **YOUR**--PROBLEM IS CALLED "DIANA OF THEMYSCIRA."

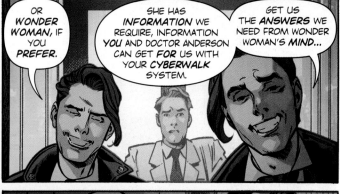

OR **WONDER WOMAN**, IF YOU **PREFER**.

SHE HAS **INFORMATION** WE REQUIRE, INFORMATION **YOU** AND DOCTOR ANDERSON CAN GET **FOR** US WITH YOUR **CYBERWALK** SYSTEM.

GET US THE **ANSWERS** WE NEED FROM WONDER WOMAN'S **MIND**...

...AND YOU'LL GET YOUR **DAUGHTER** BACK, SIMPLE AS THAT.

MIND YOURSELF, DOCTOR. YOU'RE IN THE **PRESENCE** OF GODS.

SO LET'S JUST **SKIP** THE **INCREDULITY** AND **AWE** PHASES AND GO **STRAIGHT** TO **ACCEPTANCE**, ALL RIGHT?

WHAT DO YOU WANT TO **KNOW?**

YOU CAN'T JUST **ASK** HER?

THE LOCATION OF **THEMYSCIRA**, HER HOME.

WE'VE BEEN IN HER **MIND** AND COULDN'T **FIND** IT.

AND IF TWO **GODS** CAN'T FIND IT, WHAT MAKES YOU THINK **WE** CAN?

WE BELIEVE IT'S BEEN **HIDDEN** FROM US PRECISELY **BECAUSE** WE **ARE** GODS.

AND IF **WE CAN'T** FIND IT?

THEN IZZY LEARNS A WHOLE **NEW** DIMENSION OF **FEAR**.

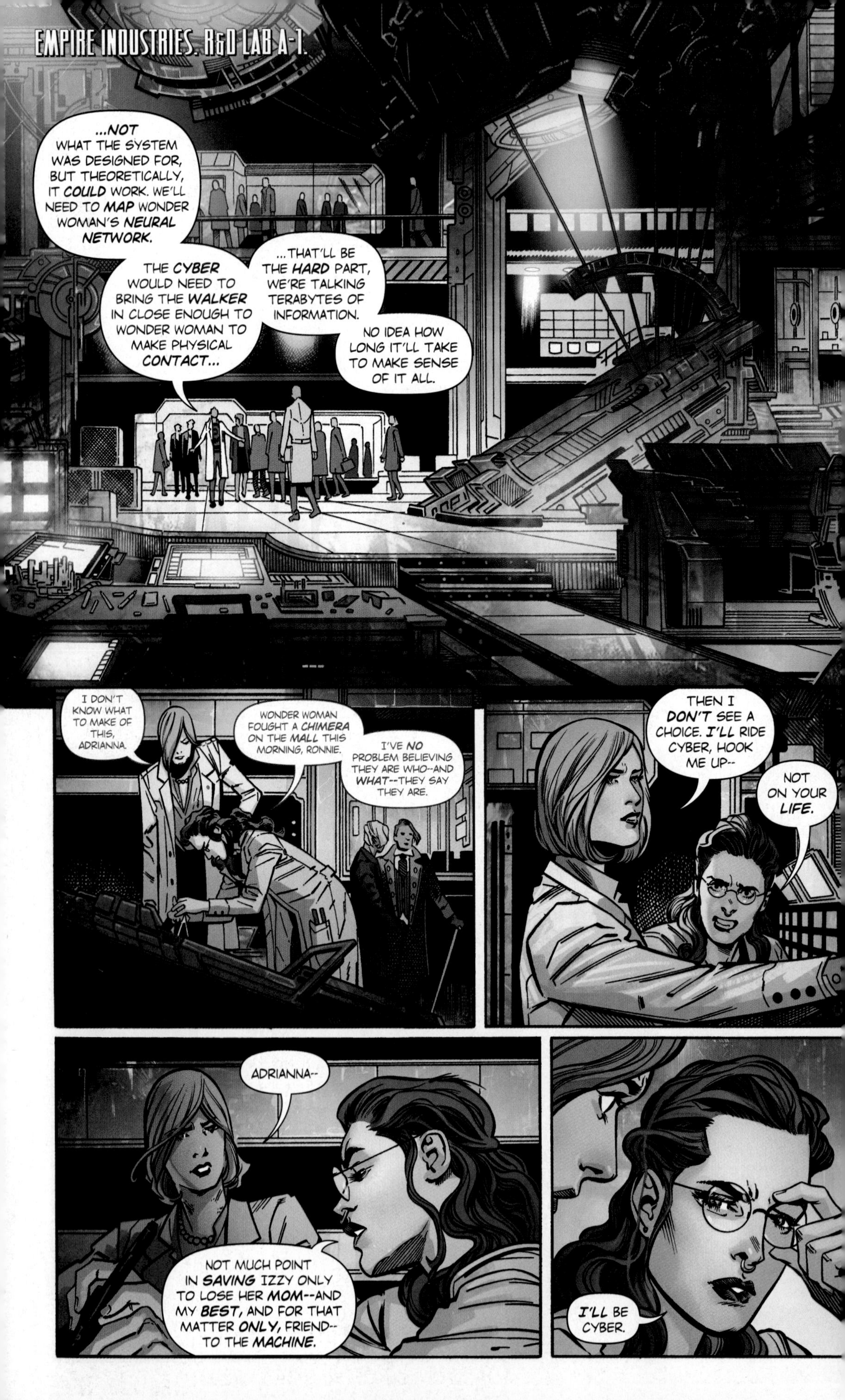
EMPIRE INDUSTRIES. R&D LAB A-1.
...NOT WHAT THE SYSTEM WAS DESIGNED FOR, BUT THEORETICALLY, IT COULD WORK. WE'LL NEED TO MAP WONDER WOMAN'S NEURAL NETWORK.
THE CYBER WOULD NEED TO BRING THE WALKER IN CLOSE ENOUGH TO WONDER WOMAN TO MAKE PHYSICAL CONTACT...
...THAT'LL BE THE HARD PART, WE'RE TALKING TERABYTES OF INFORMATION.
NO IDEA HOW LONG IT'LL TAKE TO MAKE SENSE OF IT ALL.
I DON'T KNOW WHAT TO MAKE OF THIS, ADRIANNA.
WONDER WOMAN FOUGHT A CHIMERA ON THE MALL THIS MORNING, RONNIE.
I'VE NO PROBLEM BELIEVING THEY ARE WHO--AND WHAT--THEY SAY THEY ARE.
THEN I DON'T SEE A CHOICE. I'LL RIDE CYBER, HOOK ME UP--
NOT ON YOUR LIFE.
ADRIANNA--
NOT MUCH POINT IN SAVING IZZY ONLY TO LOSE HER MOM--AND MY BEST, AND FOR THAT MATTER ONLY, FRIEND--TO THE MACHINE.
I'LL BE CYBER.

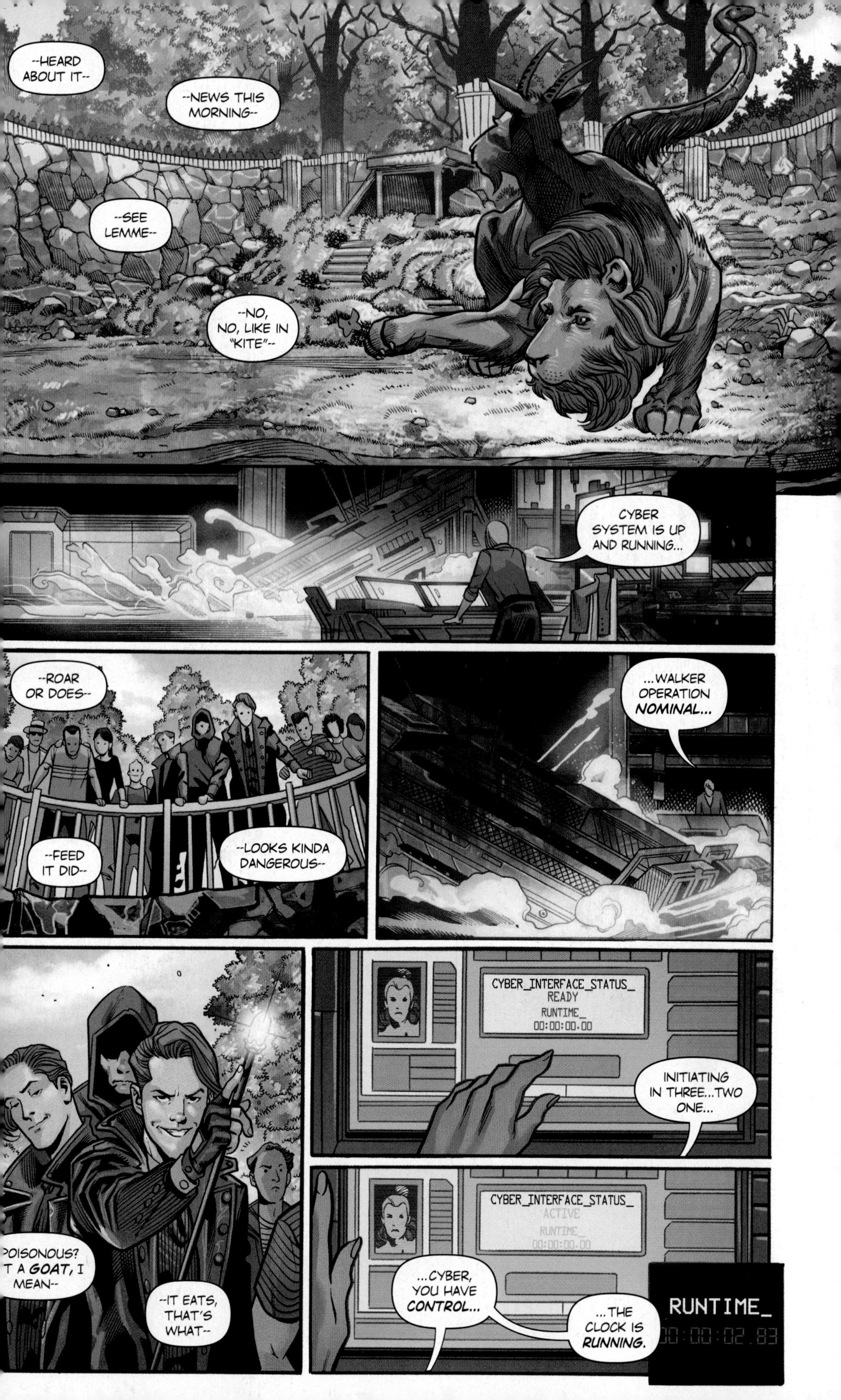
--HEARD ABOUT IT--
--NEWS THIS MORNING--
--SEE LEMME--
--NO, NO, LIKE IN "KITE"--
CYBER SYSTEM IS UP AND RUNNING...
--ROAR OR DOES--
--FEED IT DID--
--LOOKS KINDA DANGEROUS--
...WALKER OPERATION NOMINAL...
CYBER_INTERFACE_STATUS_
READY
RUNTIME_
00:00:00.00
INITIATING IN THREE...TWO ONE...
POISONOUS? T A GOAT, I MEAN--
--IT EATS, THAT'S WHAT--
CYBER_INTERFACE_STATUS_
ACTIVE
RUNTIME_
00:00:00.00
...CYBER, YOU HAVE CONTROL...
...THE CLOCK IS RUNNING.
RUNTIME_
00:00:02.83

RRRRRRRROOOOOAAAARRRRRRRRR

ASSUMING CONTROL.

--ahh!

--FIRE IT--

--BACK GET B--

--BACK, EVERYONE, STAY CALM--

--STAY--

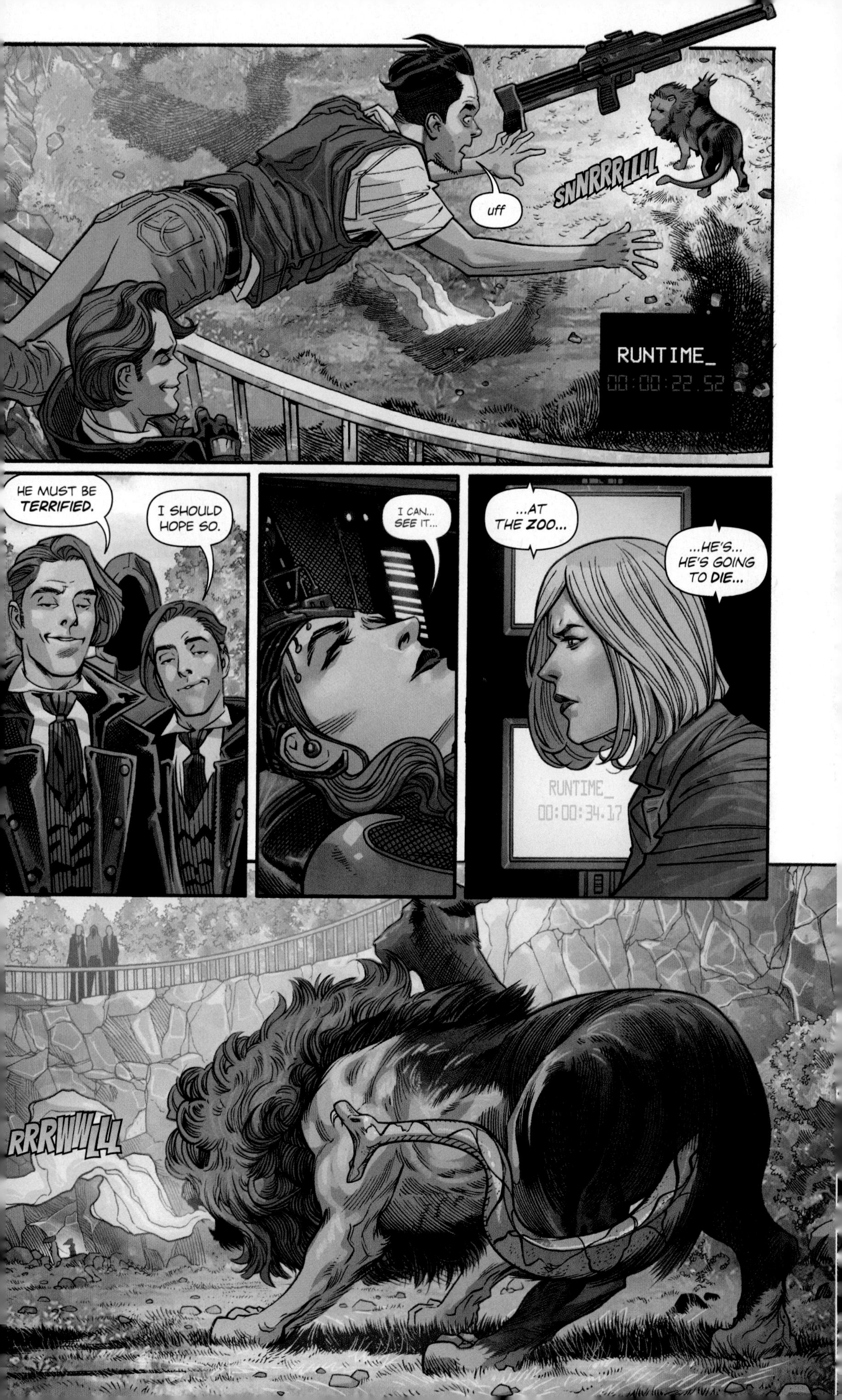

uff
SNNRRRLLLL
RUNTIME_
00:00:22.52
HE MUST BE TERRIFIED.
I SHOULD HOPE SO.
I CAN... SEE IT...
...AT THE ZOO...
...HE'S... HE'S GOING TO DIE...
RUNTIME_
00:00:34.17
RRRWWLLL

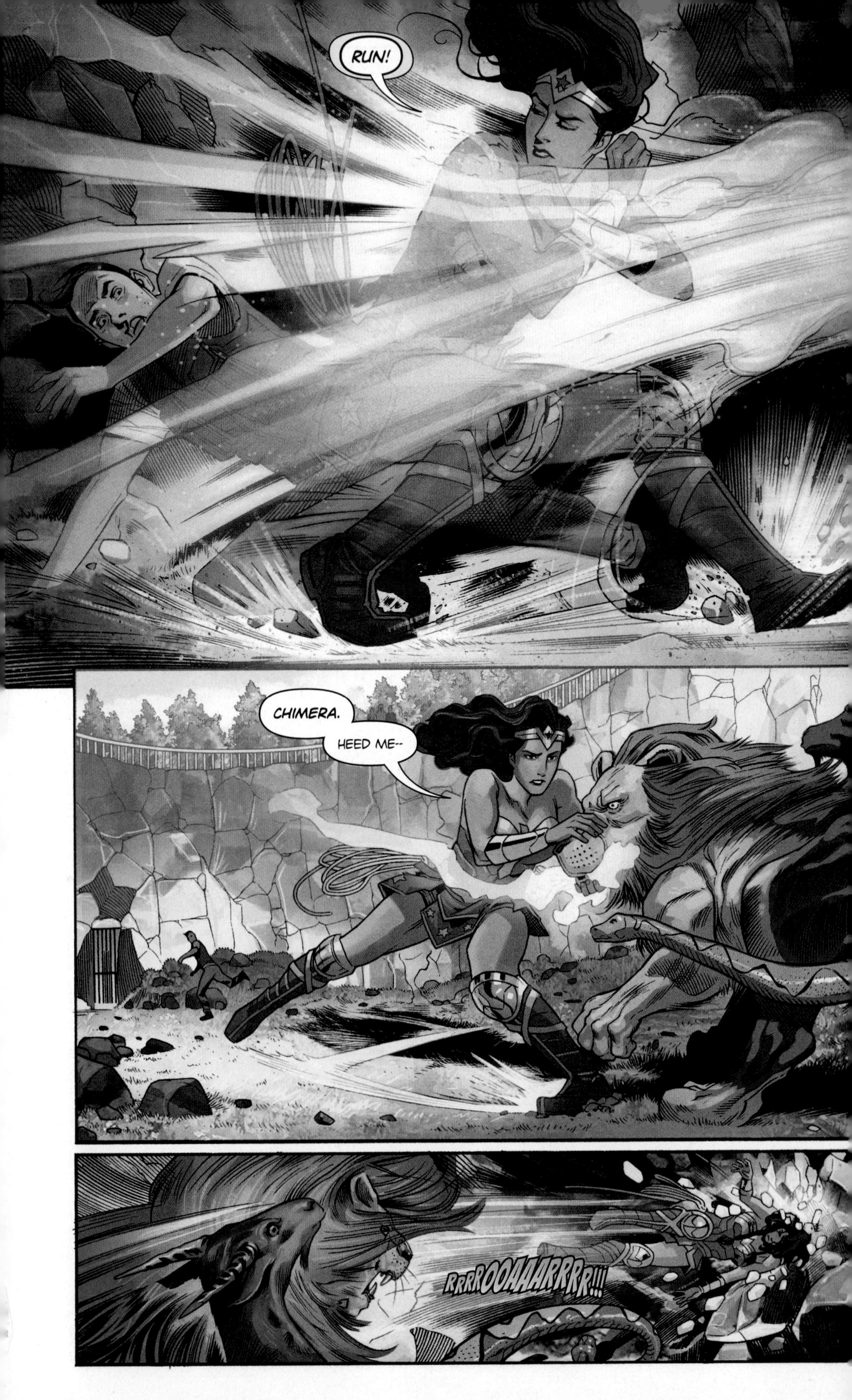
RUN!
CHIMERA.
HEED ME--
RRRROOAAAARRRR!!!

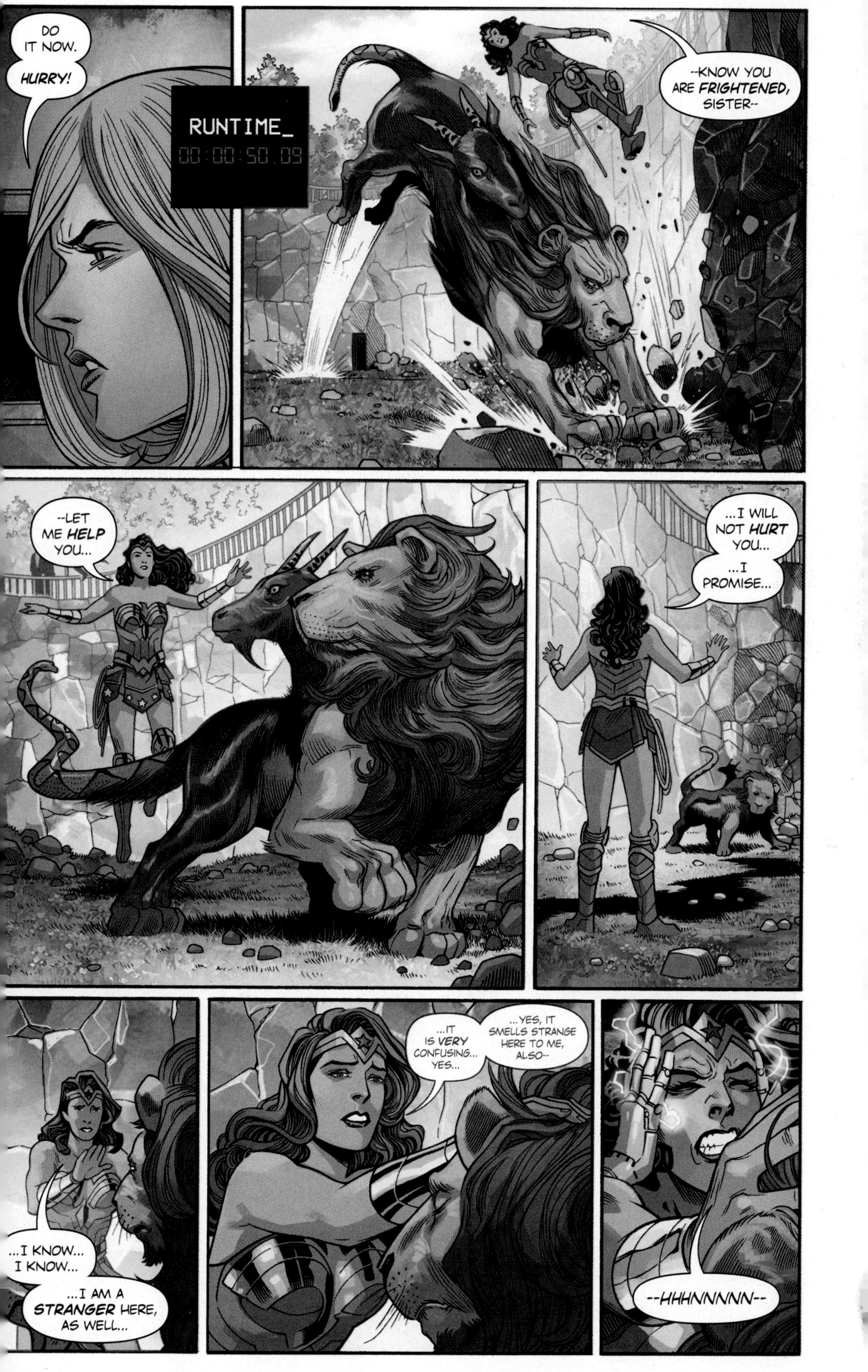
DO IT NOW. HURRY!
RUNTIME_
00:00:50.09
--KNOW YOU ARE FRIGHTENED, SISTER--
--LET ME HELP YOU...
...I WILL NOT HURT YOU...
...I PROMISE...
...I KNOW... I KNOW...
...I AM A STRANGER HERE, AS WELL...
...IT IS VERY CONFUSING... YES...
...YES, IT SMELLS STRANGE HERE TO ME, ALSO--
--HHHNNNNN--

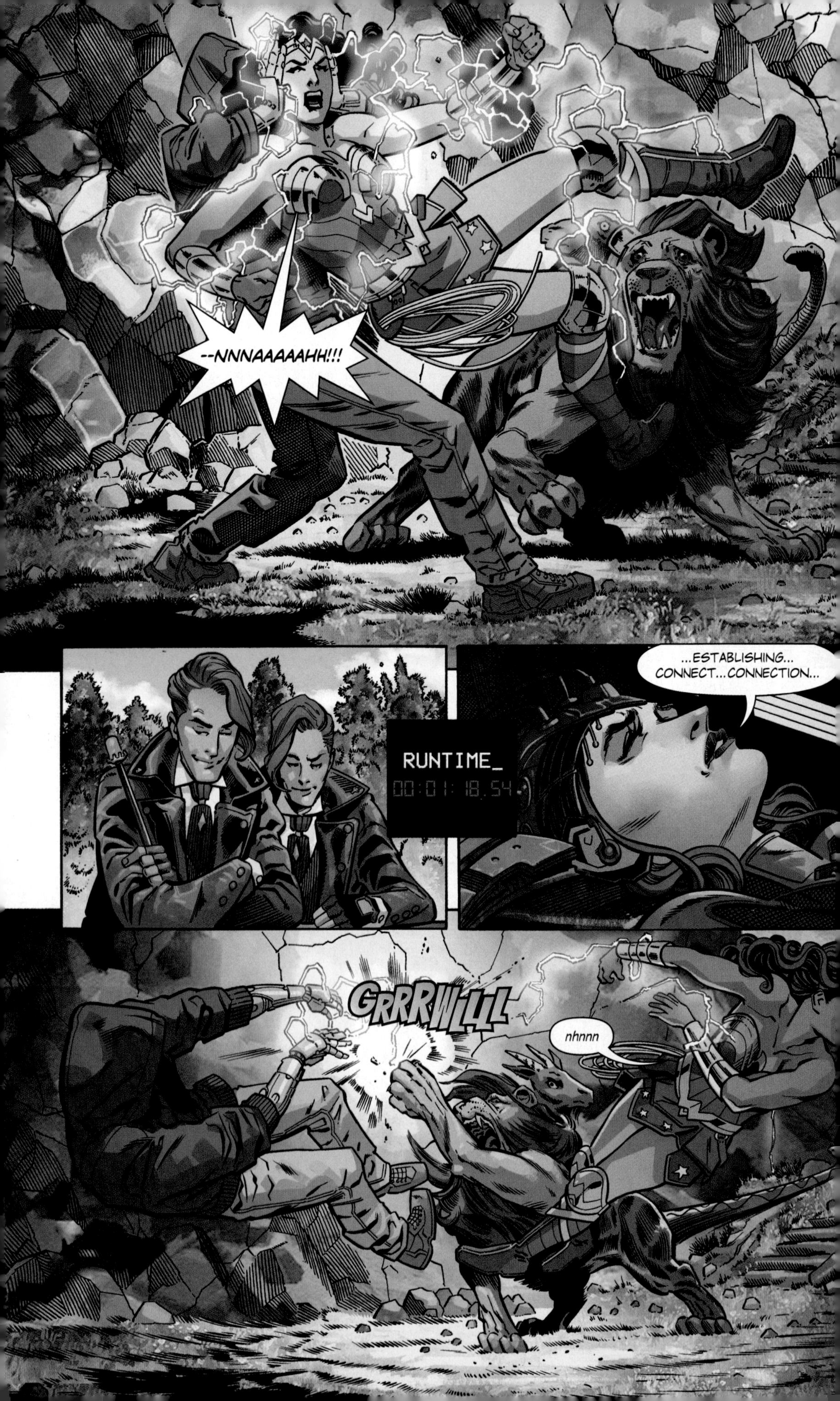
--NNNAAAAAHH!!!
RUNTIME_
00:01:18.54
...ESTABLISHING...
CONNECT...CONNECTION...
GRRRWLLL
nhnnn

hnnh

WAIT, THAT'S NOT--

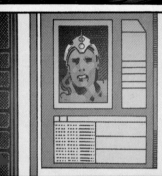

CYBER_INTERFACE_STATUS_
COMPROMISED

RUNTIME_
00:00:26.79

--RIGHT, THAT'S NOT SUPPOSED TO HAPPEN--

nnh nhnn

SNRRLLL

...W-- WAIT...

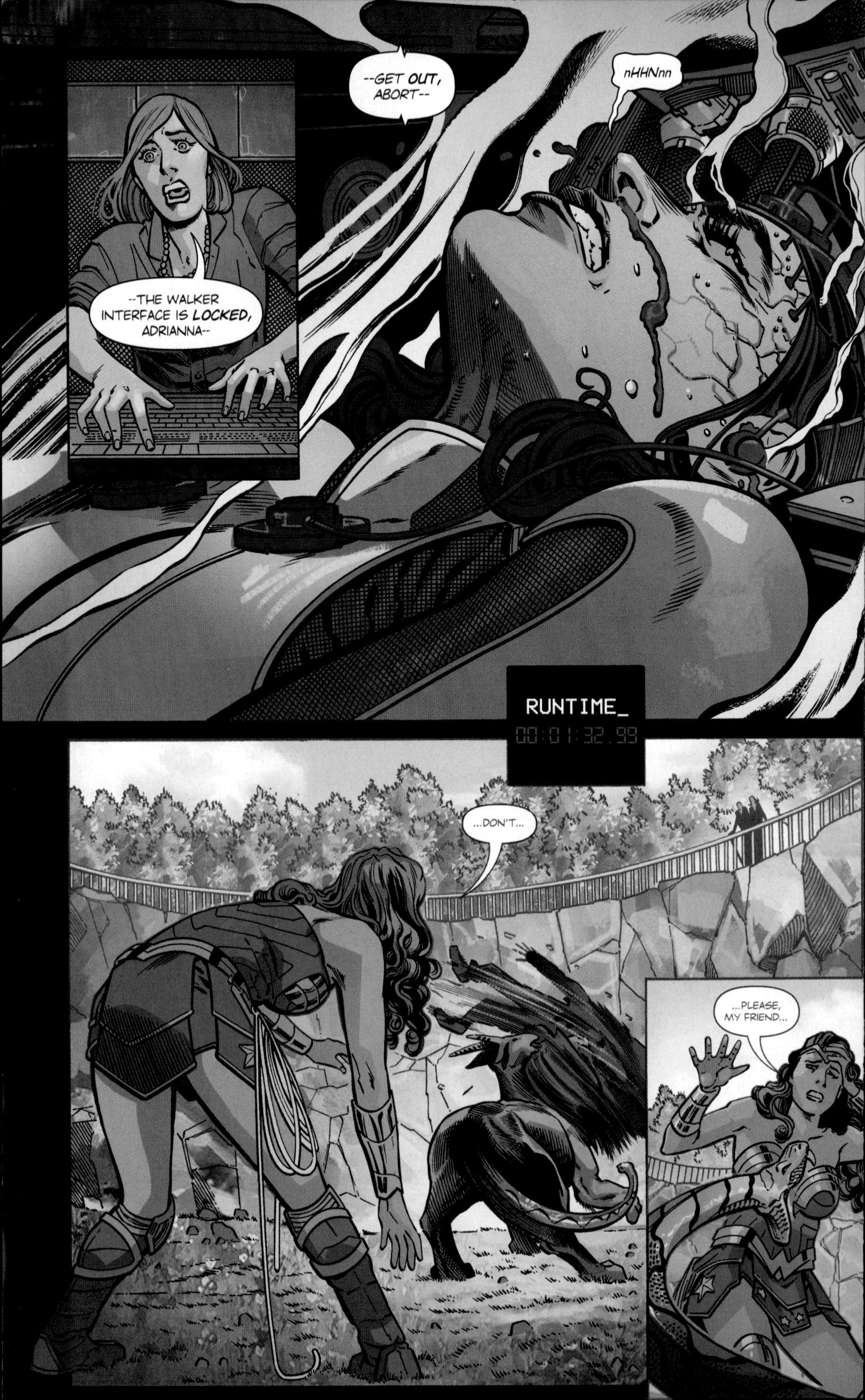
--THE WALKER INTERFACE IS LOCKED, ADRIANNA--
--GET OUT, ABORT--
nHHNnn
RUNTIME_
00:01:32.99
...DON'T...
...PLEASE, MY FRIEND...

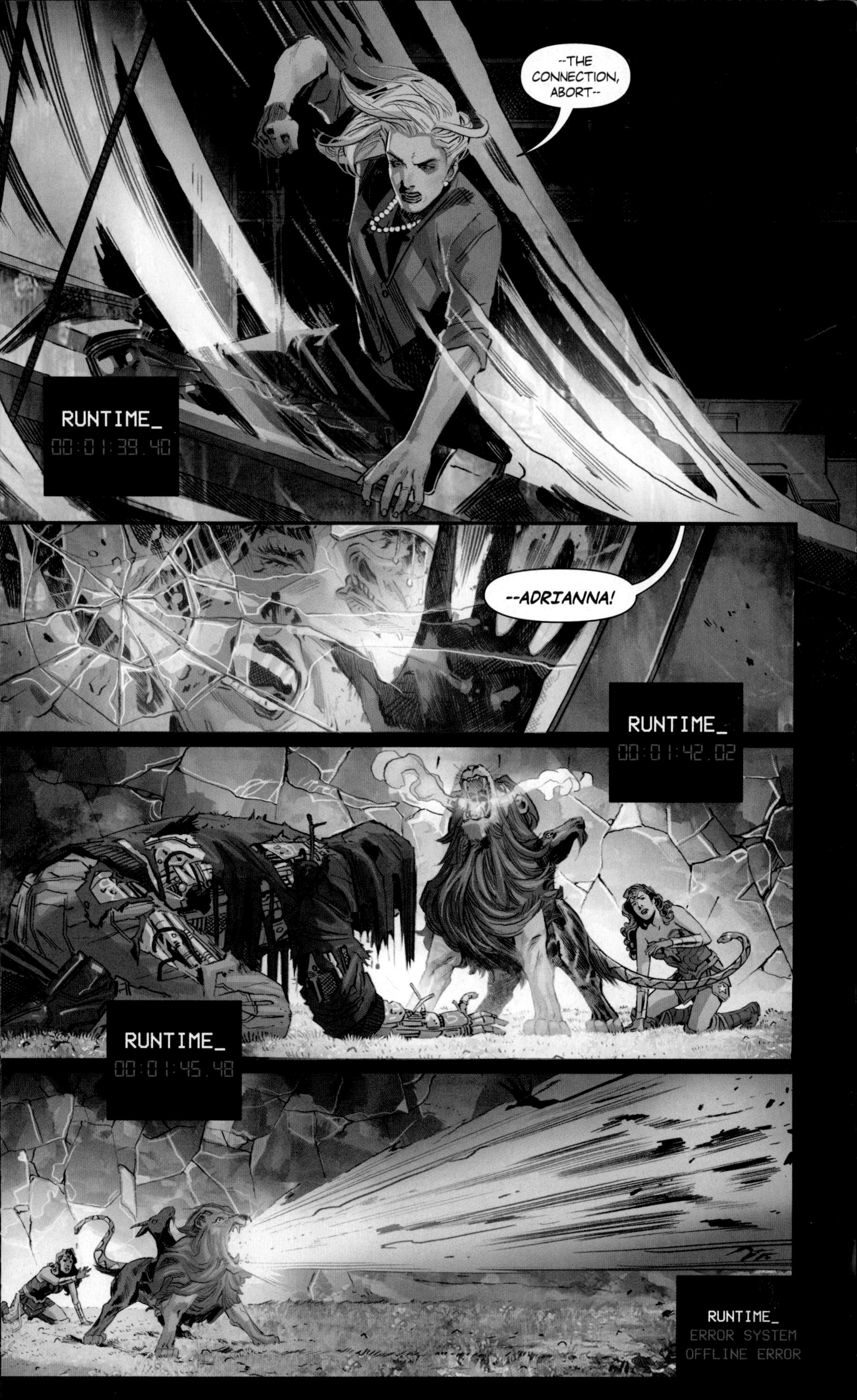

--THE CONNECTION, ABORT--
RUNTIME_
00:01:39.40
--ADRIANNA!
RUNTIME_
00:01:42.02
RUNTIME_
00:01:45.48
RUNTIME_
ERROR SYSTEM
OFFLINE ERROR

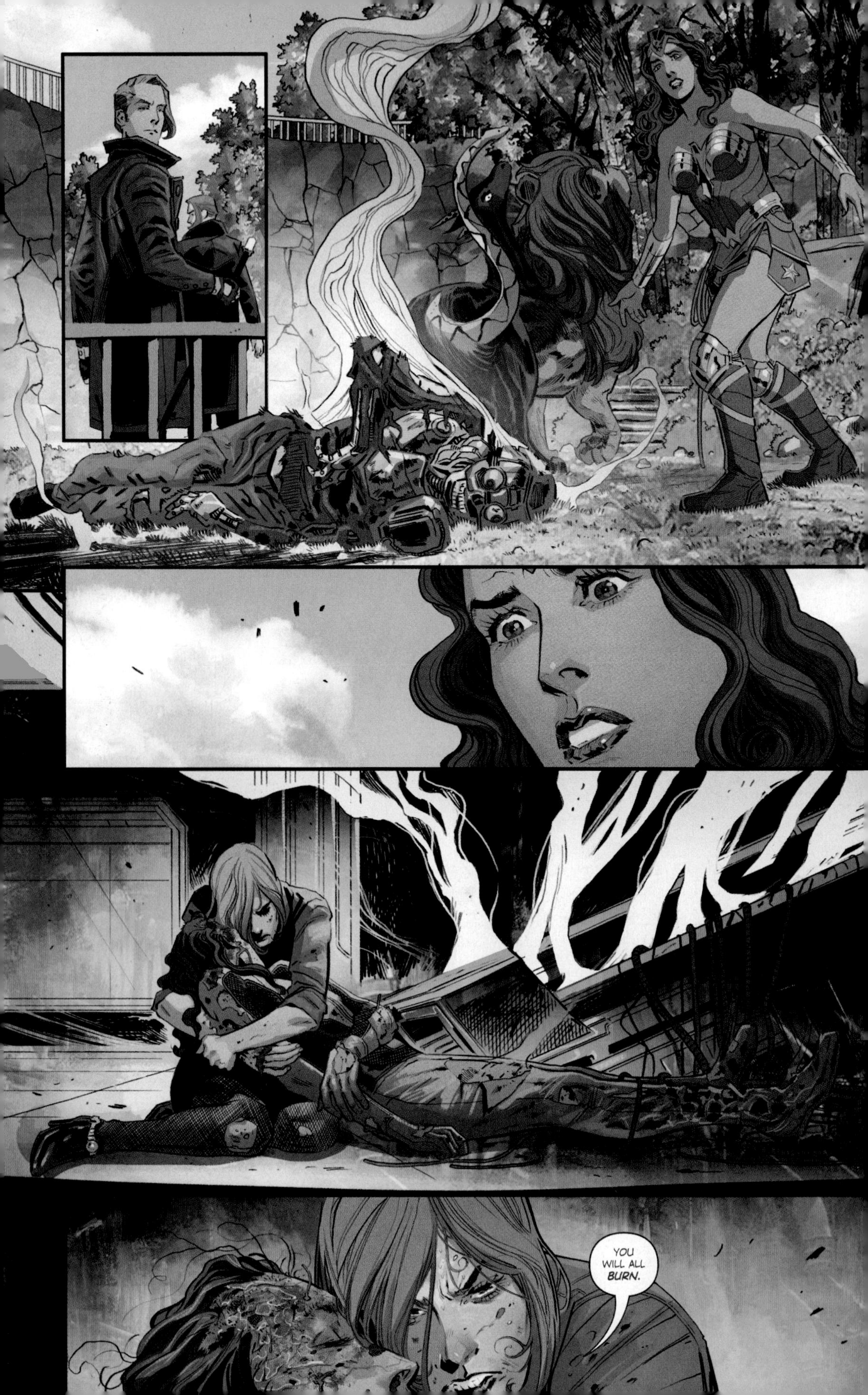
YOU WILL ALL BURN.

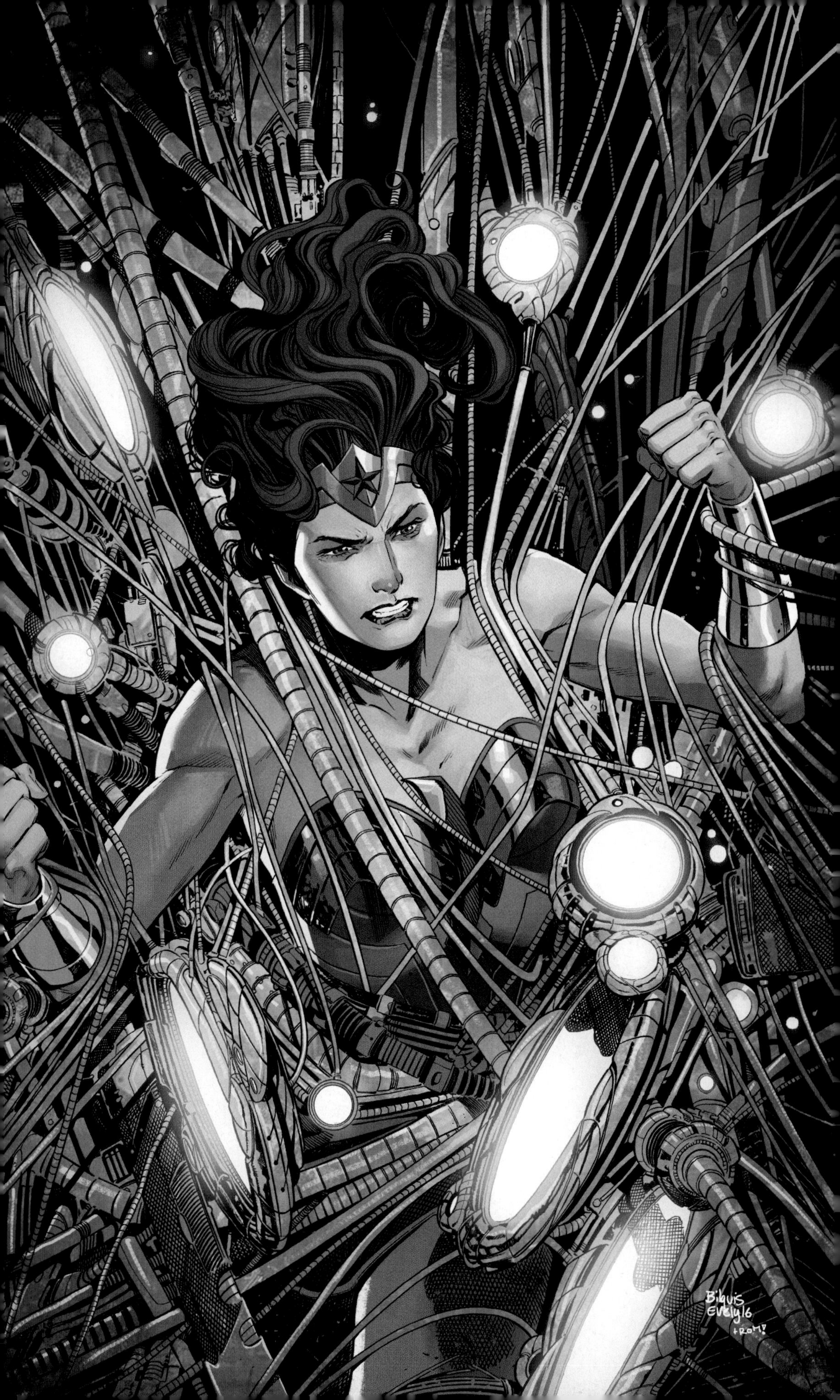
Bilquis Evely 16
+ROM!

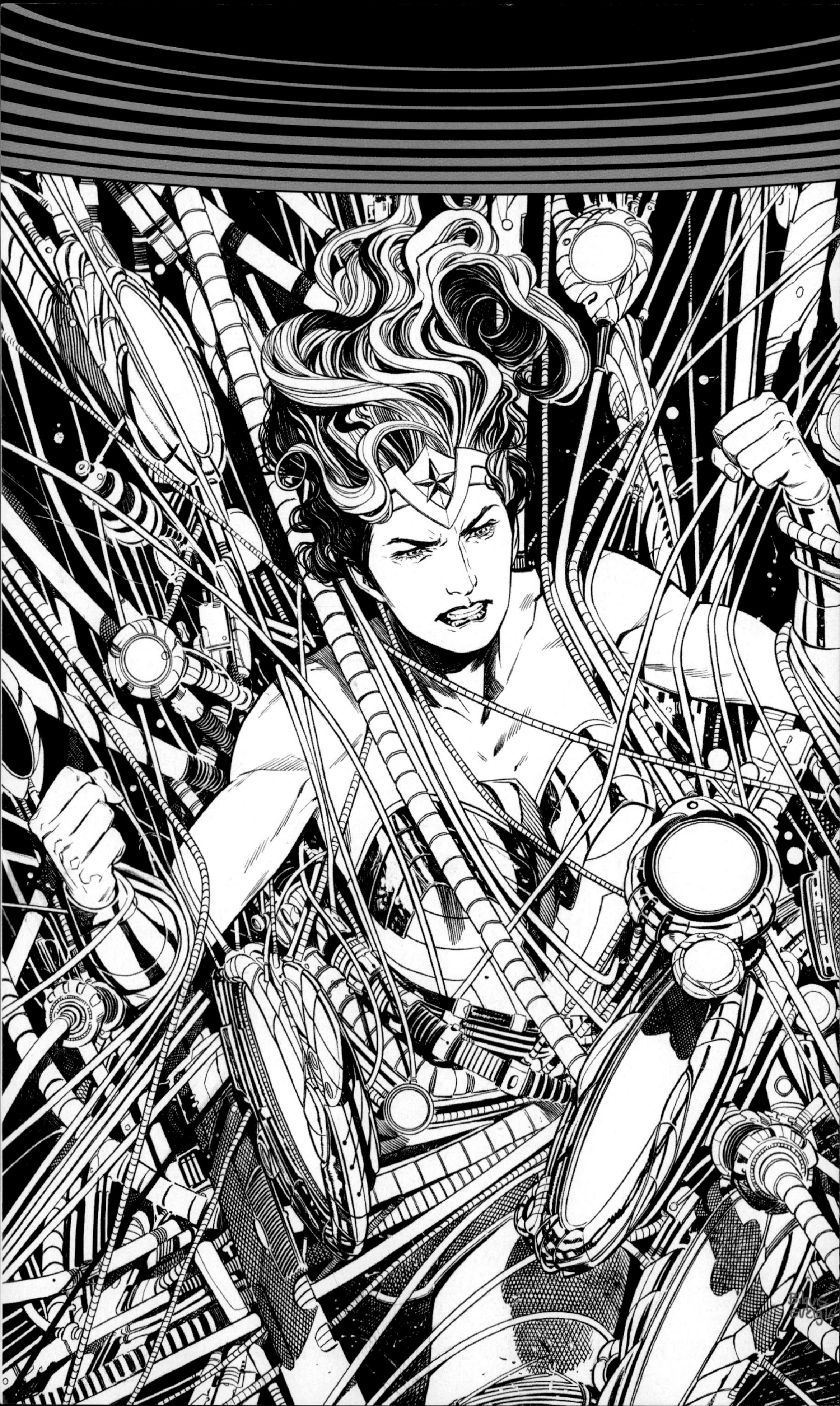

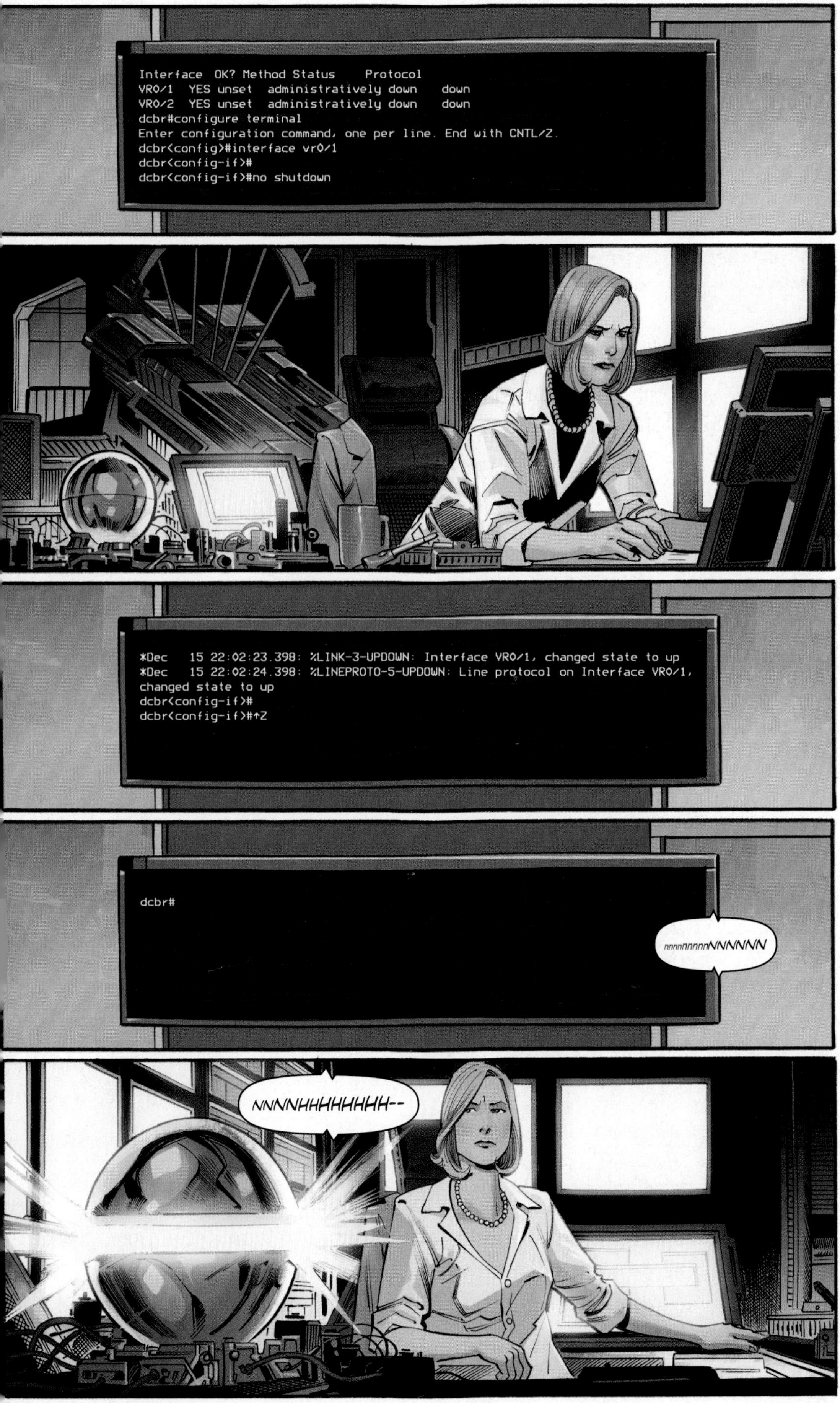

Interface OK? Method Status Protocol
VR0/1 YES unset administratively down down
VR0/2 YES unset administratively down down
dcbr#configure terminal
Enter configuration command, one per line. End with CNTL/Z.
dcbr<config>#interface vr0/1
dcbr<config-if>#
dcbr<config-if>#no shutdown
*Dec 15 22:02:23.398: %LINK-3-UPDOWN: Interface VR0/1, changed state to up
*Dec 15 22:02:24.398: %LINEPROTO-5-UPDOWN: Line protocol on Interface VR0/1, changed state to up
dcbr<config-if>#
dcbr<config-if>#^Z
dcbr#
nnnnnnnnNNNNNN
NNNNHHHHHHHH--

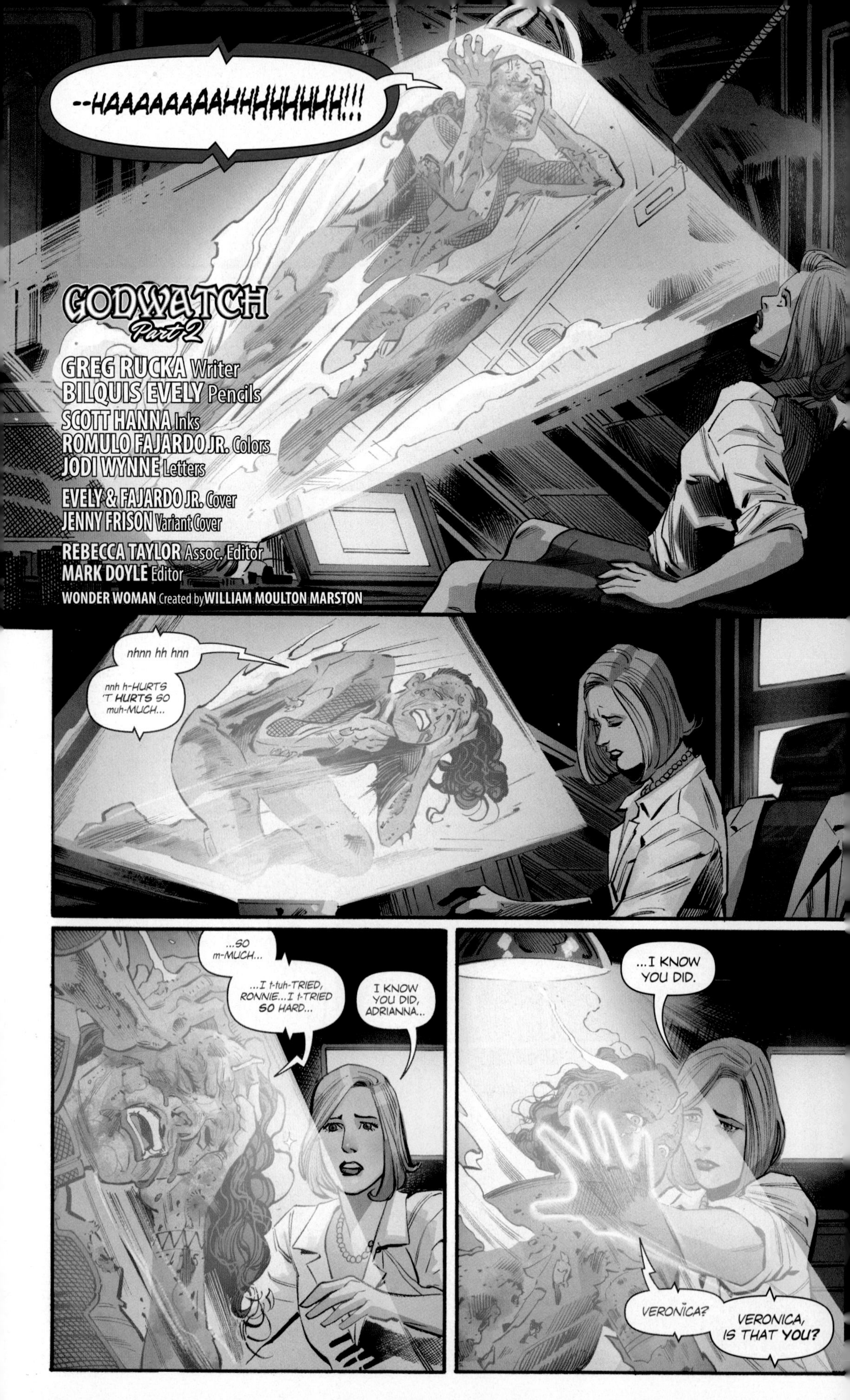
--HAAAAAAAAHHHHHHH!!!
GODWATCH
Part 2
GREG RUCKA Writer
BILQUIS EVELY Pencils
SCOTT HANNA Inks
ROMULO FAJARDO JR. Colors
JODI WYNNE Letters
EVELY & FAJARDO JR. Cover
JENNY FRISON Variant Cover
REBECCA TAYLOR Assoc. Editor
MARK DOYLE Editor
WONDER WOMAN Created by WILLIAM MOULTON MARSTON
nhnn hh hnn
nnh h-HURTS 'T HURTS SO muh-MUCH...
...SO m-MUCH...
...I t-tuh-TRIED, RONNIE...I t-TRIED SO HARD...
I KNOW YOU DID, ADRIANNA..
...I KNOW YOU DID.
VERONICA?
VERONICA, IS THAT YOU?

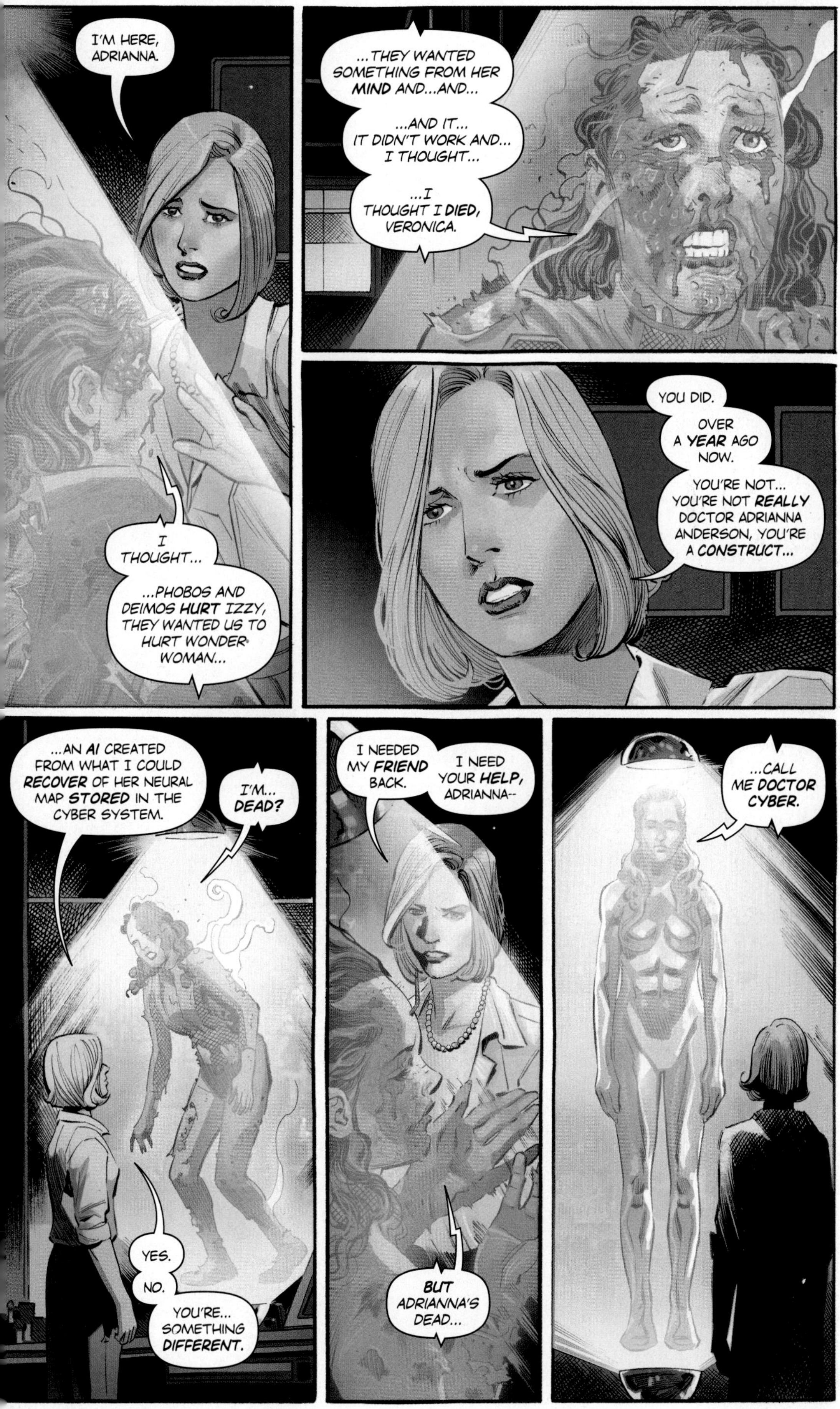
I'M HERE, ADRIANNA.
...THEY WANTED SOMETHING FROM HER MIND AND...AND...
...AND IT... IT DIDN'T WORK AND... I THOUGHT...
...I THOUGHT I DIED, VERONICA.
I THOUGHT...
...PHOBOS AND DEIMOS HURT IZZY, THEY WANTED US TO HURT WONDER WOMAN...
YOU DID.
OVER A YEAR AGO NOW.
YOU'RE NOT... YOU'RE NOT REALLY DOCTOR ADRIANNA ANDERSON, YOU'RE A CONSTRUCT...
...AN AI CREATED FROM WHAT I COULD RECOVER OF HER NEURAL MAP STORED IN THE CYBER SYSTEM.
I'M... DEAD?
YES.
NO.
YOU'RE... SOMETHING DIFFERENT.
I NEEDED MY FRIEND BACK.
I NEED YOUR HELP, ADRIANNA--
BUT ADRIANNA'S DEAD...
...CALL ME DOCTOR CYBER.

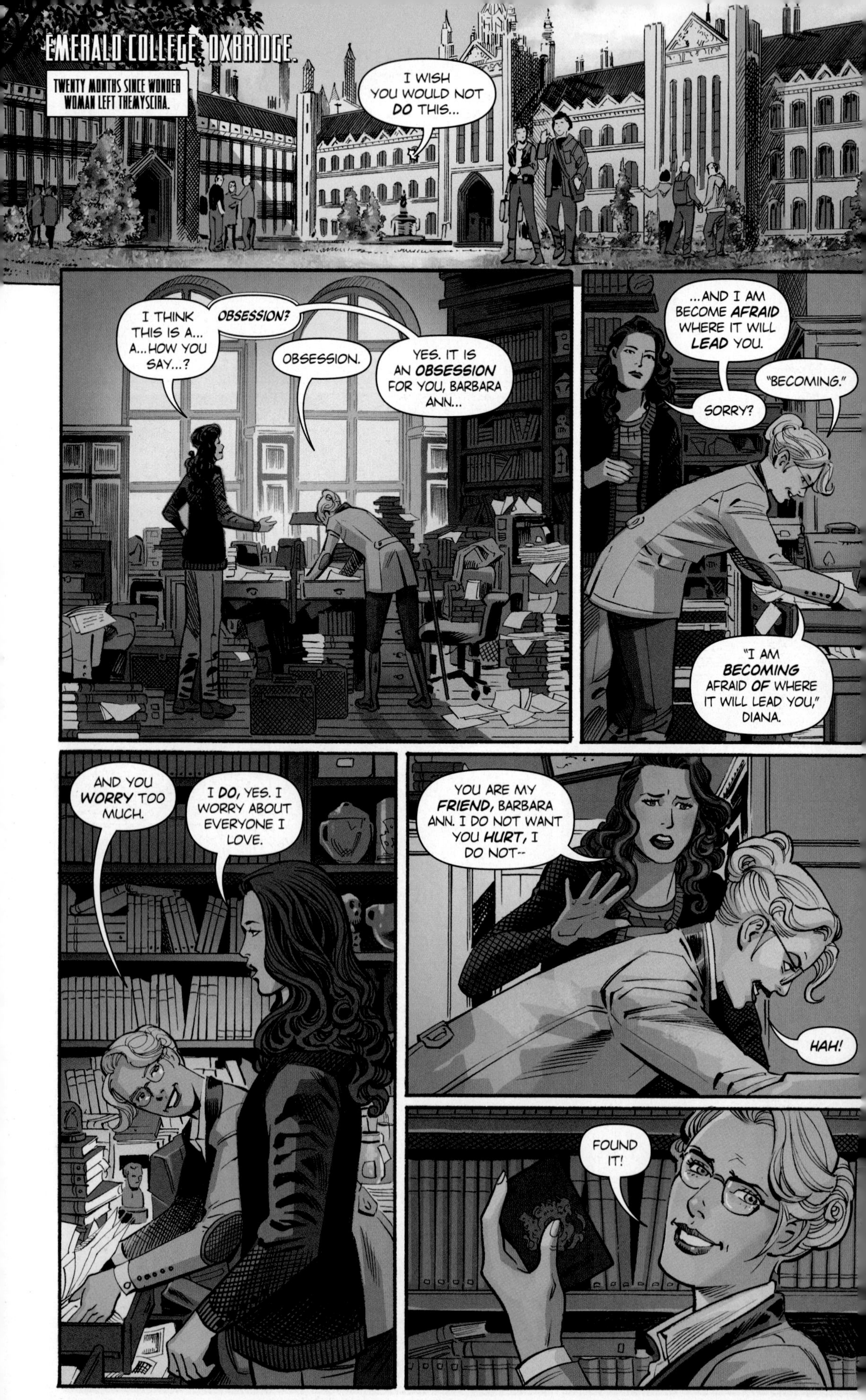
EMERALD COLLEGE, OXBRIDGE.
TWENTY MONTHS SINCE WONDER WOMAN LEFT THEMYSCIRA.
I WISH YOU WOULD NOT DO THIS...
I THINK THIS IS A... A...HOW YOU SAY...?
OBSESSION?
OBSESSION.
YES. IT IS AN OBSESSION FOR YOU, BARBARA ANN...
...AND I AM BECOME AFRAID WHERE IT WILL LEAD YOU.
SORRY?
"BECOMING."
"I AM BECOMING AFRAID OF WHERE IT WILL LEAD YOU," DIANA.
AND YOU WORRY TOO MUCH.
I DO, YES. I WORRY ABOUT EVERYONE I LOVE.
YOU ARE MY FRIEND, BARBARA ANN. I DO NOT WANT YOU HURT, I DO NOT--
HAH!
FOUND IT!

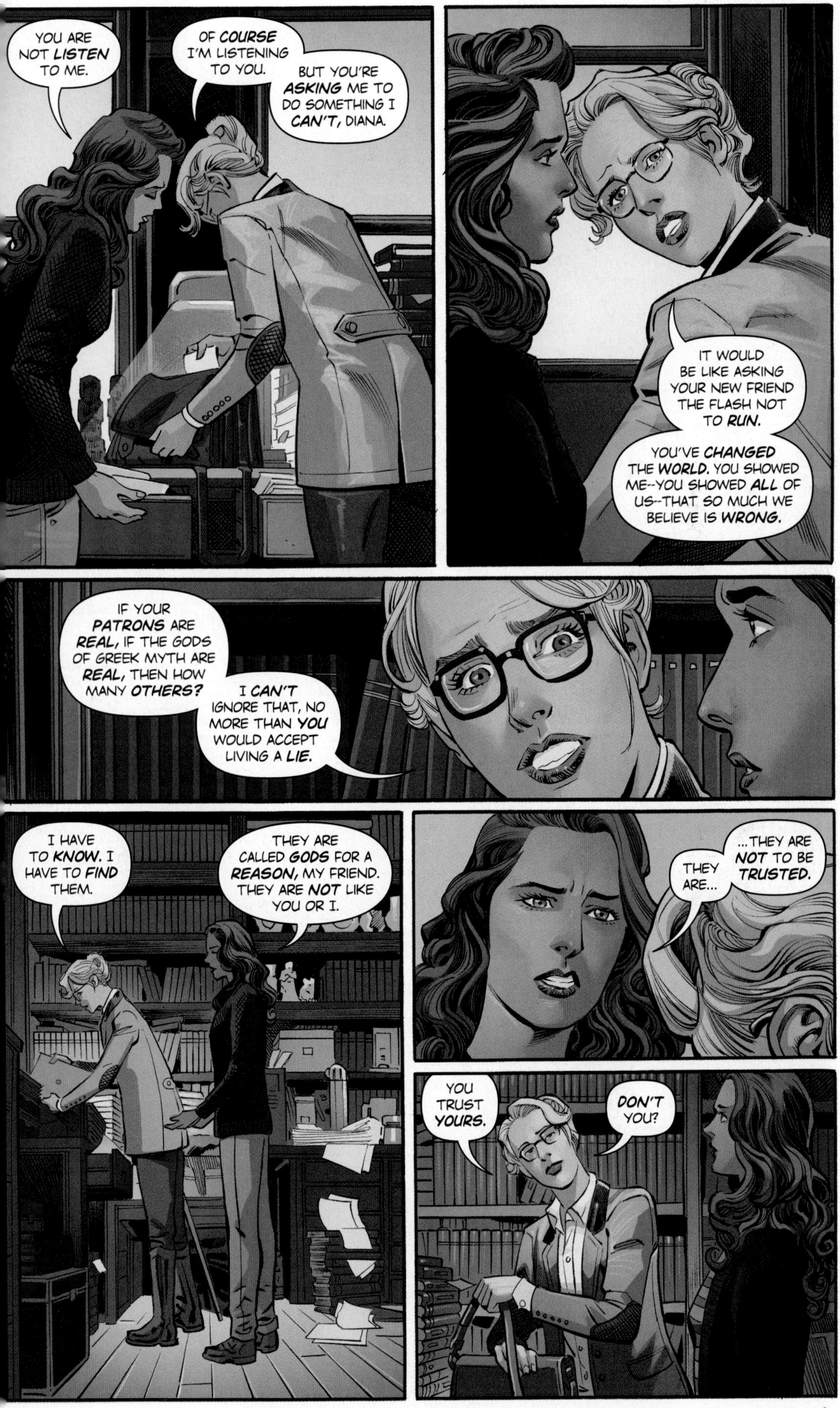
YOU ARE NOT LISTEN TO ME.
OF COURSE I'M LISTENING TO YOU.
BUT YOU'RE ASKING ME TO DO SOMETHING I CAN'T, DIANA.
IT WOULD BE LIKE ASKING YOUR NEW FRIEND THE FLASH NOT TO RUN.
YOU'VE CHANGED THE WORLD. YOU SHOWED ME--YOU SHOWED ALL OF US--THAT SO MUCH WE BELIEVE IS WRONG.
IF YOUR PATRONS ARE REAL, IF THE GODS OF GREEK MYTH ARE REAL, THEN HOW MANY OTHERS?
I CAN'T IGNORE THAT, NO MORE THAN YOU WOULD ACCEPT LIVING A LIE.
I HAVE TO KNOW. I HAVE TO FIND THEM.
THEY ARE CALLED GODS FOR A REASON, MY FRIEND. THEY ARE NOT LIKE YOU OR I.
THEY ARE...
...THEY ARE NOT TO BE TRUSTED.
YOU TRUST YOURS.
DON'T YOU?

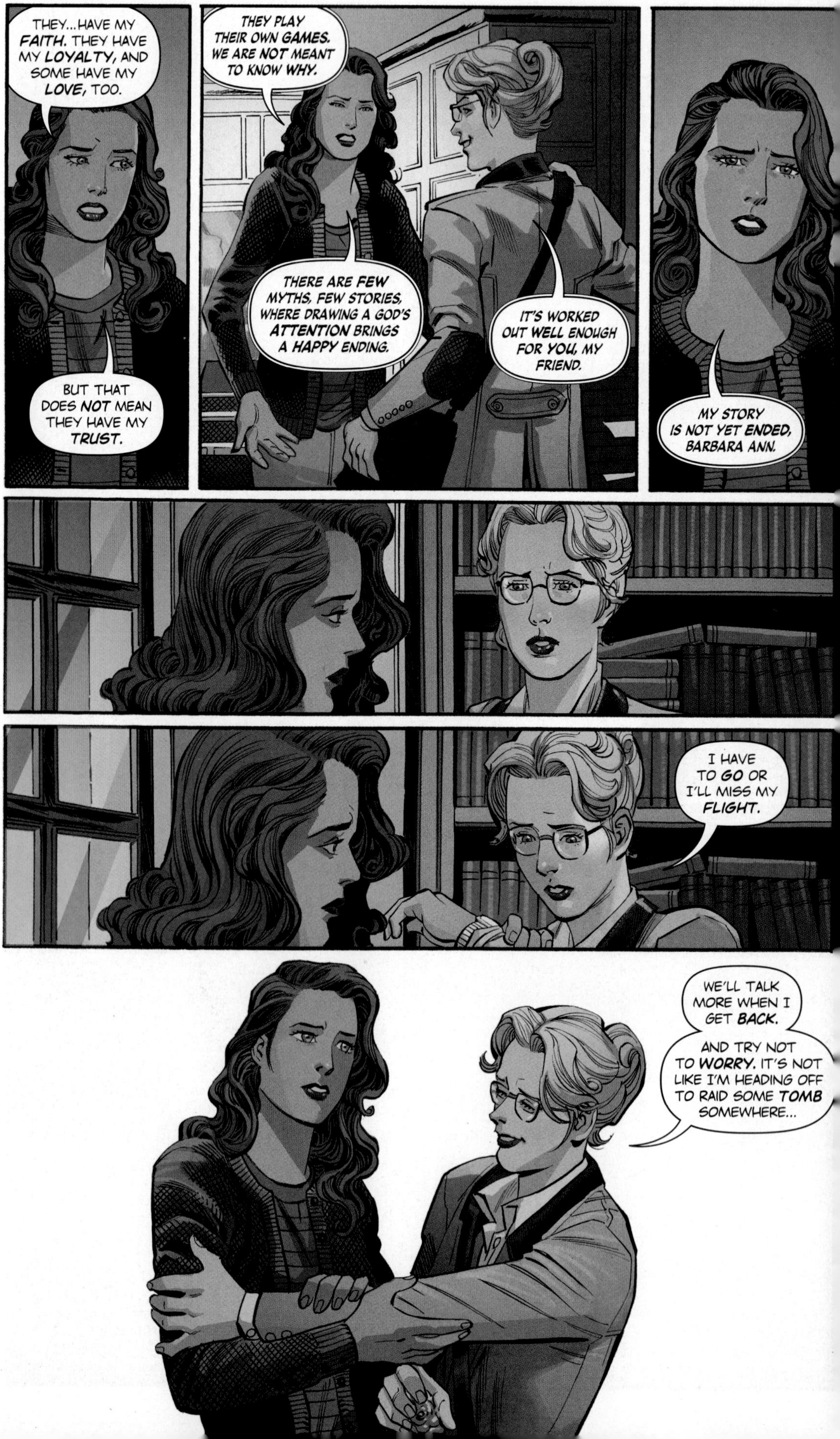
THEY...HAVE MY FAITH. THEY HAVE MY LOYALTY, AND SOME HAVE MY LOVE, TOO.
BUT THAT DOES NOT MEAN THEY HAVE MY TRUST.
THEY PLAY THEIR OWN GAMES. WE ARE NOT MEANT TO KNOW WHY.
THERE ARE FEW MYTHS, FEW STORIES, WHERE DRAWING A GOD'S ATTENTION BRINGS A HAPPY ENDING.
IT'S WORKED OUT WELL ENOUGH FOR YOU, MY FRIEND.
MY STORY IS NOT YET ENDED, BARBARA ANN.
I HAVE TO GO OR I'LL MISS MY FLIGHT.
WE'LL TALK MORE WHEN I GET BACK.
AND TRY NOT TO WORRY. IT'S NOT LIKE I'M HEADING OFF TO RAID SOME TOMB SOMEWHERE...

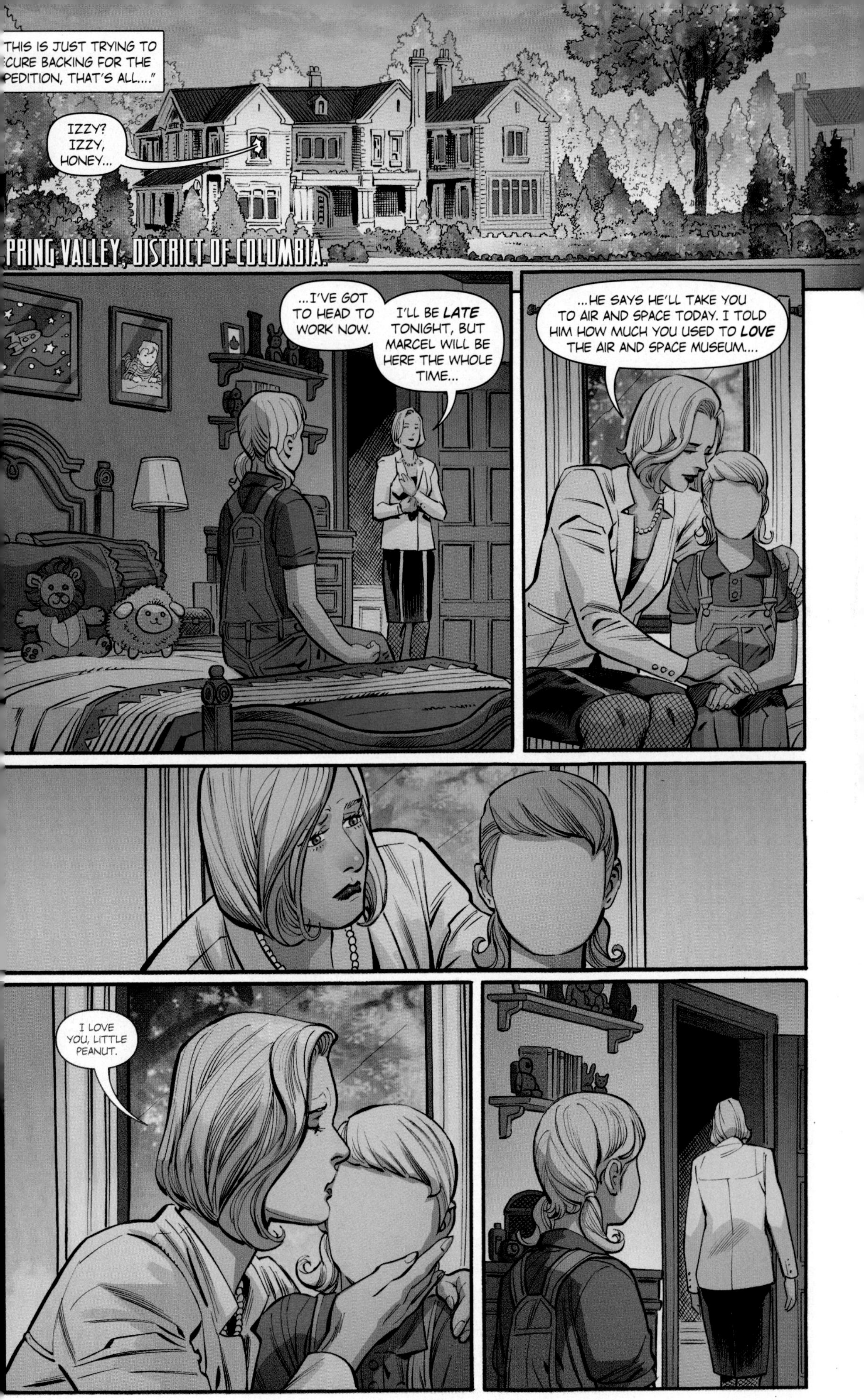
THIS IS JUST TRYING TO
CURE BACKING FOR THE
PEDITION, THAT'S ALL...."
IZZY? IZZY, HONEY...
PRING VALLEY, DISTRICT OF COLUMBIA.
...I'VE GOT TO HEAD TO WORK NOW.
I'LL BE LATE TONIGHT, BUT MARCEL WILL BE HERE THE WHOLE TIME...
...HE SAYS HE'LL TAKE YOU TO AIR AND SPACE TODAY. I TOLD HIM HOW MUCH YOU USED TO LOVE THE AIR AND SPACE MUSEUM....
I LOVE YOU, LITTLE PEANUT.

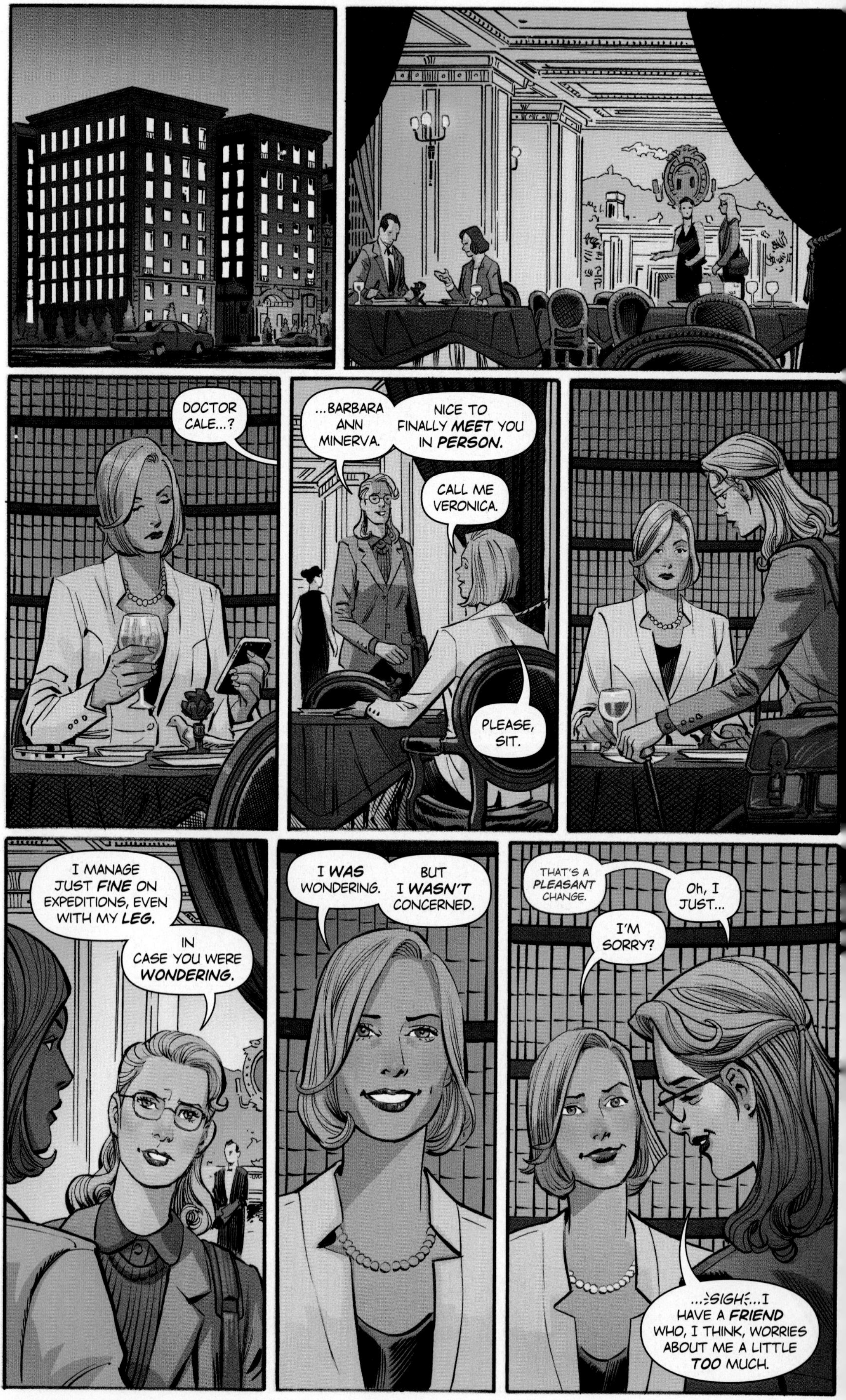
DOCTOR CALE...?
...BARBARA ANN MINERVA.
NICE TO FINALLY MEET YOU IN PERSON.
CALL ME VERONICA.
PLEASE, SIT.
I MANAGE JUST FINE ON EXPEDITIONS, EVEN WITH MY LEG.
IN CASE YOU WERE WONDERING.
I WAS WONDERING.
BUT I WASN'T CONCERNED.
THAT'S A PLEASANT CHANGE.
Oh, I JUST...
I'M SORRY?
...SIGH...I HAVE A FRIEND WHO, I THINK, WORRIES ABOUT ME A LITTLE TOO MUCH.

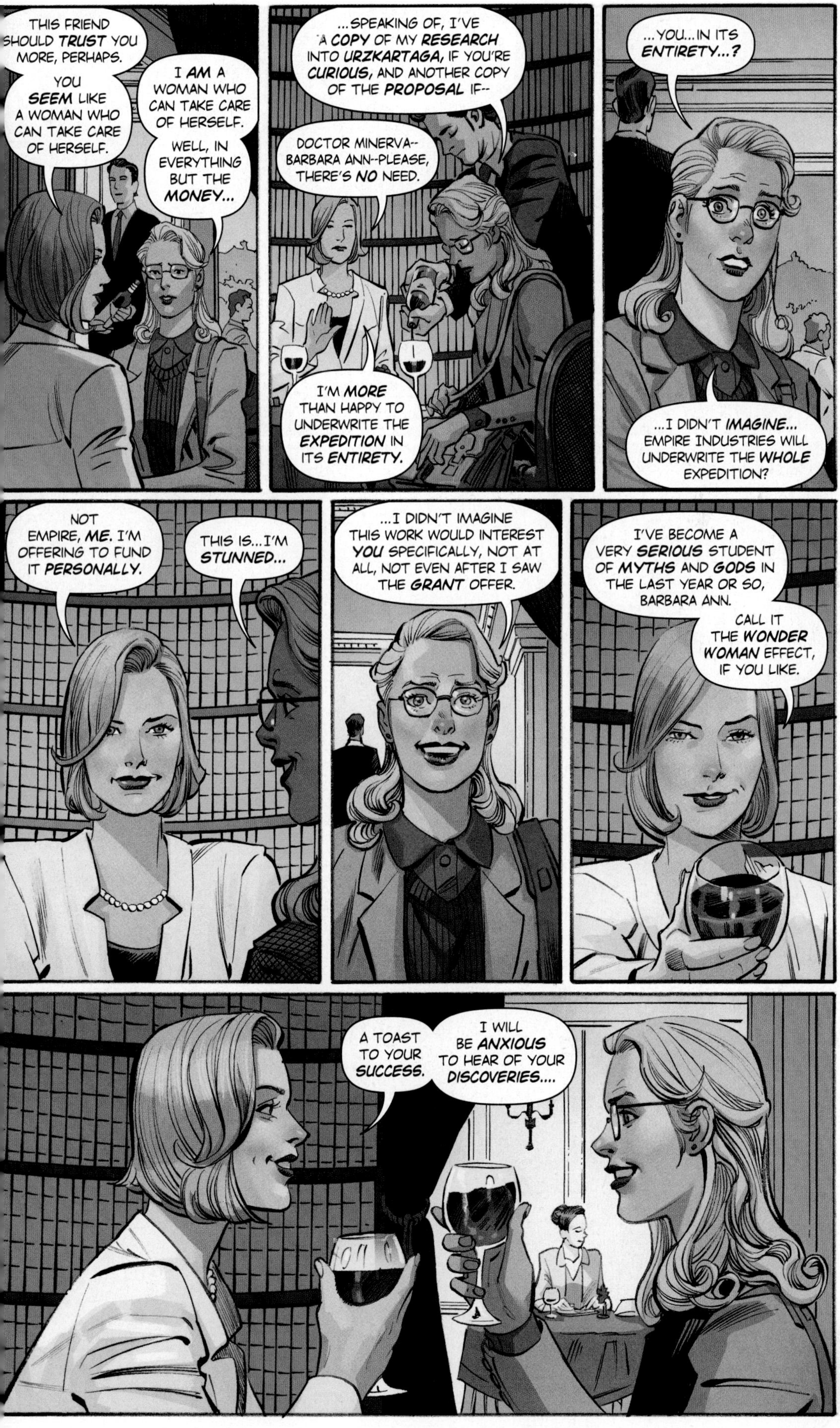
THIS FRIEND SHOULD TRUST YOU MORE, PERHAPS.
YOU SEEM LIKE A WOMAN WHO CAN TAKE CARE OF HERSELF.
I AM A WOMAN WHO CAN TAKE CARE OF HERSELF.
WELL, IN EVERYTHING BUT THE MONEY...
...SPEAKING OF, I'VE A COPY OF MY RESEARCH INTO URZKARTAGA, IF YOU'RE CURIOUS, AND ANOTHER COPY OF THE PROPOSAL IF--
DOCTOR MINERVA--BARBARA ANN--PLEASE, THERE'S NO NEED.
I'M MORE THAN HAPPY TO UNDERWRITE THE EXPEDITION IN ITS ENTIRETY.
...YOU...IN ITS ENTIRETY...?
...I DIDN'T IMAGINE... EMPIRE INDUSTRIES WILL UNDERWRITE THE WHOLE EXPEDITION?
NOT EMPIRE, ME. I'M OFFERING TO FUND IT PERSONALLY.
THIS IS...I'M STUNNED...
...I DIDN'T IMAGINE THIS WORK WOULD INTEREST YOU SPECIFICALLY, NOT AT ALL, NOT EVEN AFTER I SAW THE GRANT OFFER.
I'VE BECOME A VERY SERIOUS STUDENT OF MYTHS AND GODS IN THE LAST YEAR OR SO, BARBARA ANN.
CALL IT THE WONDER WOMAN EFFECT, IF YOU LIKE.
A TOAST TO YOUR SUCCESS.
I WILL BE ANXIOUS TO HEAR OF YOUR DISCOVERIES....

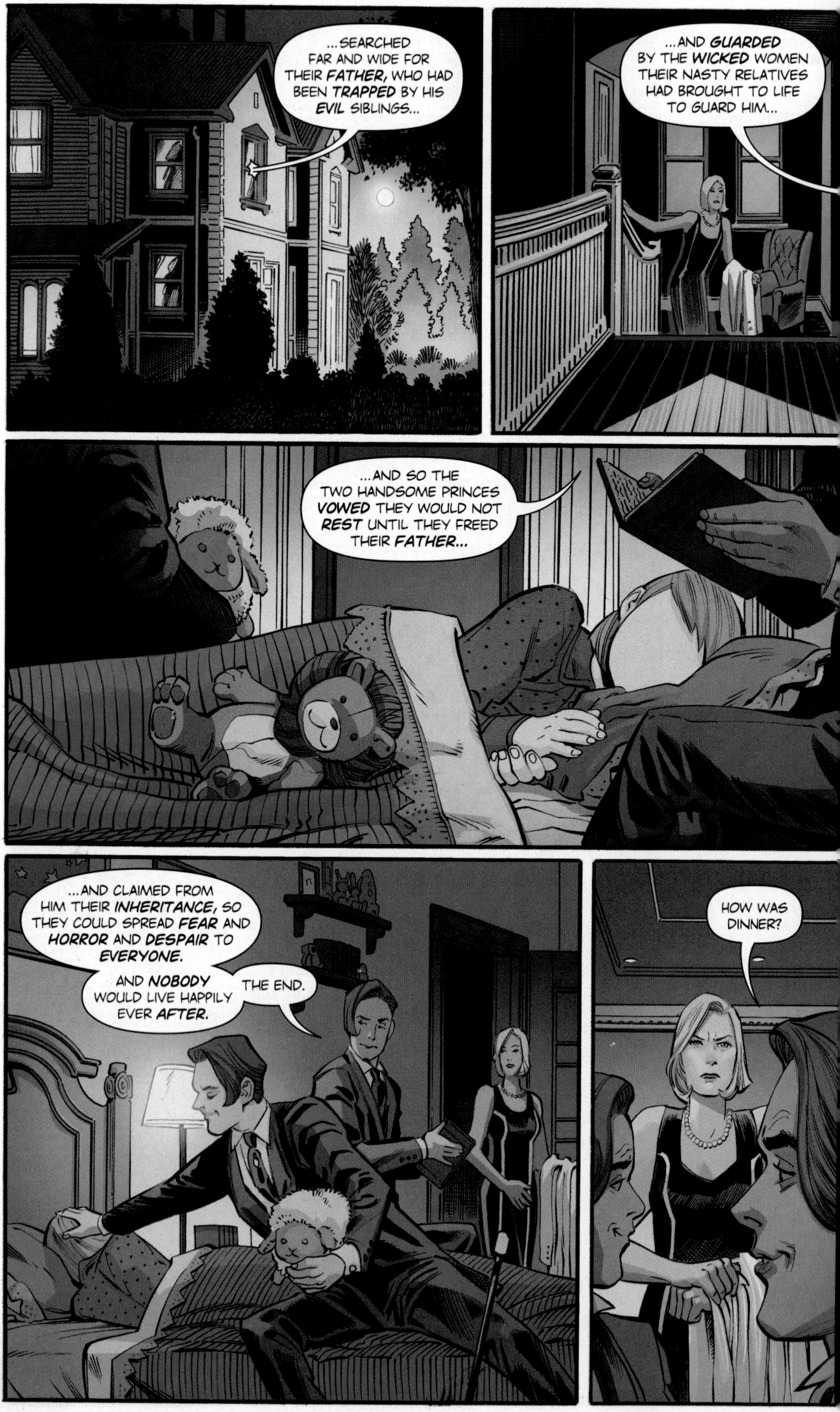
...SEARCHED FAR AND WIDE FOR THEIR FATHER, WHO HAD BEEN TRAPPED BY HIS EVIL SIBLINGS...
...AND GUARDED BY THE WICKED WOMEN THEIR NASTY RELATIVES HAD BROUGHT TO LIFE TO GUARD HIM...
...AND SO THE TWO HANDSOME PRINCES VOWED THEY WOULD NOT REST UNTIL THEY FREED THEIR FATHER...
...AND CLAIMED FROM HIM THEIR INHERITANCE, SO THEY COULD SPREAD FEAR AND HORROR AND DESPAIR TO EVERYONE.
AND NOBODY WOULD LIVE HAPPILY EVER AFTER.
THE END.
HOW WAS DINNER?

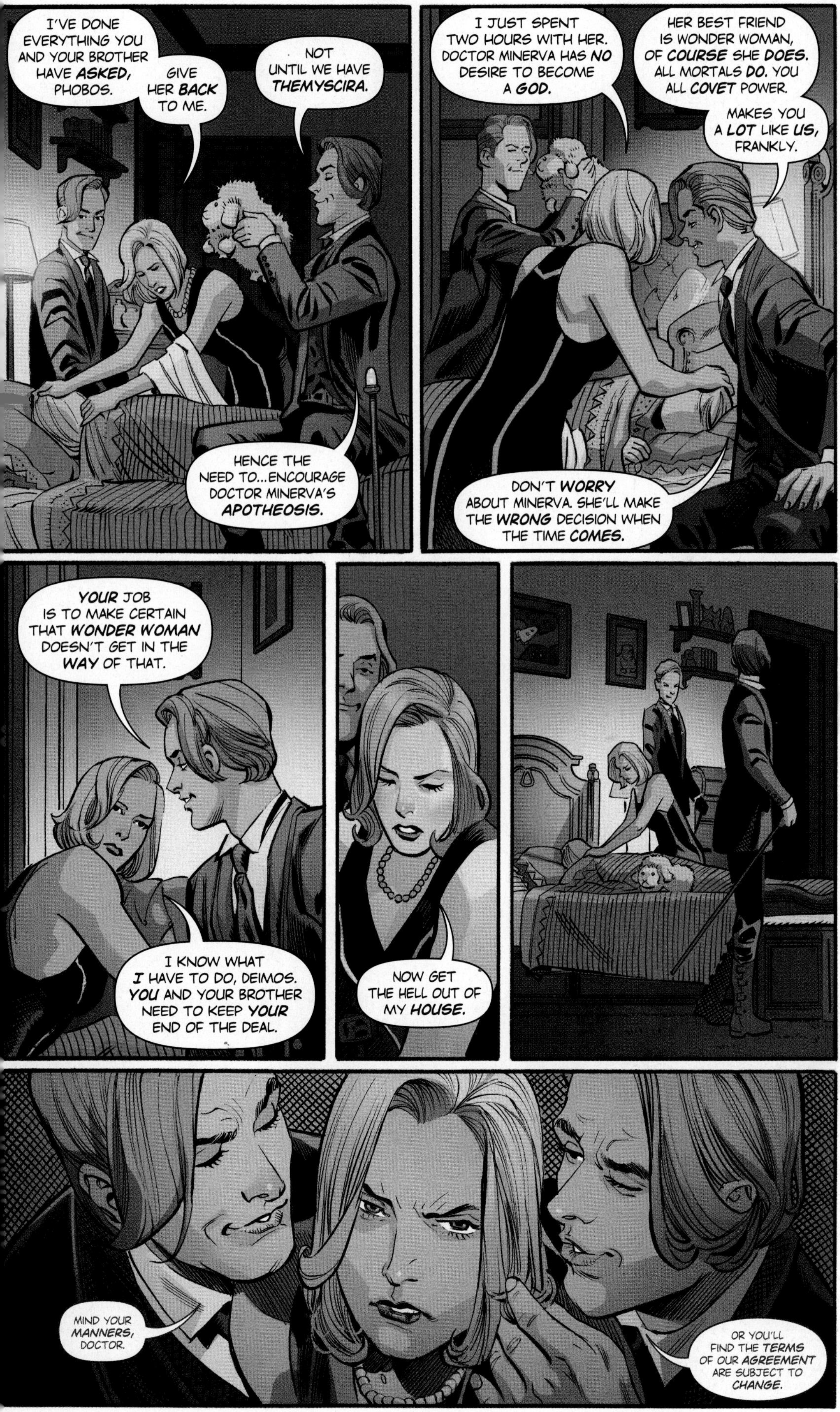
I'VE DONE EVERYTHING YOU AND YOUR BROTHER HAVE ASKED, PHOBOS.
GIVE HER BACK TO ME.
NOT UNTIL WE HAVE THEMYSCIRA.
HENCE THE NEED TO...ENCOURAGE DOCTOR MINERVA'S APOTHEOSIS.
I JUST SPENT TWO HOURS WITH HER. DOCTOR MINERVA HAS NO DESIRE TO BECOME A GOD.
HER BEST FRIEND IS WONDER WOMAN, OF COURSE SHE DOES. ALL MORTALS DO. YOU ALL COVET POWER.
MAKES YOU A LOT LIKE US, FRANKLY.
DON'T WORRY ABOUT MINERVA. SHE'LL MAKE THE WRONG DECISION WHEN THE TIME COMES.
YOUR JOB IS TO MAKE CERTAIN THAT WONDER WOMAN DOESN'T GET IN THE WAY OF THAT.
I KNOW WHAT I HAVE TO DO, DEIMOS. YOU AND YOUR BROTHER NEED TO KEEP YOUR END OF THE DEAL.
NOW GET THE HELL OUT OF MY HOUSE.
MIND YOUR MANNERS, DOCTOR.
OR YOU'LL FIND THE TERMS OF OUR AGREEMENT ARE SUBJECT TO CHANGE.

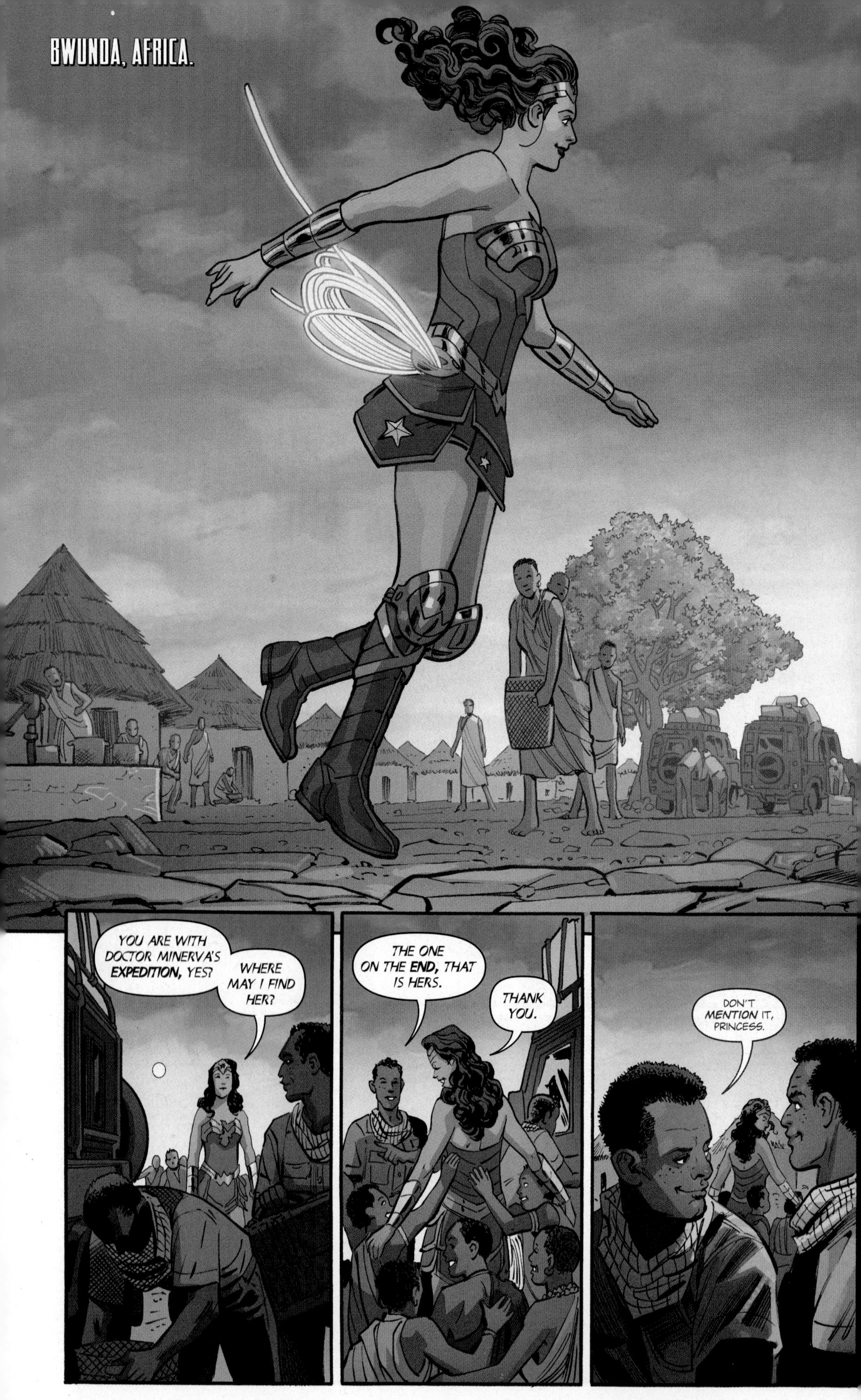
BWUNDA, AFRICA.
YOU ARE WITH DOCTOR MINERVA'S EXPEDITION, YES?
WHERE MAY I FIND HER?
THE ONE ON THE END, THAT IS HERS.
THANK YOU.
DON'T MENTION IT, PRINCESS.

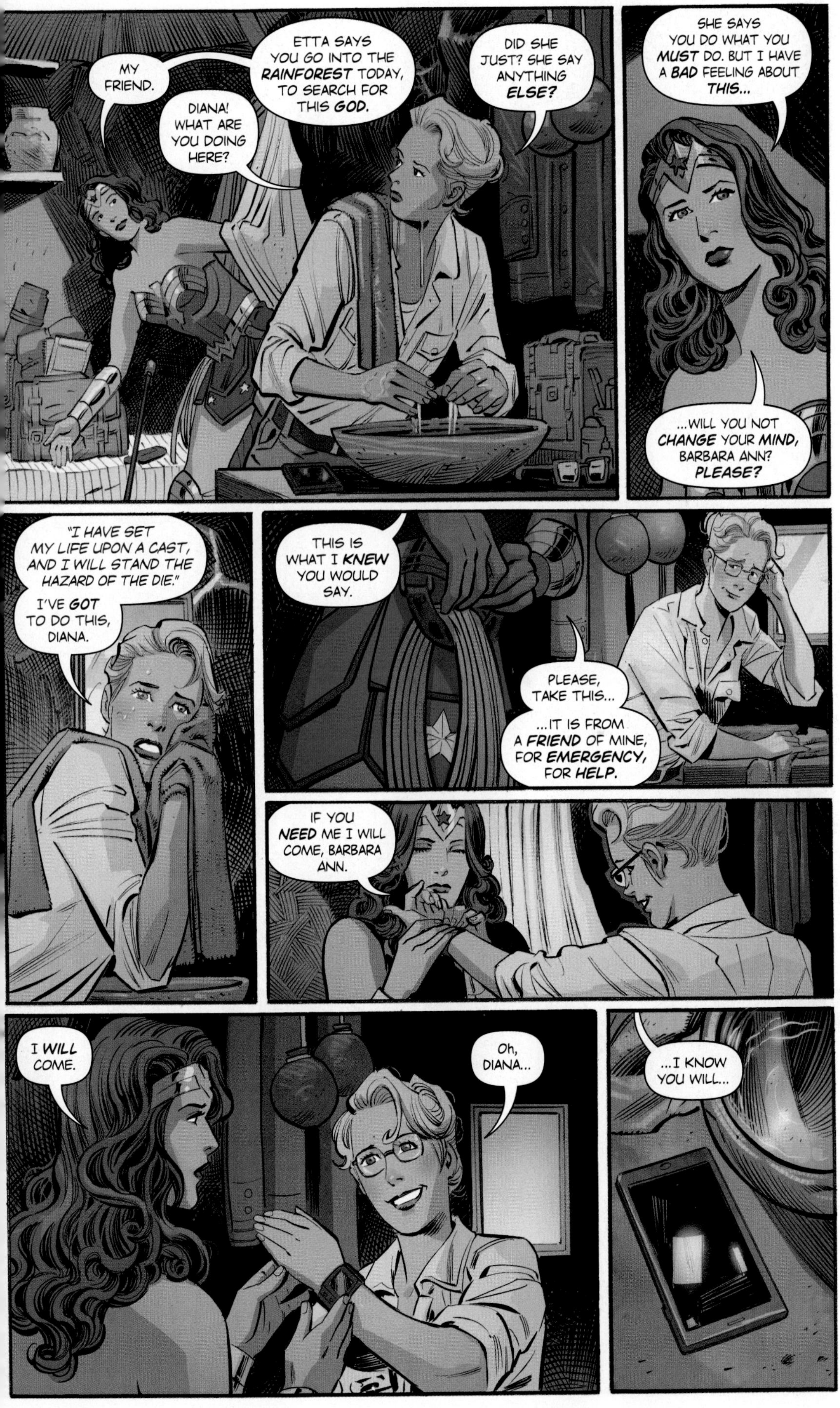
MY FRIEND.
DIANA! WHAT ARE YOU DOING HERE?
ETTA SAYS YOU GO INTO THE RAINFOREST TODAY, TO SEARCH FOR THIS GOD.
DID SHE JUST? SHE SAY ANYTHING ELSE?
SHE SAYS YOU DO WHAT YOU MUST DO. BUT I HAVE A BAD FEELING ABOUT THIS...
...WILL YOU NOT CHANGE YOUR MIND, BARBARA ANN? PLEASE?
"I HAVE SET MY LIFE UPON A CAST, AND I WILL STAND THE HAZARD OF THE DIE."
I'VE GOT TO DO THIS, DIANA.
THIS IS WHAT I KNEW YOU WOULD SAY.
PLEASE, TAKE THIS...
...IT IS FROM A FRIEND OF MINE, FOR EMERGENCY, FOR HELP.
IF YOU NEED ME I WILL COME, BARBARA ANN.
I WILL COME.
Oh, DIANA...
...I KNOW YOU WILL...

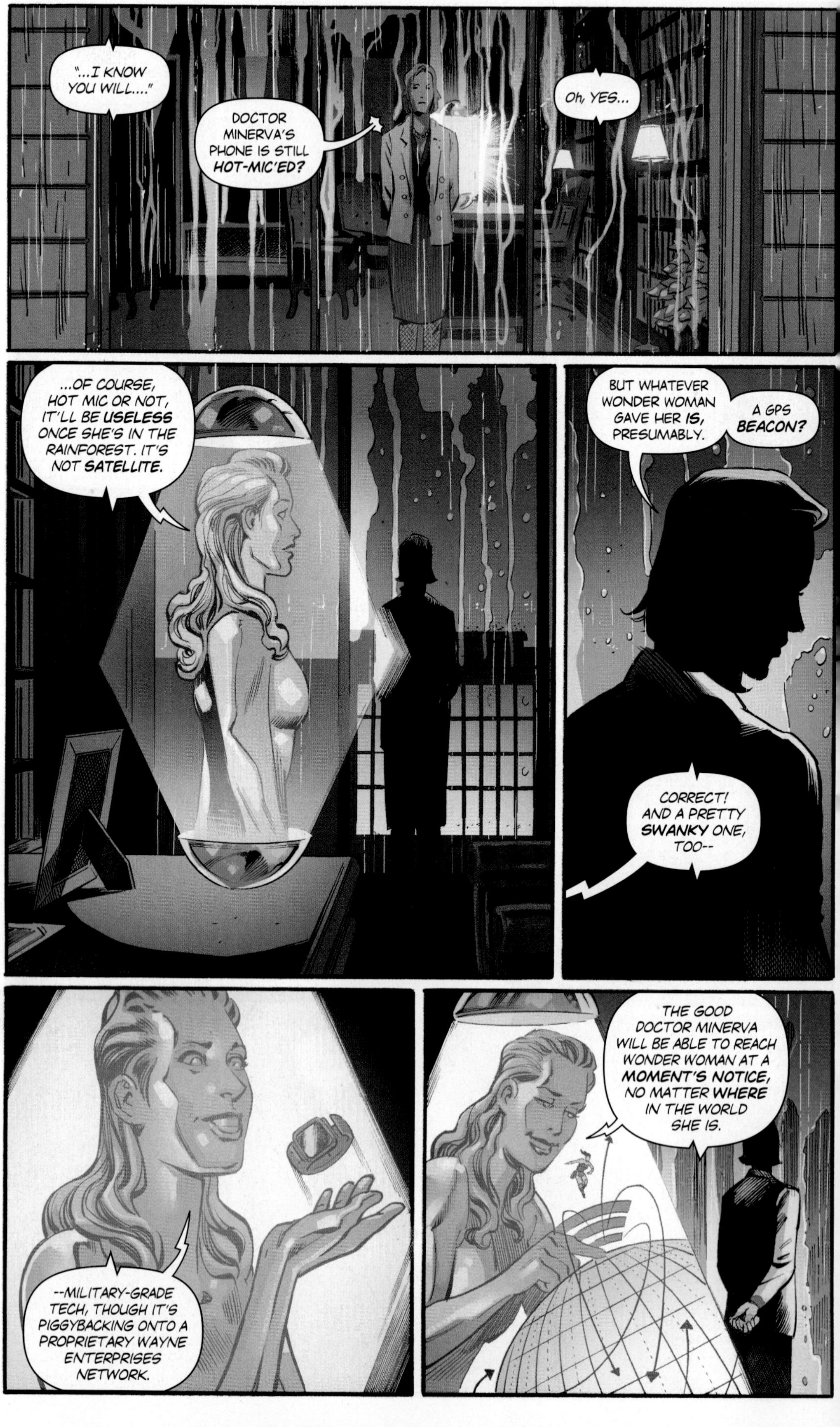
"...I KNOW YOU WILL..."
DOCTOR MINERVA'S PHONE IS STILL HOT-MIC'ED?
Oh, YES...
...OF COURSE, HOT MIC OR NOT, IT'LL BE USELESS ONCE SHE'S IN THE RAINFOREST. IT'S NOT SATELLITE.
BUT WHATEVER WONDER WOMAN GAVE HER IS, PRESUMABLY.
A GPS BEACON?
CORRECT! AND A PRETTY SWANKY ONE, TOO--
--MILITARY-GRADE TECH, THOUGH IT'S PIGGYBACKING ONTO A PROPRIETARY WAYNE ENTERPRISES NETWORK.
THE GOOD DOCTOR MINERVA WILL BE ABLE TO REACH WONDER WOMAN AT A MOMENT'S NOTICE, NO MATTER WHERE IN THE WORLD SHE IS.

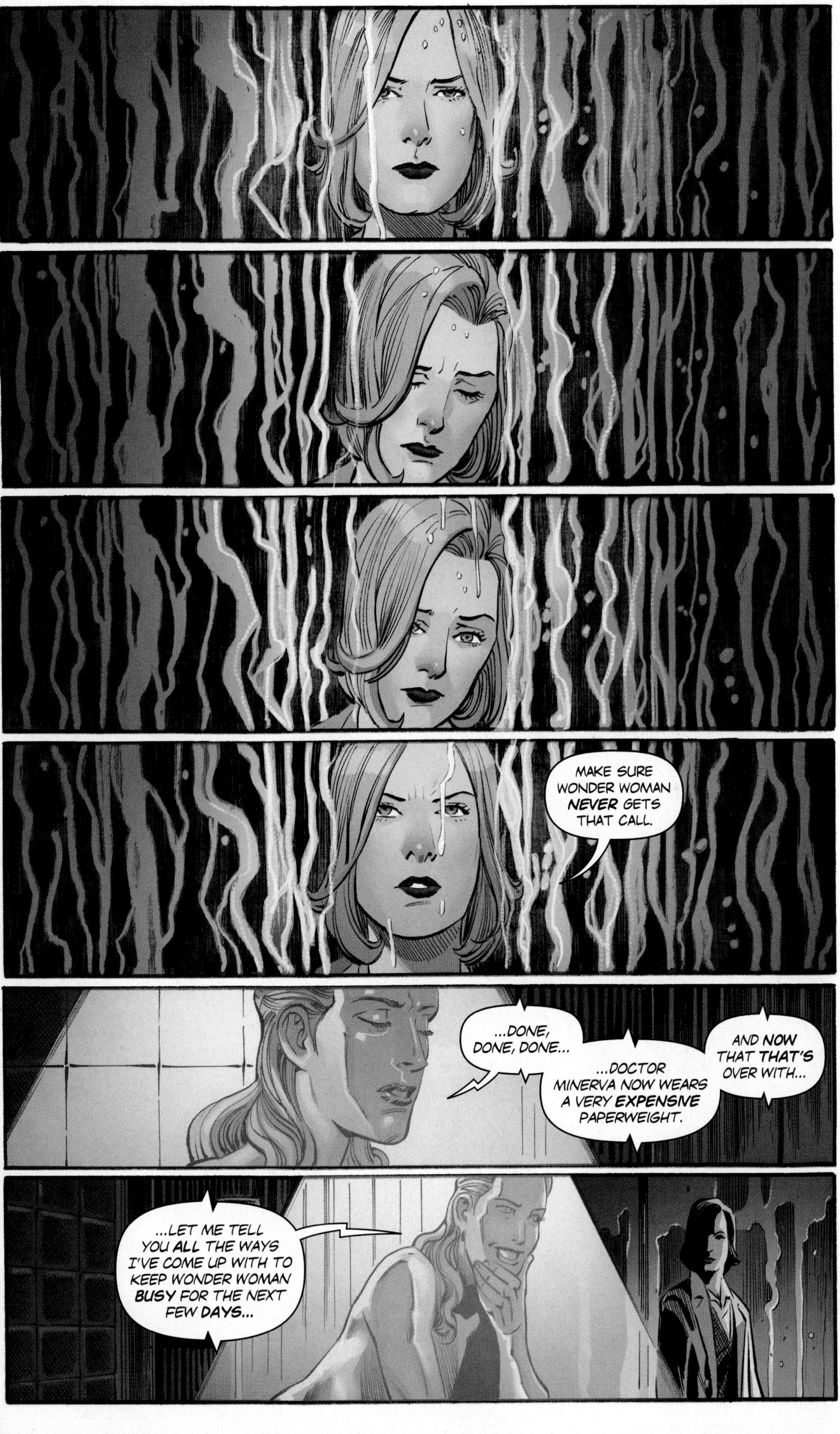

MAKE SURE WONDER WOMAN **NEVER** GETS THAT CALL.
...DONE, DONE, DONE...
...DOCTOR MINERVA NOW WEARS A VERY **EXPENSIVE** PAPERWEIGHT.
AND **NOW** THAT **THAT'S** OVER WITH...
...LET ME TELL YOU **ALL** THE WAYS I'VE COME UP WITH TO KEEP WONDER WOMAN **BUSY** FOR THE NEXT FEW **DAYS**...

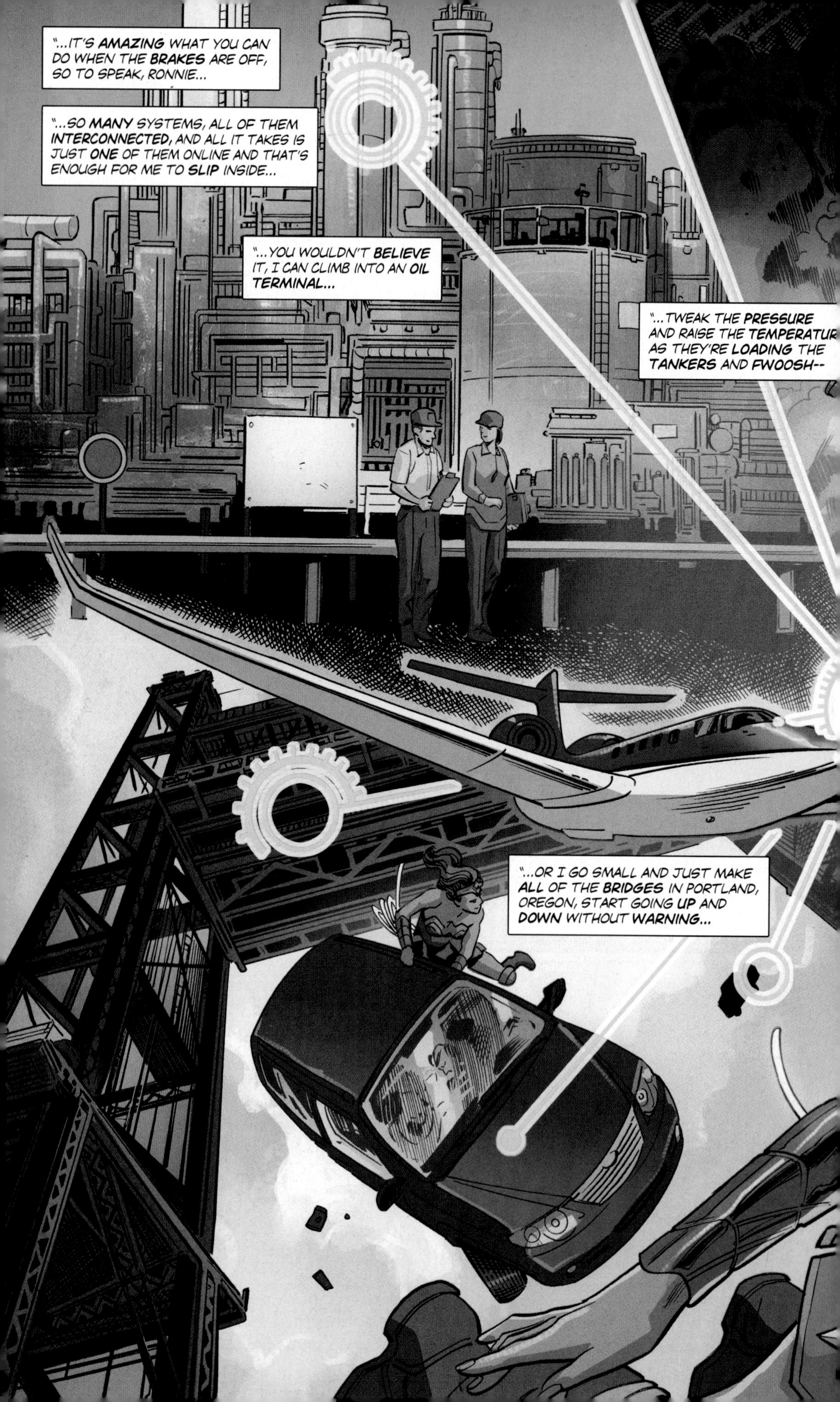

"...IT'S AMAZING WHAT YOU CAN DO WHEN THE BRAKES ARE OFF, SO TO SPEAK, RONNIE...
"...SO MANY SYSTEMS, ALL OF THEM INTERCONNECTED, AND ALL IT TAKES IS JUST ONE OF THEM ONLINE AND THAT'S ENOUGH FOR ME TO SLIP INSIDE...
"...YOU WOULDN'T BELIEVE IT, I CAN CLIMB INTO AN OIL TERMINAL...
"...TWEAK THE PRESSURE AND RAISE THE TEMPERATUR AS THEY'RE LOADING THE TANKERS AND FWOOSH--
"...OR I GO SMALL AND JUST MAKE ALL OF THE BRIDGES IN PORTLAND, OREGON, START GOING UP AND DOWN WITHOUT WARNING...

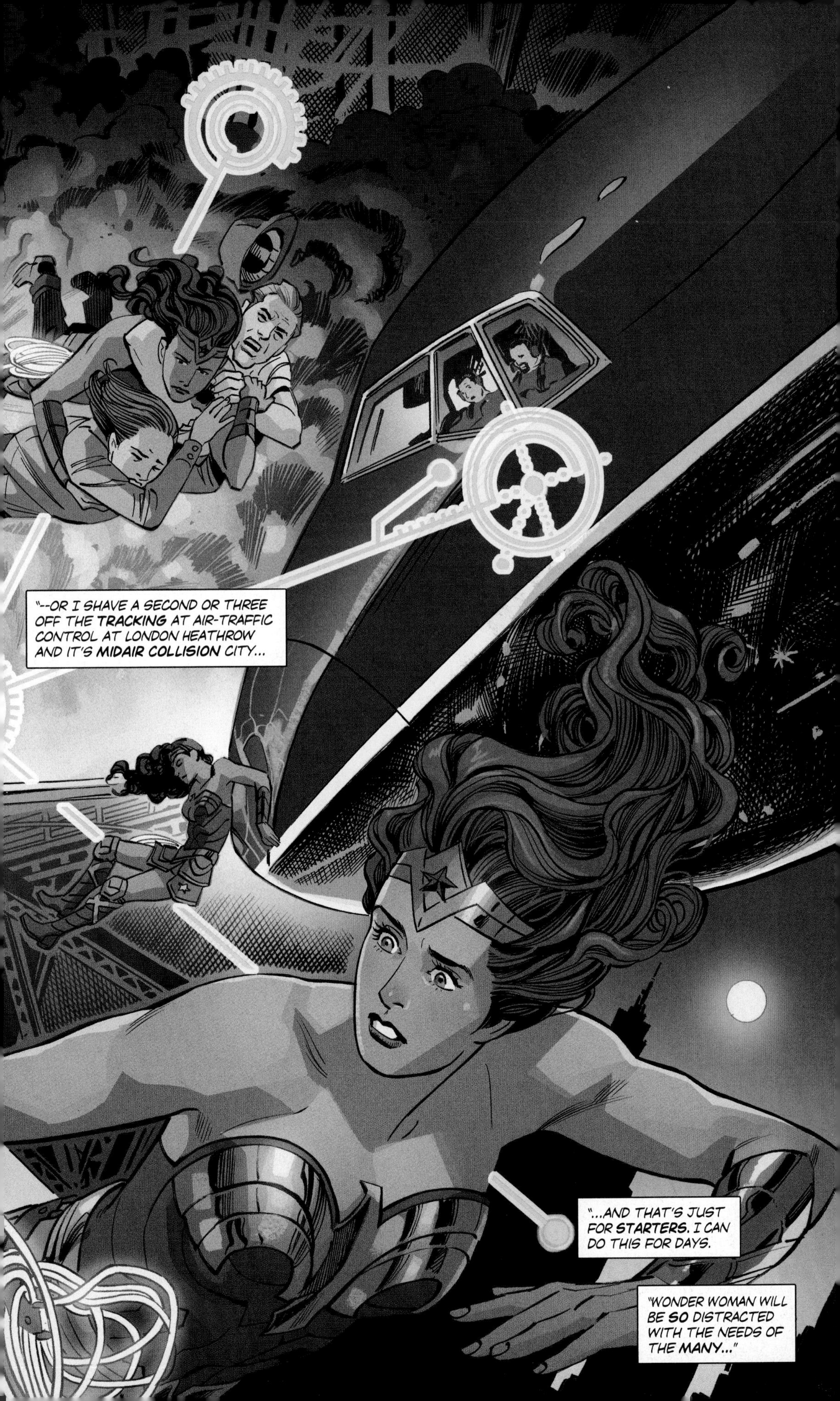
"--OR I SHAVE A SECOND OR THREE OFF THE TRACKING AT AIR-TRAFFIC CONTROL AT LONDON HEATHROW AND IT'S MIDAIR COLLISION CITY...
"...AND THAT'S JUST FOR STARTERS. I CAN DO THIS FOR DAYS.
"WONDER WOMAN WILL BE SO DISTRACTED WITH THE NEEDS OF THE MANY..."

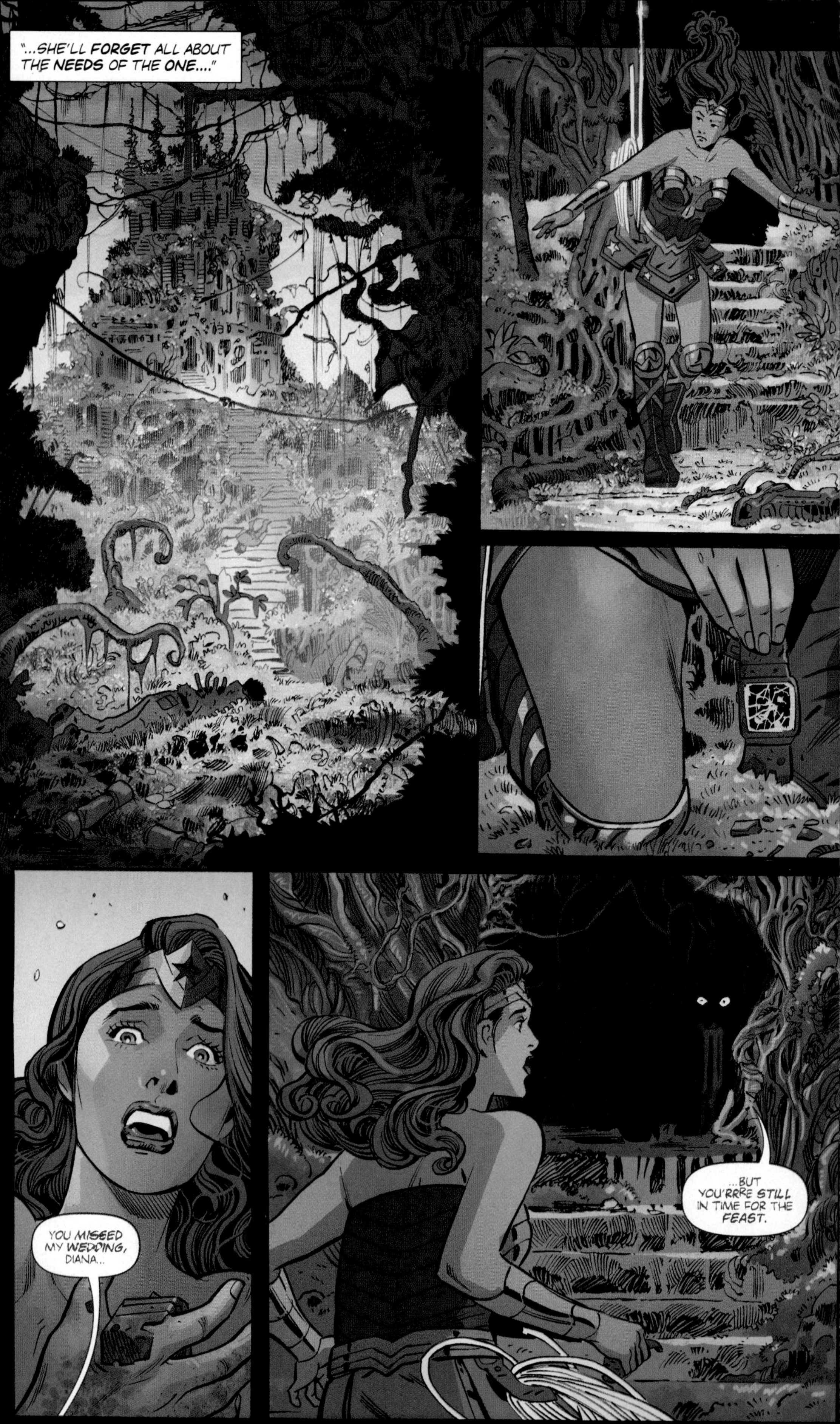
"...SHE'LL FORGET ALL ABOUT THE NEEDS OF THE ONE...."
YOU MISEED MY WEDDING, DIANA...
...BUT YOU'RRRE STILL IN TIME FOR THE FEAST.

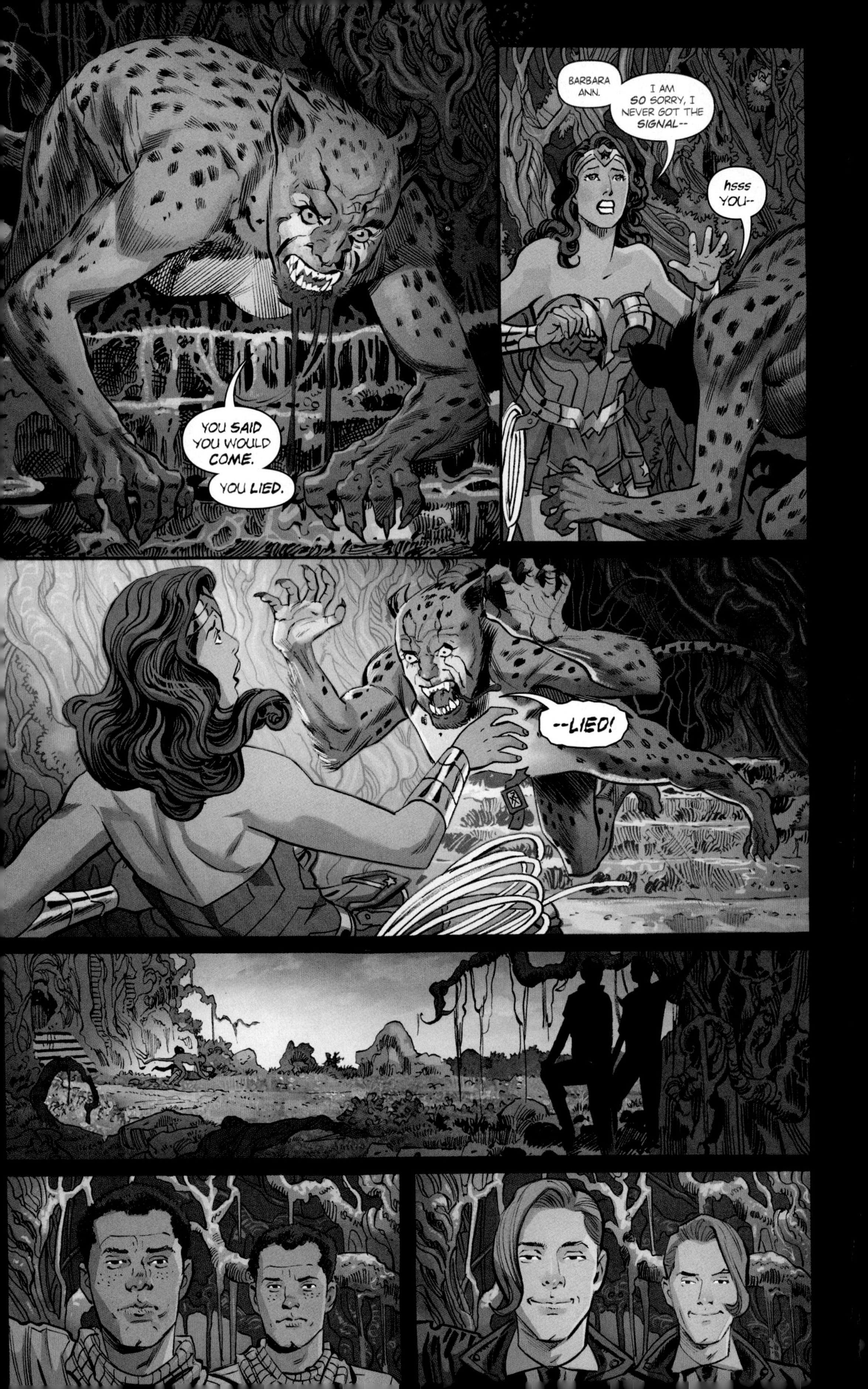
YOU SAID YOU WOULD COME.
YOU LIED.
BARBARA ANN.
I AM SO SORRY, I NEVER GOT THE SIGNAL--
hsss YOU--
--LIED!

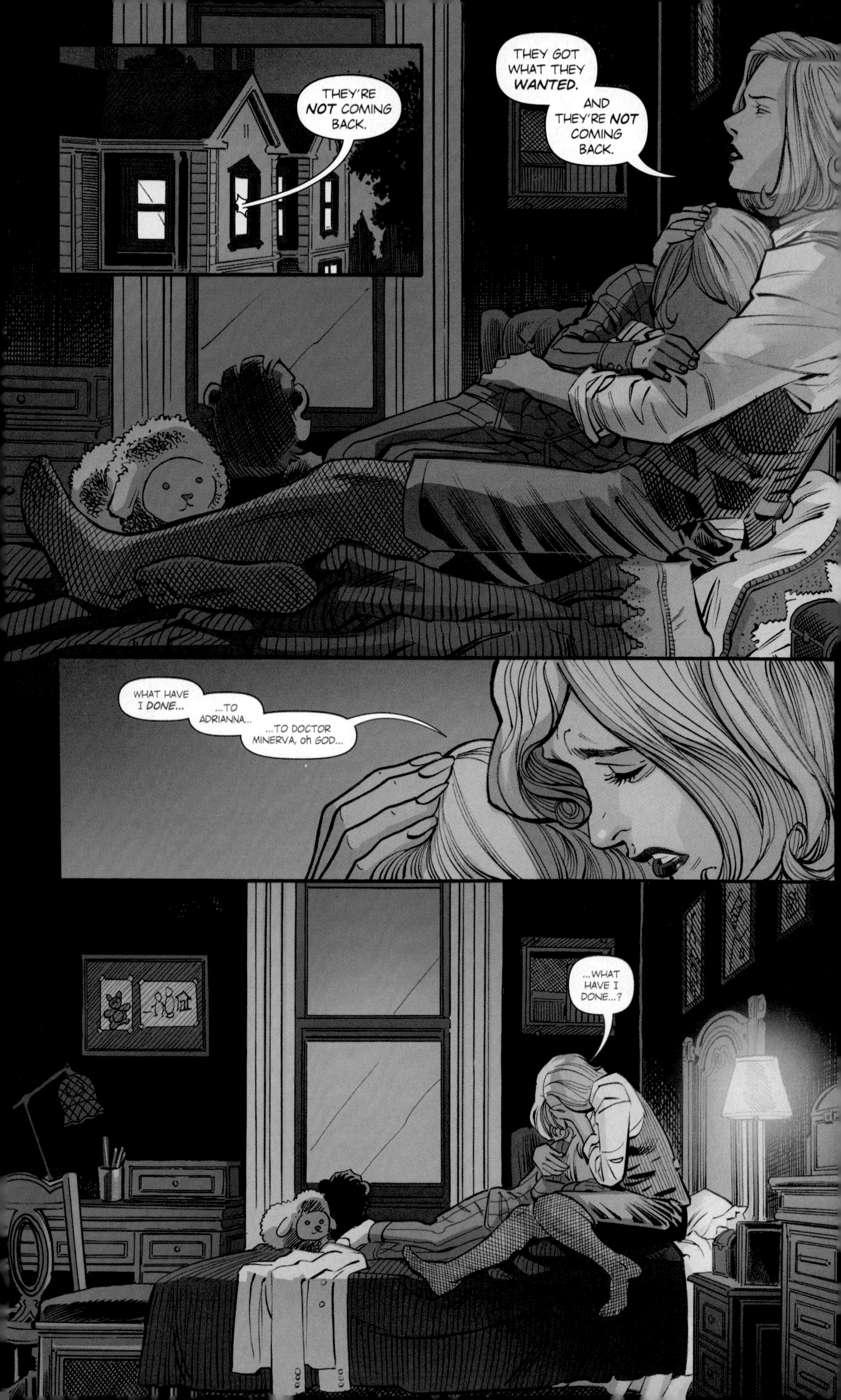
THEY'RE NOT COMING BACK.
THEY GOT WHAT THEY WANTED.
AND THEY'RE NOT COMING BACK.
WHAT HAVE I DONE...
...TO ADRIANNA...
...TO DOCTOR MINERVA, oh GOD...
...WHAT HAVE I DONE...?

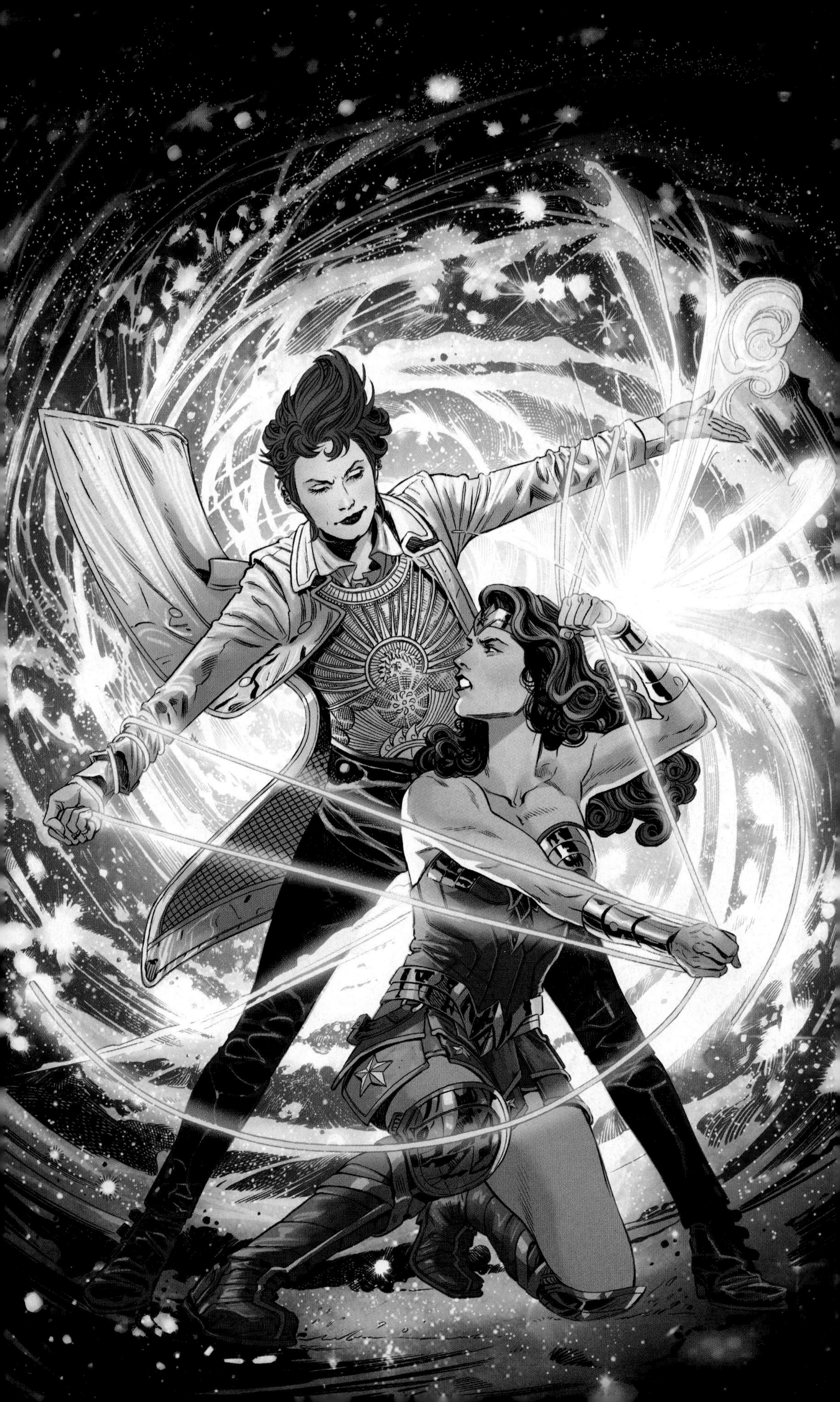

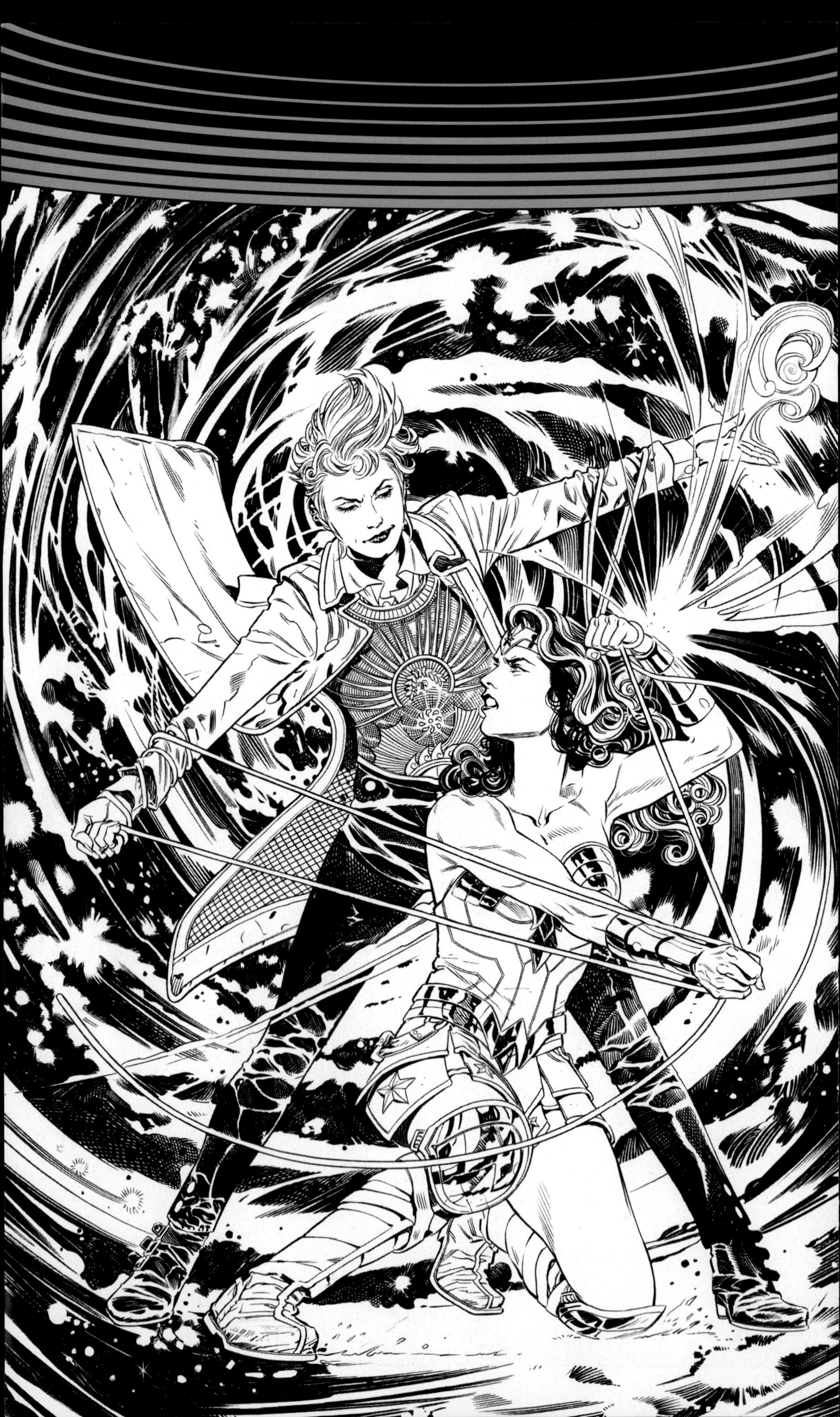

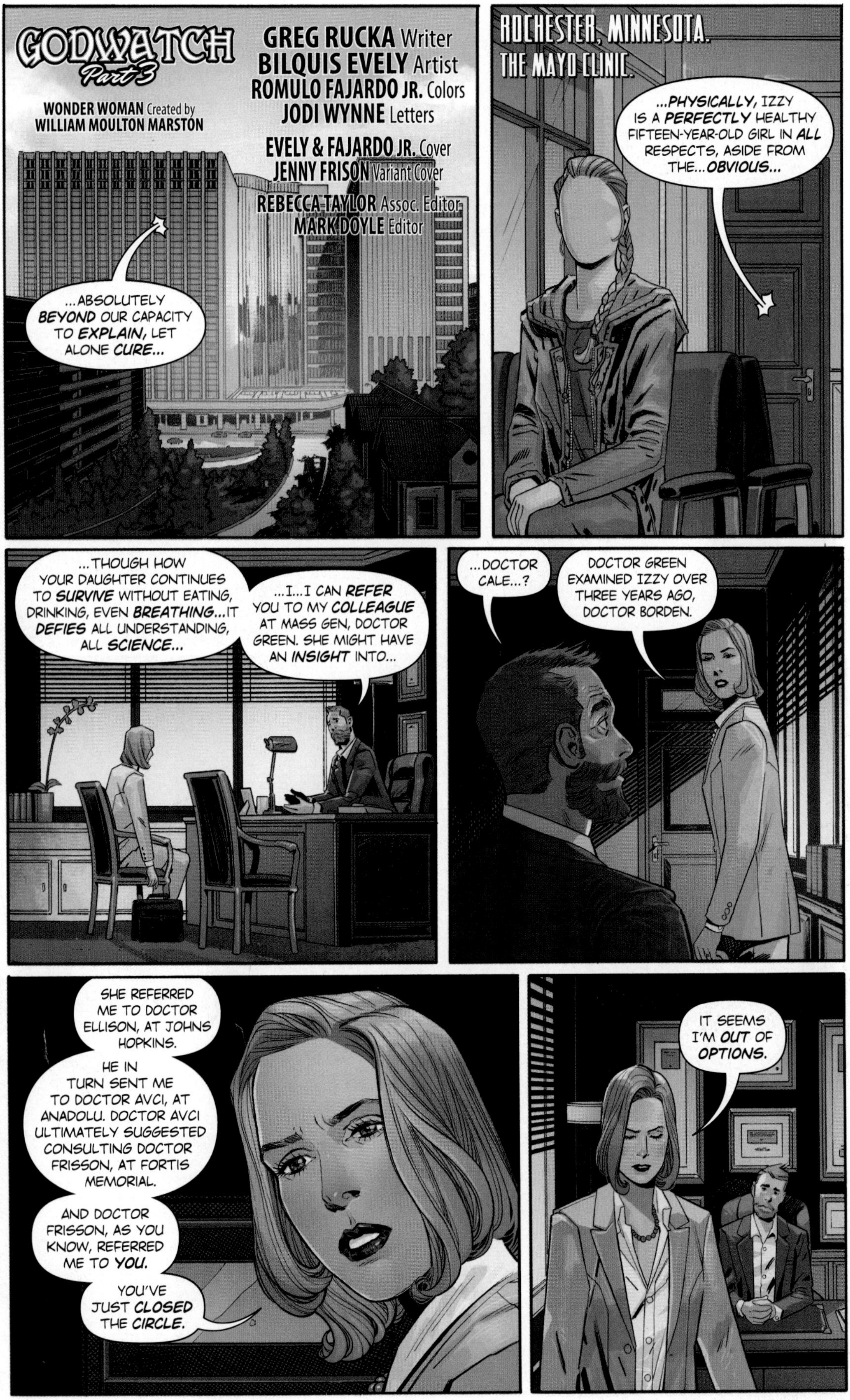
GODWATCH Part 3
GREG RUCKA Writer
BILQUIS EVELY Artist
ROMULO FAJARDO JR. Colors
JODI WYNNE Letters
WONDER WOMAN Created by WILLIAM MOULTON MARSTON
EVELY & FAJARDO JR. Cover
JENNY FRISON Variant Cover
REBECCA TAYLOR Assoc. Editor
MARK DOYLE Editor
ROCHESTER, MINNESOTA. THE MAYO CLINIC.
...PHYSICALLY, IZZY IS A PERFECTLY HEALTHY FIFTEEN-YEAR-OLD GIRL IN ALL RESPECTS, ASIDE FROM THE...OBVIOUS...
...ABSOLUTELY BEYOND OUR CAPACITY TO EXPLAIN, LET ALONE CURE...
...THOUGH HOW YOUR DAUGHTER CONTINUES TO SURVIVE WITHOUT EATING, DRINKING, EVEN BREATHING...IT DEFIES ALL UNDERSTANDING, ALL SCIENCE...
...I...I CAN REFER YOU TO MY COLLEAGUE AT MASS GEN, DOCTOR GREEN. SHE MIGHT HAVE AN INSIGHT INTO...
...DOCTOR CALE...?
DOCTOR GREEN EXAMINED IZZY OVER THREE YEARS AGO, DOCTOR BORDEN.
SHE REFERRED ME TO DOCTOR ELLISON, AT JOHNS HOPKINS.
HE IN TURN SENT ME TO DOCTOR AVCI, AT ANADOLU. DOCTOR AVCI ULTIMATELY SUGGESTED CONSULTING DOCTOR FRISSON, AT FORTIS MEMORIAL.
AND DOCTOR FRISSON, AS YOU KNOW, REFERRED ME TO YOU.
YOU'VE JUST CLOSED THE CIRCLE.
IT SEEMS I'M OUT OF OPTIONS.

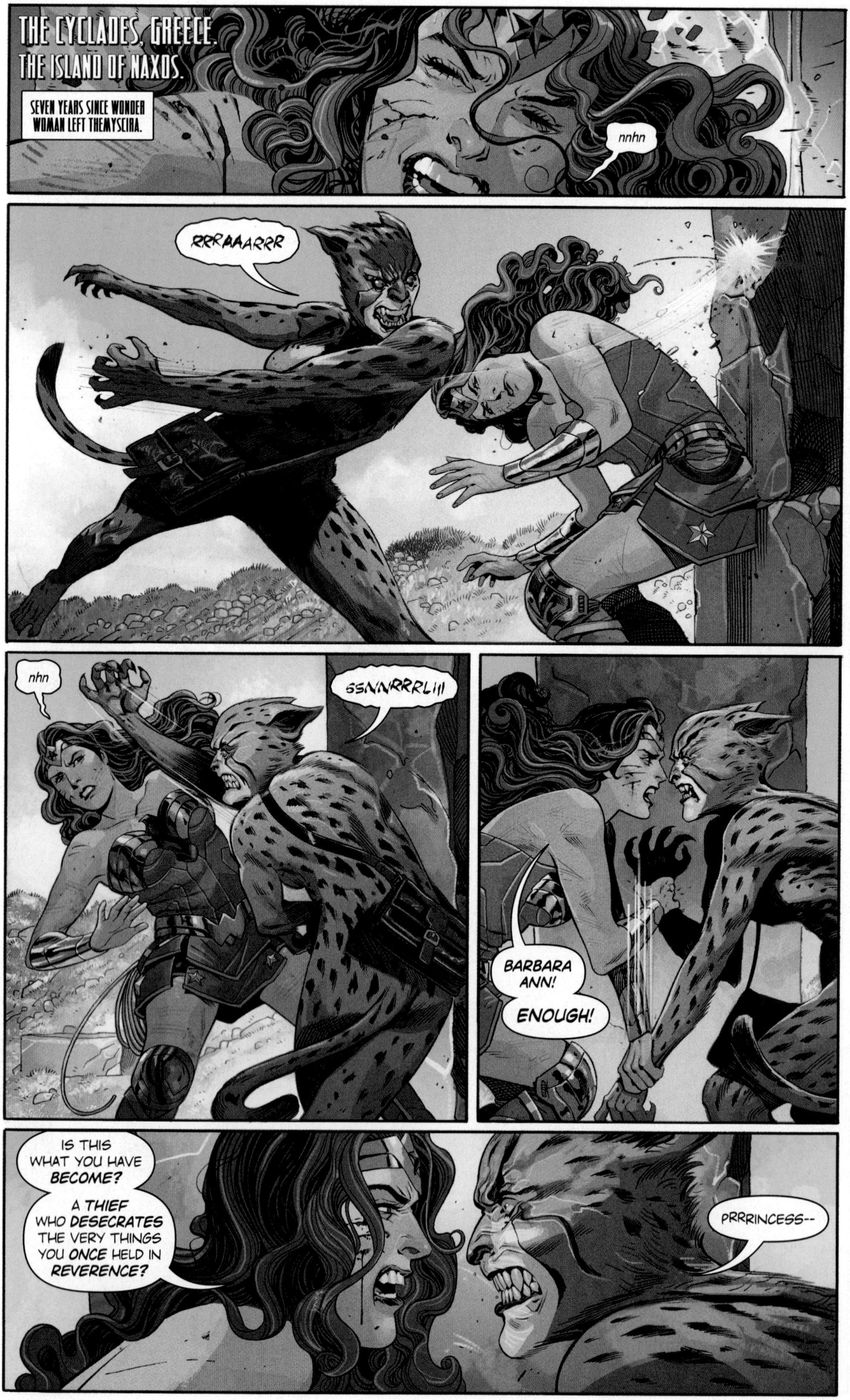
THE CYCLADES, GREECE.
THE ISLAND OF NAXOS.
SEVEN YEARS SINCE WONDER WOMAN LEFT THEMYSCIRA.
nnhn
RRRAAARRR
nhn
SSNNRRRLII
BARBARA ANN!
ENOUGH!
IS THIS WHAT YOU HAVE BECOME?
A THIEF WHO DESECRATES THE VERY THINGS YOU ONCE HELD IN REVERENCE?
PRRRINCESS--

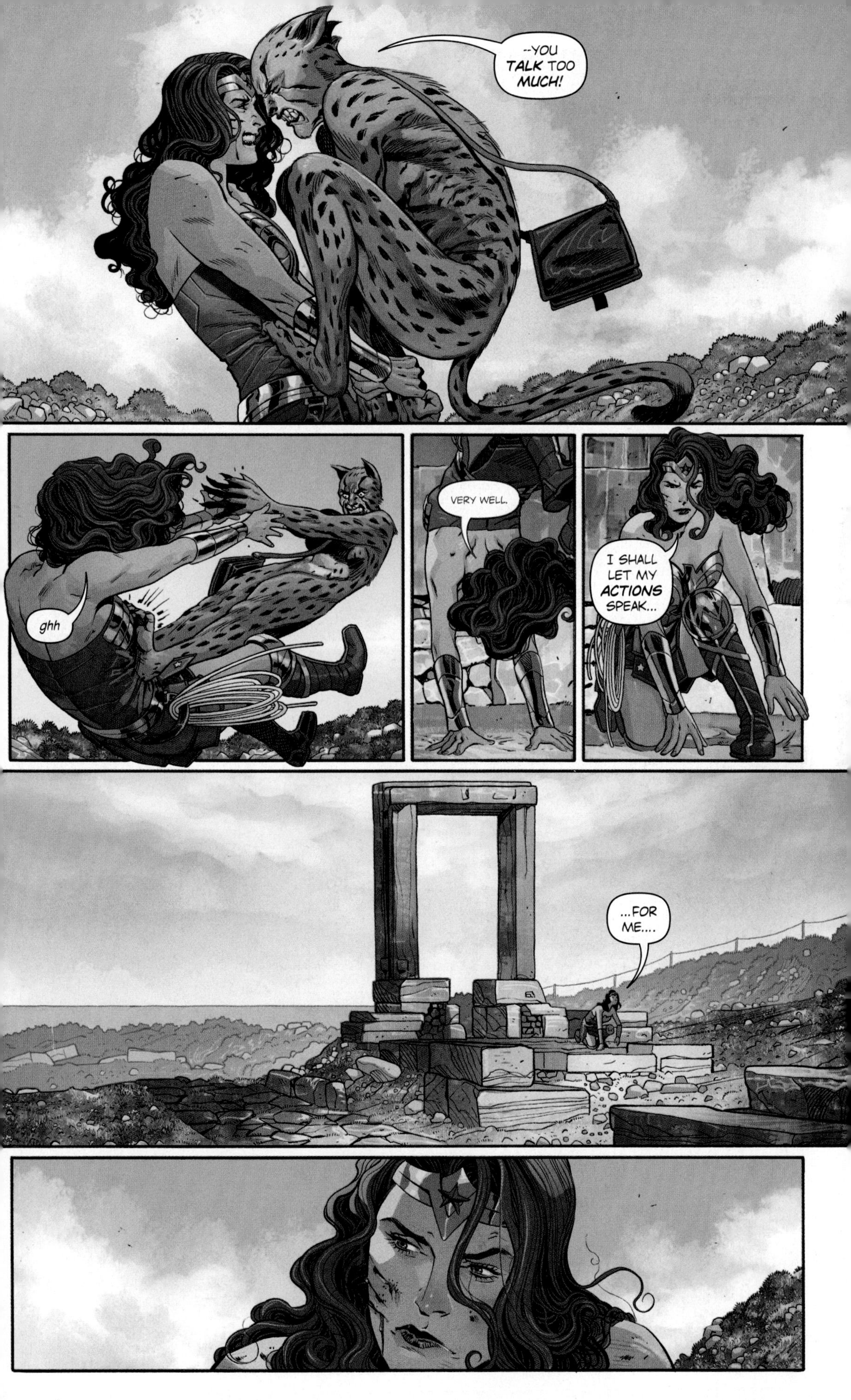
--YOU TALK TOO MUCH!
ghh
VERY WELL.
I SHALL LET MY ACTIONS SPEAK...
...FOR ME....

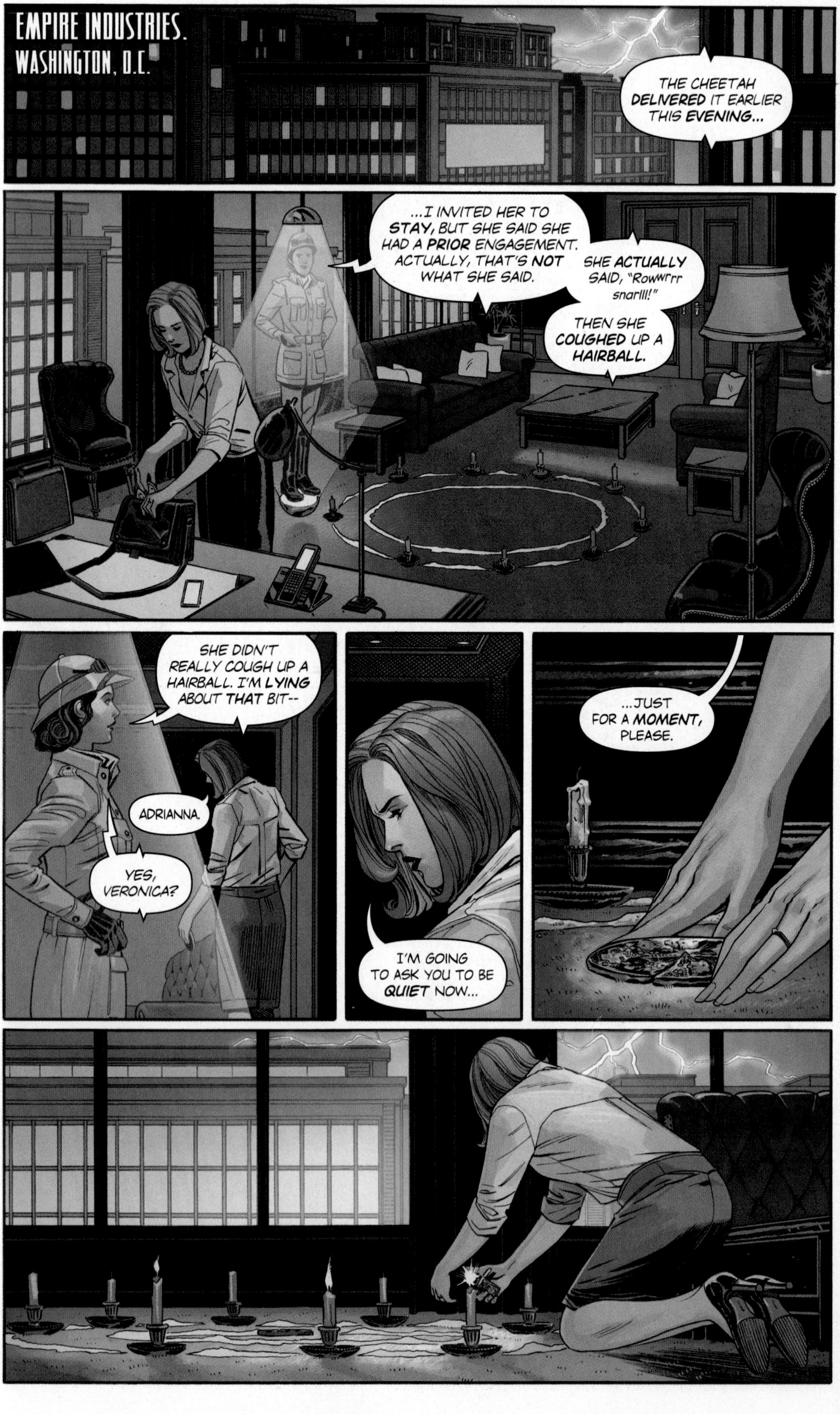
EMPIRE INDUSTRIES. WASHINGTON, D.C.
THE CHEETAH DELIVERED IT EARLIER THIS EVENING...
...I INVITED HER TO STAY, BUT SHE SAID SHE HAD A PRIOR ENGAGEMENT. ACTUALLY, THAT'S NOT WHAT SHE SAID.
SHE ACTUALLY SAID, "Rowwrrr snarlll!"
THEN SHE COUGHED UP A HAIRBALL.
SHE DIDN'T REALLY COUGH UP A HAIRBALL. I'M LYING ABOUT THAT BIT--
ADRIANNA.
YES, VERONICA?
I'M GOING TO ASK YOU TO BE QUIET NOW...
...JUST FOR A MOMENT, PLEASE.

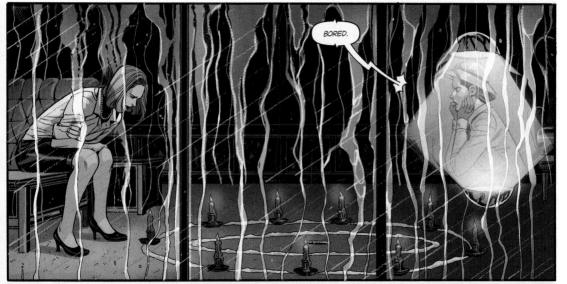

BORED.

BORED BORED BORED BORED BORED.

BORED.

WE'VE BEEN **RESEARCHING** THIS FOR **YEARS**.

WHAT DID WE DO **WRONG?**

WE DIDN'T DO **ANYTHING** WRONG, RONNIE!

THIS **SHOULD** BE WORKING, THIS **SHOULD** DO IT! THE CANDLES, THE **SALT**, THE **DIRT**, THE SACRED **SEAL**, HIDDEN IN THE LOST TEMPLE OF APOLLO...

...EVERYTHING I **LEARNED**, THIS IS **HOW** YOU'RE SUPPOSED TO **SUMMON HER!**

OR, ALTERNATIVELY, YOU COULD'VE JUST, Y'KNOW, **PICKED** UP THE **PHONE**...

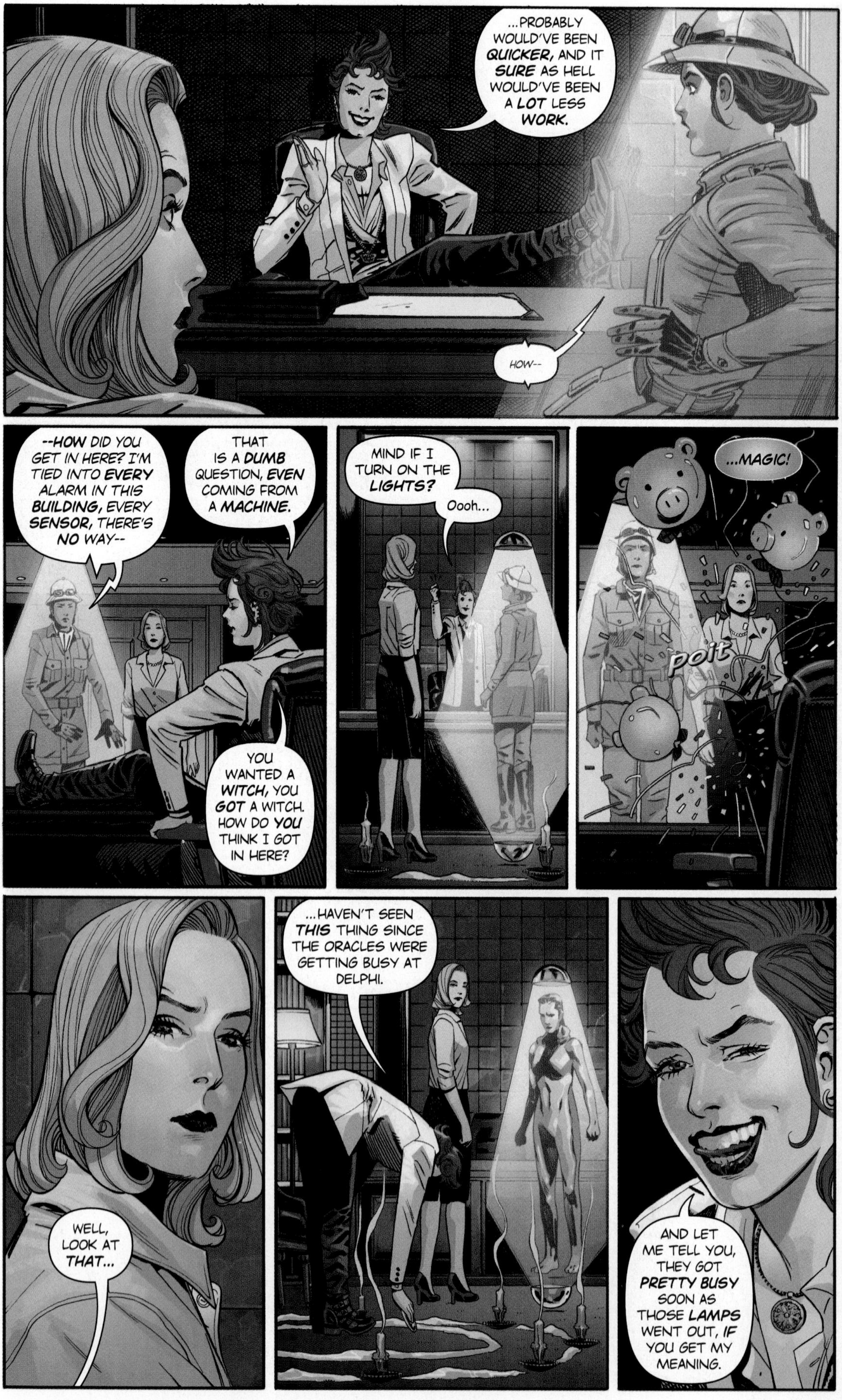

...PROBABLY WOULD'VE BEEN QUICKER, AND IT SURE AS HELL WOULD'VE BEEN A LOT LESS WORK.
HOW--
--HOW DID YOU GET IN HERE? I'M TIED INTO EVERY ALARM IN THIS BUILDING, EVERY SENSOR, THERE'S NO WAY--
THAT IS A DUMB QUESTION, EVEN COMING FROM A MACHINE.
YOU WANTED A WITCH, YOU GOT A WITCH. HOW DO YOU THINK I GOT IN HERE?
MIND IF I TURN ON THE LIGHTS?
Oooh...
...MAGIC!
poit
WELL, LOOK AT THAT...
...HAVEN'T SEEN THIS THING SINCE THE ORACLES WERE GETTING BUSY AT DELPHI.
AND LET ME TELL YOU, THEY GOT PRETTY BUSY SOON AS THOSE LAMPS WENT OUT, IF YOU GET MY MEANING.

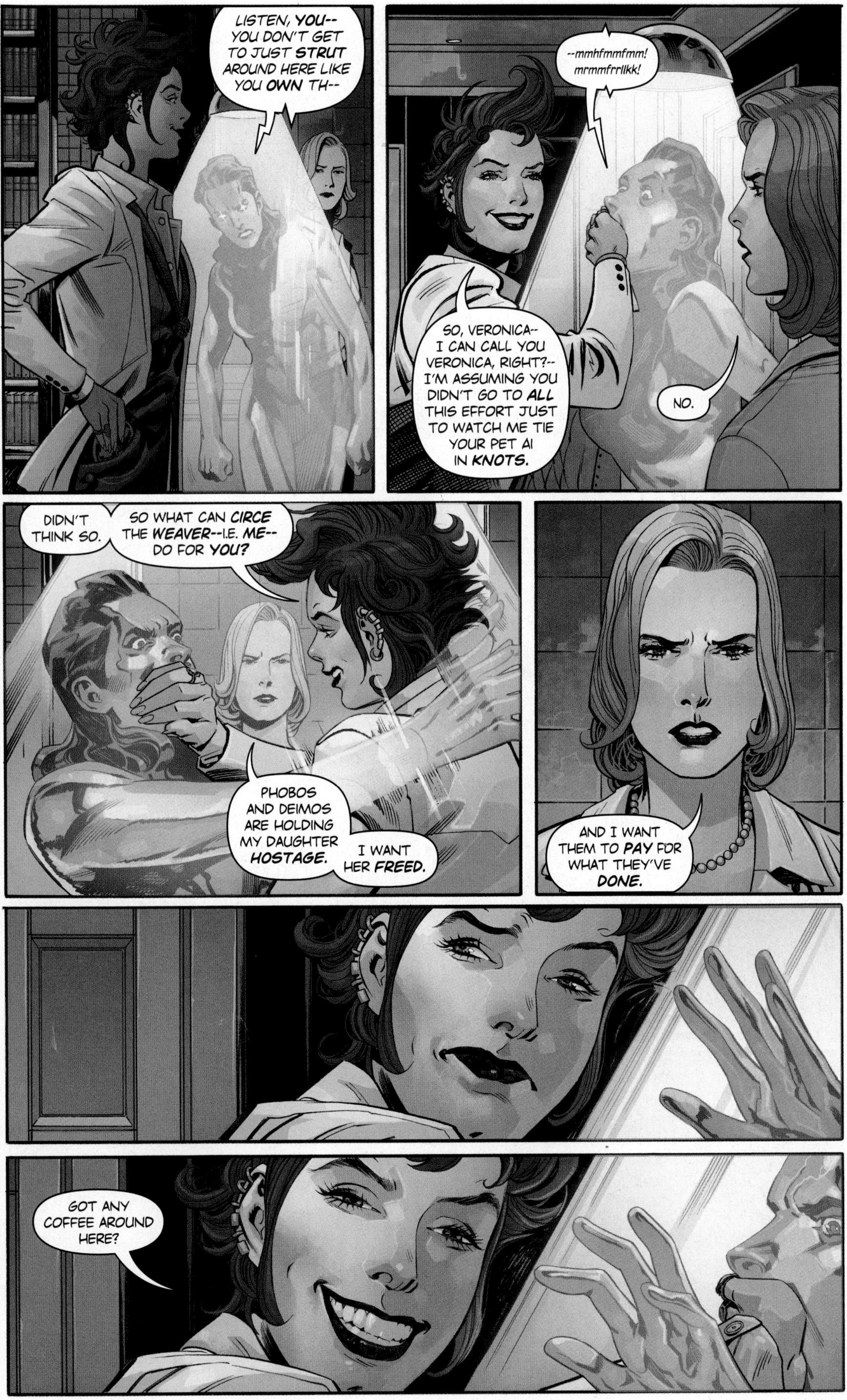
LISTEN, YOU--
YOU DON'T GET TO JUST STRUT AROUND HERE LIKE YOU OWN TH--
--mmhfmmfmm! mrmmfrrllkk!
SO, VERONICA-- I CAN CALL YOU VERONICA, RIGHT?-- I'M ASSUMING YOU DIDN'T GO TO ALL THIS EFFORT JUST TO WATCH ME TIE YOUR PET AI IN KNOTS.
NO.
DIDN'T THINK SO.
SO WHAT CAN CIRCE THE WEAVER--I.E. ME-- DO FOR YOU?
PHOBOS AND DEIMOS ARE HOLDING MY DAUGHTER HOSTAGE.
I WANT HER FREED.
AND I WANT THEM TO PAY FOR WHAT THEY'VE DONE.
GOT ANY COFFEE AROUND HERE?

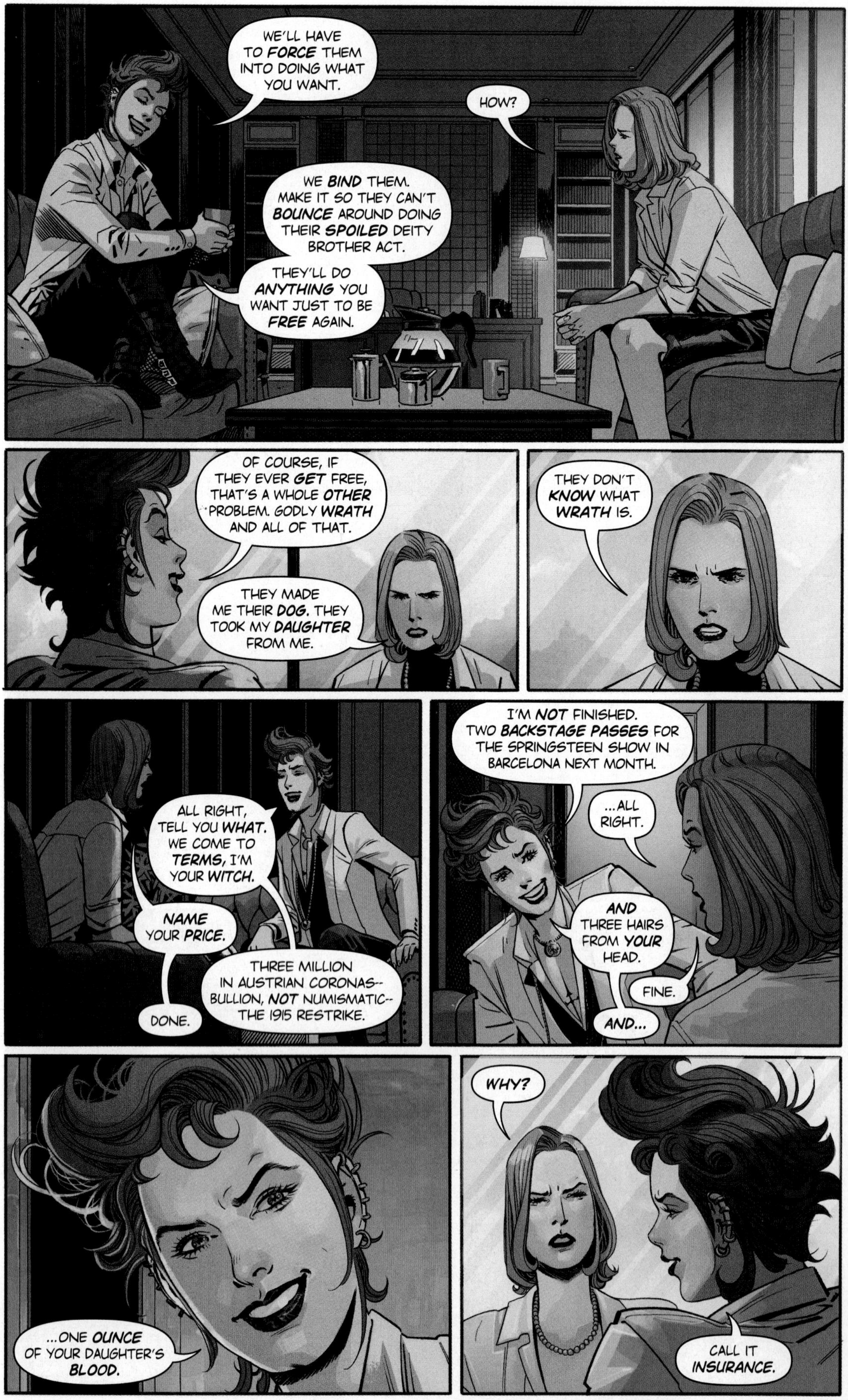
WE'LL HAVE TO FORCE THEM INTO DOING WHAT YOU WANT.
HOW?
WE BIND THEM. MAKE IT SO THEY CAN'T BOUNCE AROUND DOING THEIR SPOILED DEITY BROTHER ACT.
THEY'LL DO ANYTHING YOU WANT JUST TO BE FREE AGAIN.
OF COURSE, IF THEY EVER GET FREE, THAT'S A WHOLE OTHER PROBLEM. GODLY WRATH AND ALL OF THAT.
THEY MADE ME THEIR DOG. THEY TOOK MY DAUGHTER FROM ME.
THEY DON'T KNOW WHAT WRATH IS.
ALL RIGHT, TELL YOU WHAT. WE COME TO TERMS, I'M YOUR WITCH.
NAME YOUR PRICE.
THREE MILLION IN AUSTRIAN CORONAS-- BULLION, NOT NUMISMATIC-- THE 1915 RESTRIKE.
DONE.
I'M NOT FINISHED. TWO BACKSTAGE PASSES FOR THE SPRINGSTEEN SHOW IN BARCELONA NEXT MONTH.
...ALL RIGHT.
AND THREE HAIRS FROM YOUR HEAD.
FINE.
AND...
...ONE OUNCE OF YOUR DAUGHTER'S BLOOD.
WHY?
CALL IT INSURANCE.

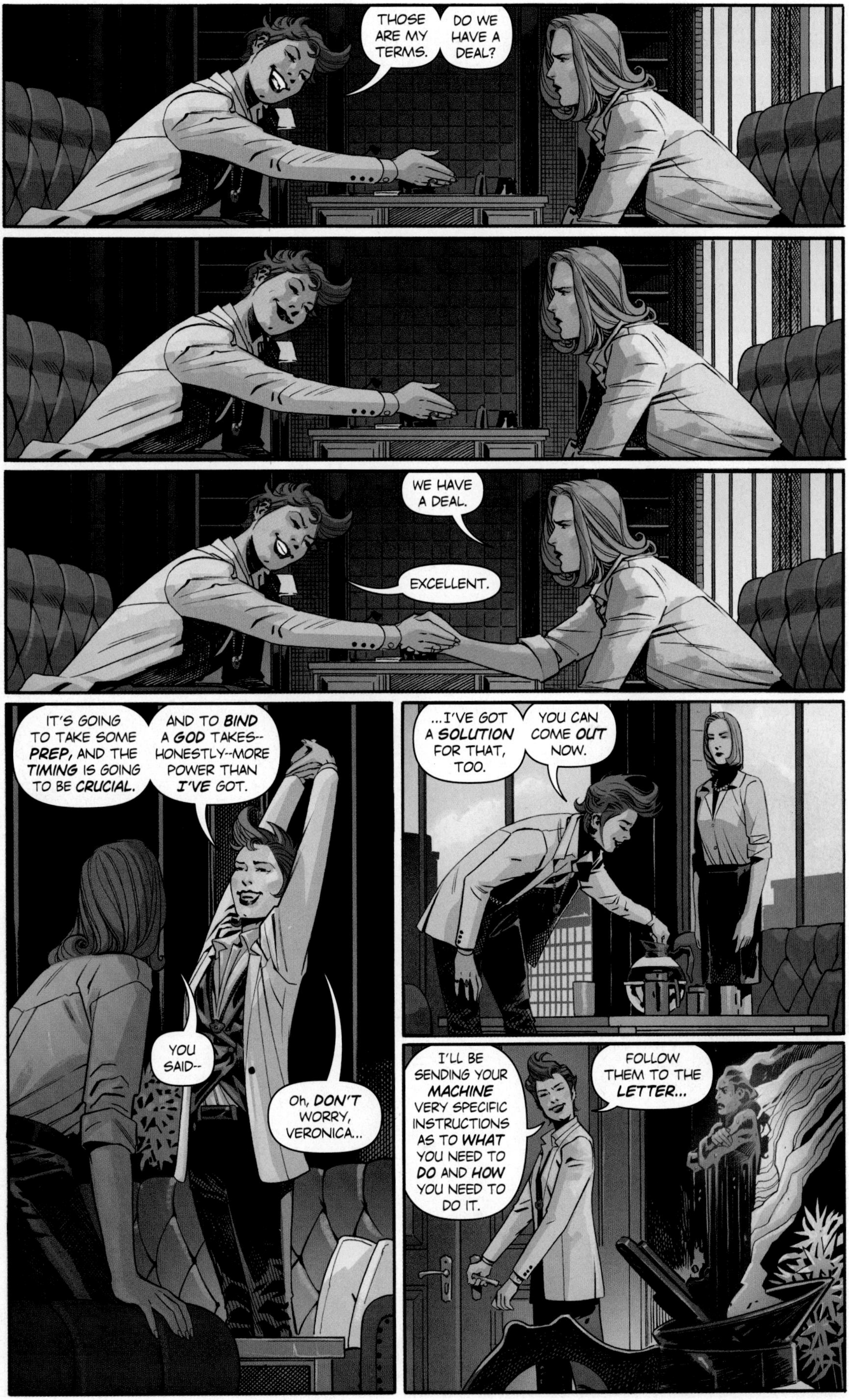
THOSE ARE MY TERMS.
DO WE HAVE A DEAL?
WE HAVE A DEAL.
EXCELLENT.
IT'S GOING TO TAKE SOME PREP, AND THE TIMING IS GOING TO BE CRUCIAL.
AND TO BIND A GOD TAKES--HONESTLY--MORE POWER THAN I'VE GOT.
YOU SAID--
Oh, DON'T WORRY, VERONICA...
...I'VE GOT A SOLUTION FOR THAT, TOO.
YOU CAN COME OUT NOW.
I'LL BE SENDING YOUR MACHINE VERY SPECIFIC INSTRUCTIONS AS TO WHAT YOU NEED TO DO AND HOW YOU NEED TO DO IT.
FOLLOW THEM TO THE LETTER...

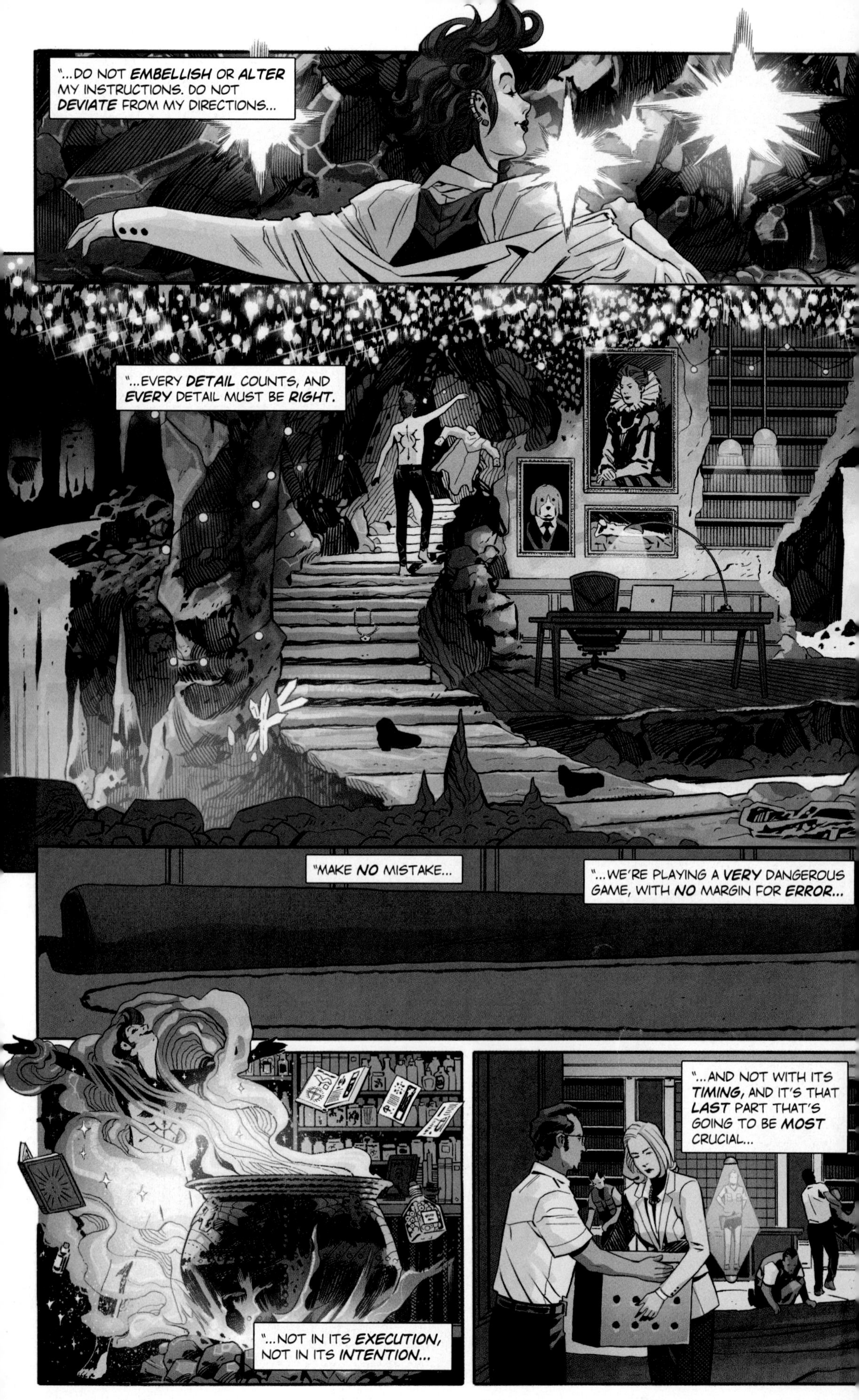
"...DO NOT EMBELLISH OR ALTER MY INSTRUCTIONS. DO NOT DEVIATE FROM MY DIRECTIONS...
"...EVERY DETAIL COUNTS, AND EVERY DETAIL MUST BE RIGHT.
"MAKE NO MISTAKE...
"...WE'RE PLAYING A VERY DANGEROUS GAME, WITH NO MARGIN FOR ERROR...
"...NOT IN ITS EXECUTION, NOT IN ITS INTENTION...
"...AND NOT WITH ITS TIMING, AND IT'S THAT LAST PART THAT'S GOING TO BE MOST CRUCIAL...

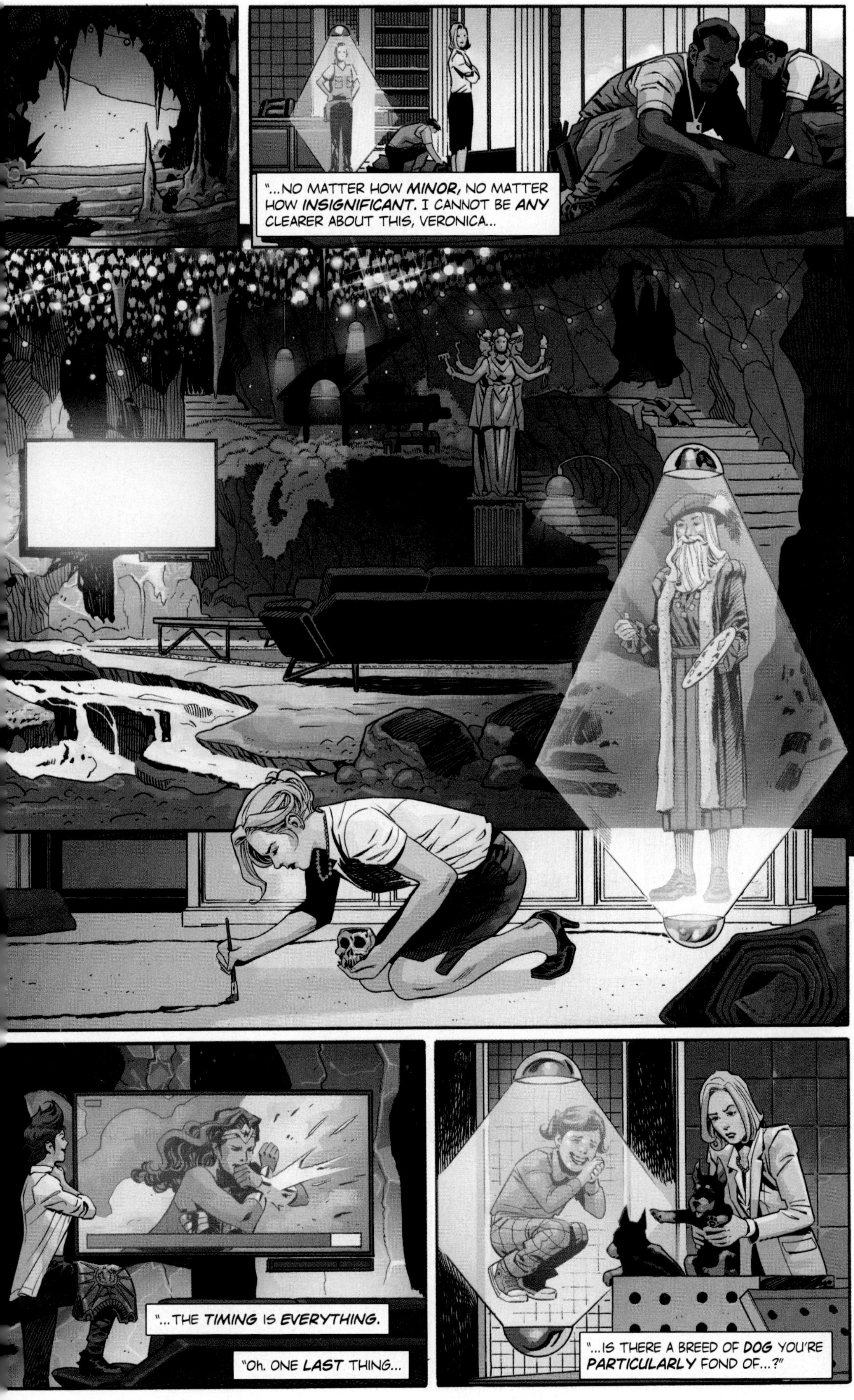
"...NO MATTER HOW MINOR, NO MATTER HOW INSIGNIFICANT. I CANNOT BE ANY CLEARER ABOUT THIS, VERONICA...
"...THE TIMING IS EVERYTHING.
"Oh. ONE LAST THING...
"...IS THERE A BREED OF DOG YOU'RE PARTICULARLY FOND OF...?"

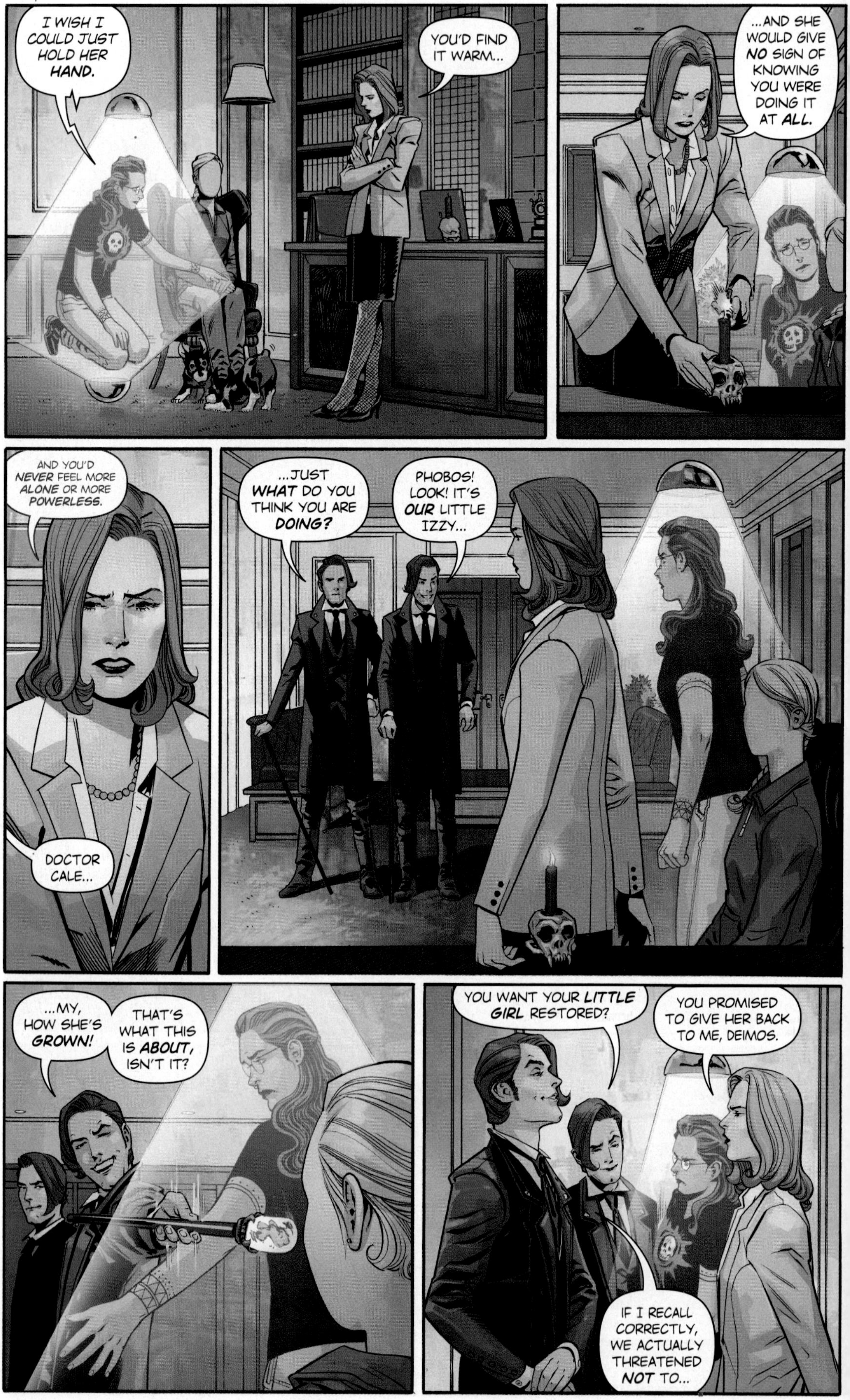
I WISH I COULD JUST HOLD HER HAND.
YOU'D FIND IT WARM...
...AND SHE WOULD GIVE NO SIGN OF KNOWING YOU WERE DOING IT AT ALL.
AND YOU'D NEVER FEEL MORE ALONE OR MORE POWERLESS.
DOCTOR CALE...
...JUST WHAT DO YOU THINK YOU ARE DOING?
PHOBOS! LOOK! IT'S OUR LITTLE IZZY...
...MY, HOW SHE'S GROWN!
THAT'S WHAT THIS IS ABOUT, ISN'T IT?
YOU WANT YOUR LITTLE GIRL RESTORED?
YOU PROMISED TO GIVE HER BACK TO ME, DEIMOS.
IF I RECALL CORRECTLY, WE ACTUALLY THREATENED NOT TO...

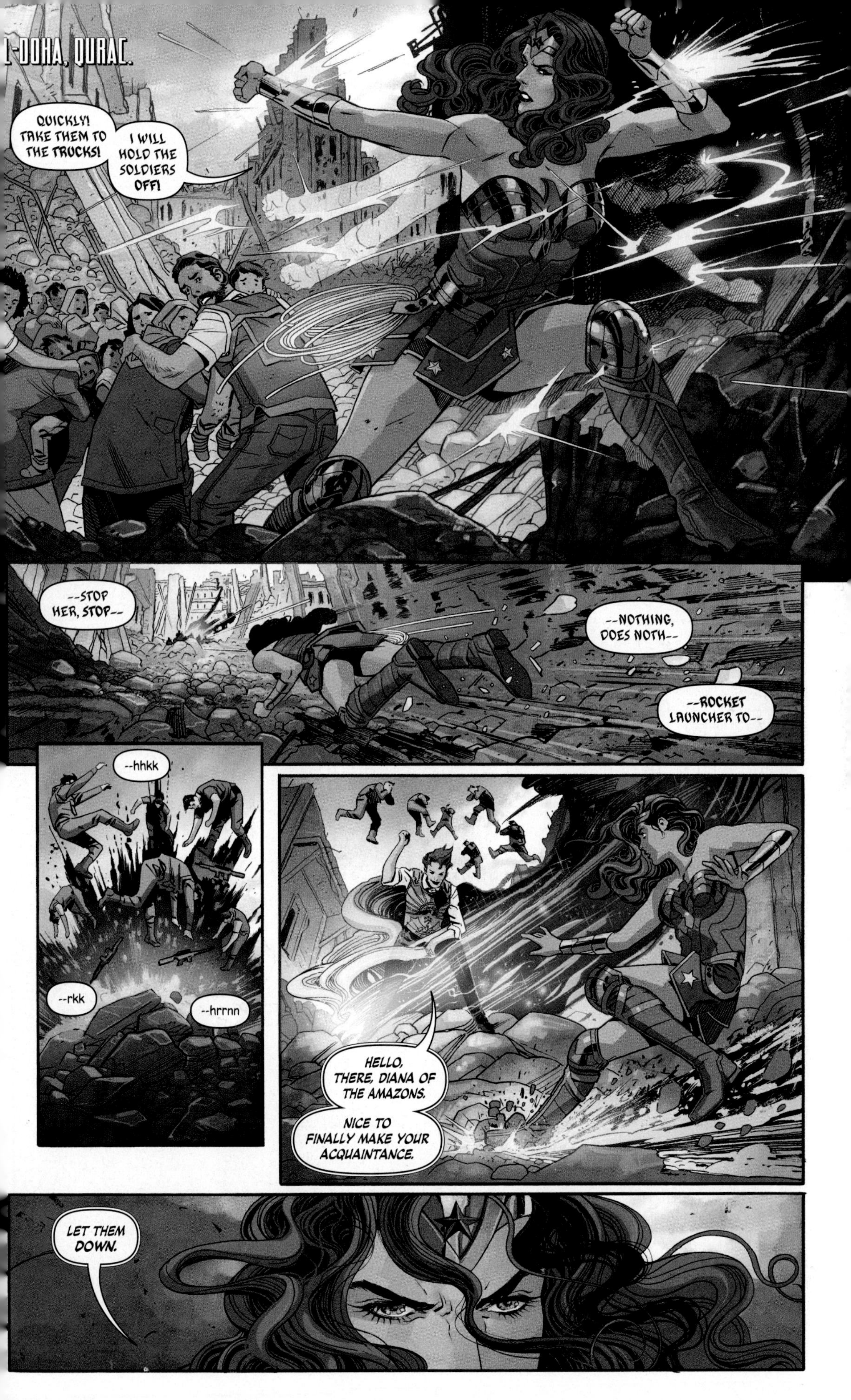
L-DOHA, QURAC.
QUICKLY! TAKE THEM TO THE TRUCKS!
I WILL HOLD THE SOLDIERS OFF!
--STOP HER, STOP--
--NOTHING, DOES NOTH--
--ROCKET LAUNCHER TO--
--hhkk
--rkk
--hrrnn
HELLO, THERE, DIANA OF THE AMAZONS.
NICE TO FINALLY MAKE YOUR ACQUAINTANCE.
LET THEM DOWN.

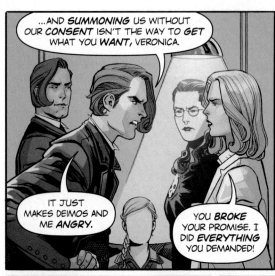

...AND **SUMMONING** US WITHOUT OUR **CONSENT** ISN'T THE WAY TO **GET** WHAT YOU **WANT**, VERONICA.

IT JUST MAKES DEIMOS AND ME **ANGRY**.

YOU **BROKE** YOUR PROMISE. I DID **EVERYTHING** YOU DEMANDED!

AND **YOU** WERE SUPPOSED TO DELIVER US **THEMYSCIRA**.

IT'S BEEN **YEARS** AND STILL WE ARE **NO CLOSER**.

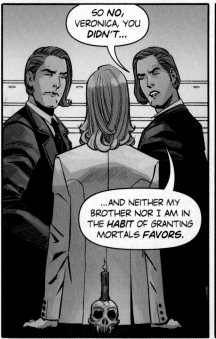

SO **NO**, VERONICA, YOU **DIDN'T**...

...AND NEITHER MY BROTHER NOR I AM IN THE **HABIT** OF GRANTING MORTALS **FAVORS**.

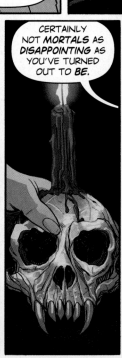

CERTAINLY NOT **MORTALS** AS **DISAPPOINTING** AS YOU'VE TURNED OUT TO BE.

SHE'S MADE **CONTACT**. DO IT **NOW**.

DO **WHAT** NOW, YOU PATHETIC WOMAN?

THIS.

KSSSH

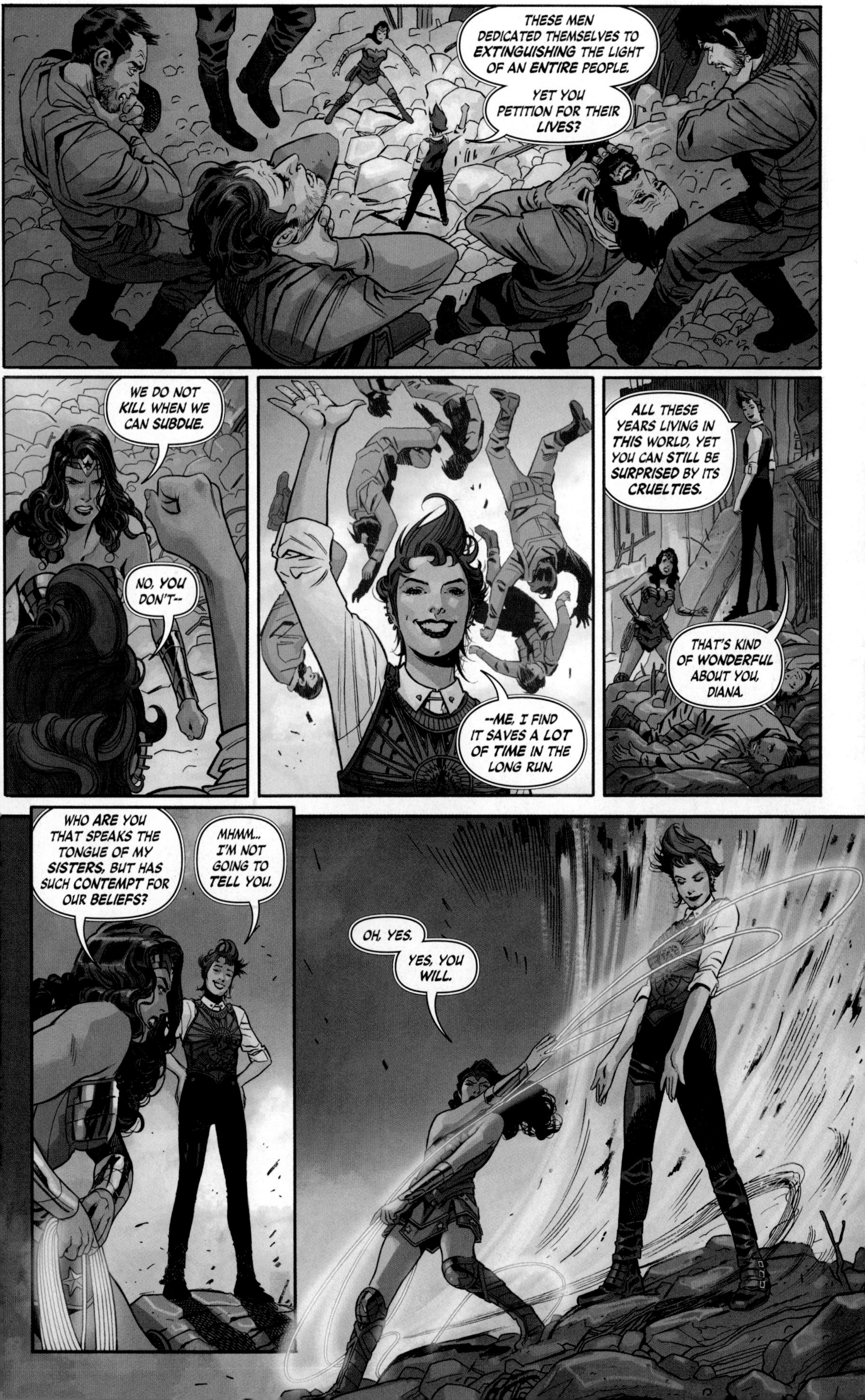

THESE MEN DEDICATED THEMSELVES TO EXTINGUISHING THE LIGHT OF AN ENTIRE PEOPLE.
YET YOU PETITION FOR THEIR LIVES?
WE DO NOT KILL WHEN WE CAN SUBDUE.
NO, YOU DON'T--
--ME, I FIND IT SAVES A LOT OF TIME IN THE LONG RUN.
ALL THESE YEARS LIVING IN THIS WORLD, YET YOU CAN STILL BE SURPRISED BY ITS CRUELTIES.
THAT'S KIND OF WONDERFUL ABOUT YOU, DIANA.
WHO ARE YOU THAT SPEAKS THE TONGUE OF MY SISTERS, BUT HAS SUCH CONTEMPT FOR OUR BELIEFS?
MHMM... I'M NOT GOING TO TELL YOU.
OH, YES.
YES, YOU WILL.

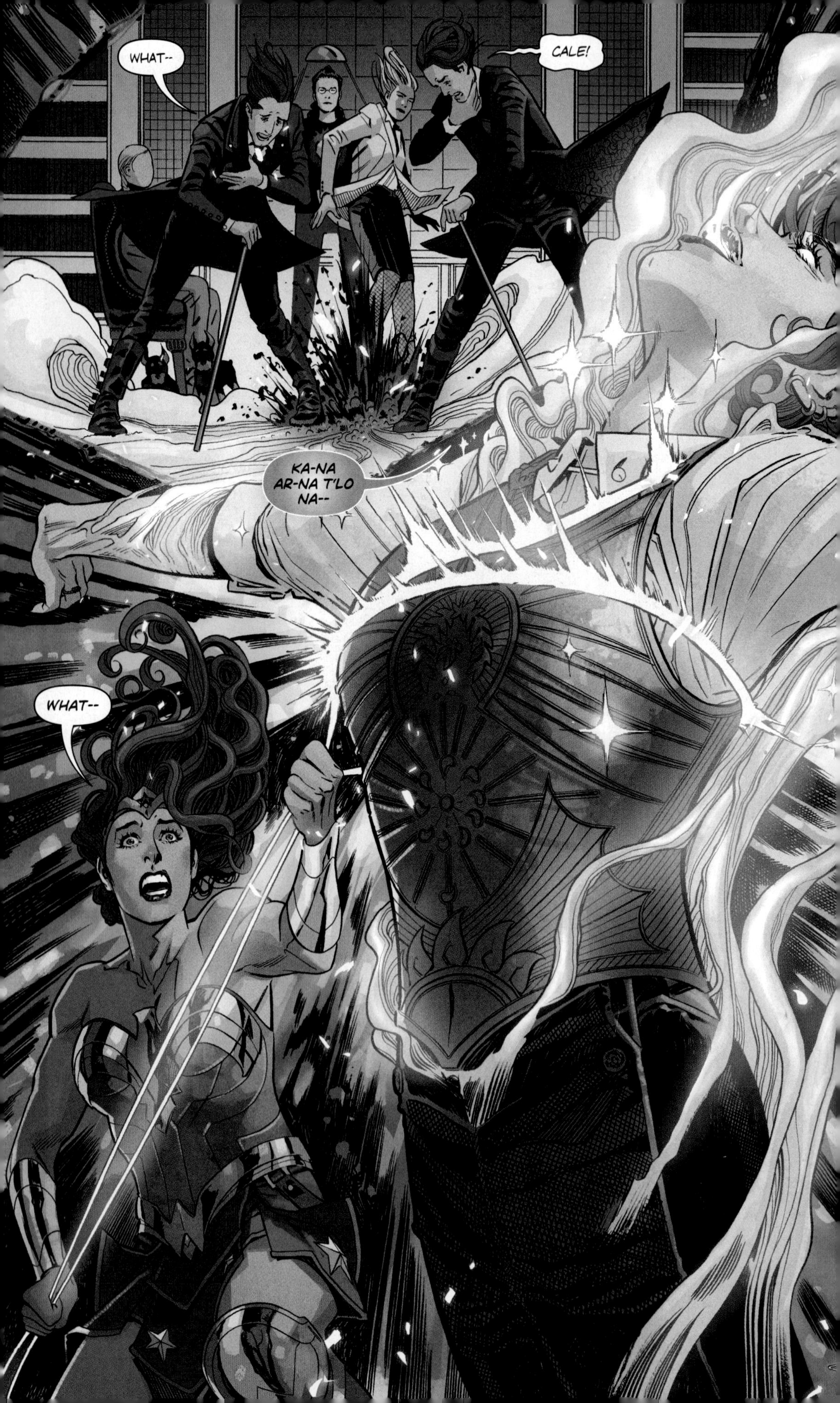
WHAT--
CALE!
KA-NA AR-NA T'LO NA--
WHAT--

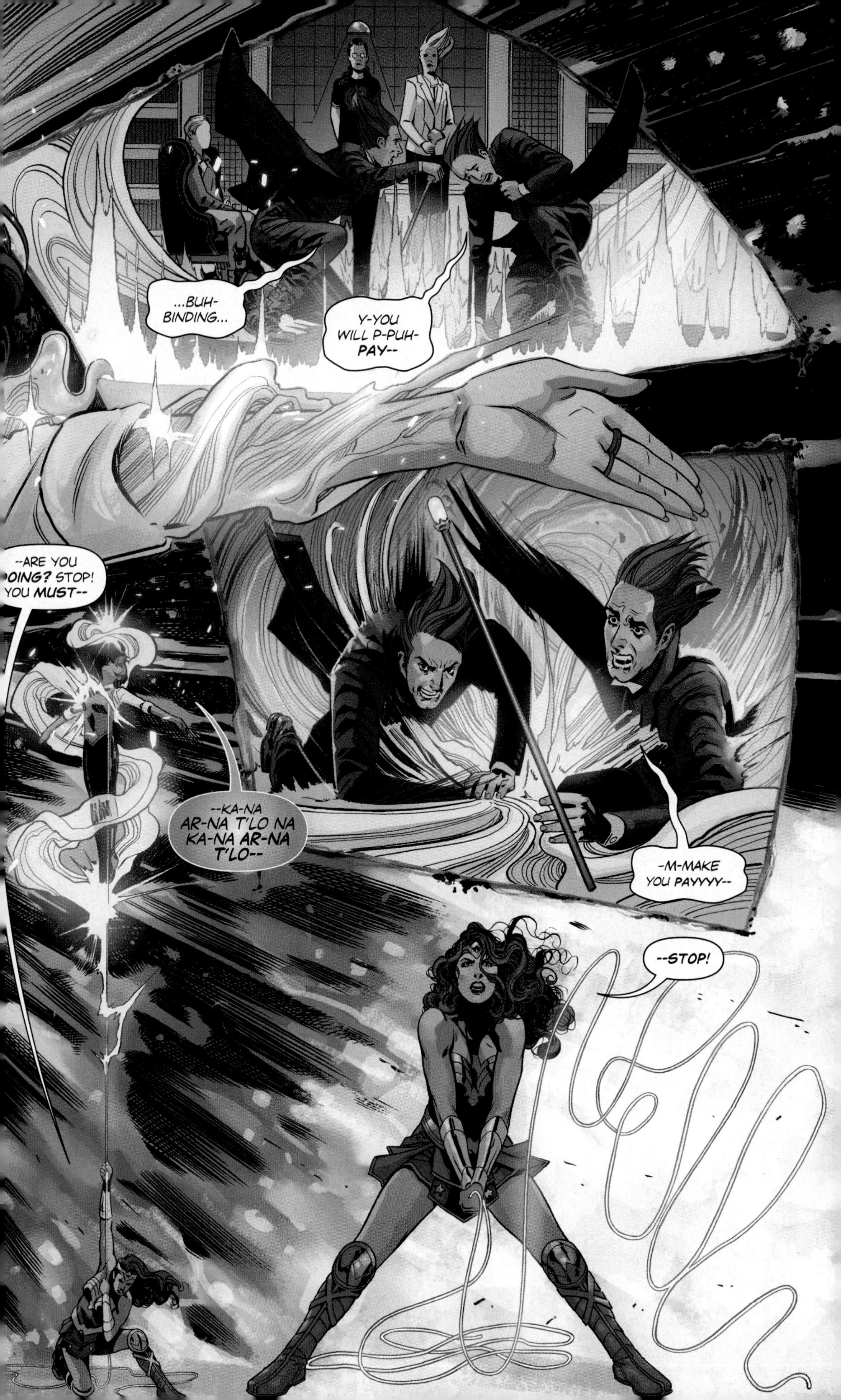
...BUH-BINDING...
Y-YOU WILL P-PUH-PAY--
--ARE YOU DOING? STOP! YOU MUST--
--KA-NA AR-NA T'LO NA KA-NA AR-NA T'LO--
-M-MAKE YOU PAYYYY--
--STOP!

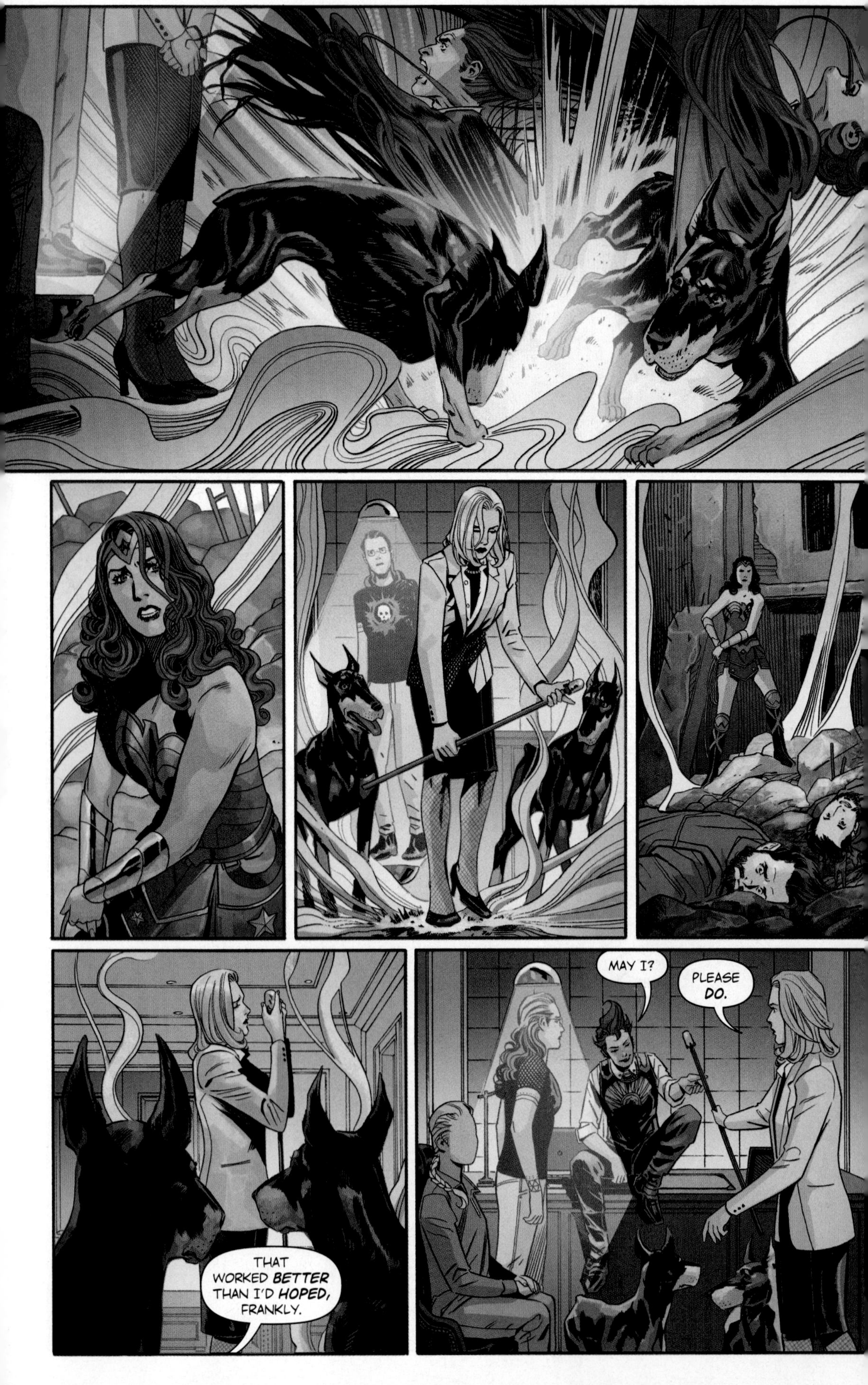
THAT WORKED BETTER THAN I'D HOPED, FRANKLY.
MAY I?
PLEASE DO.

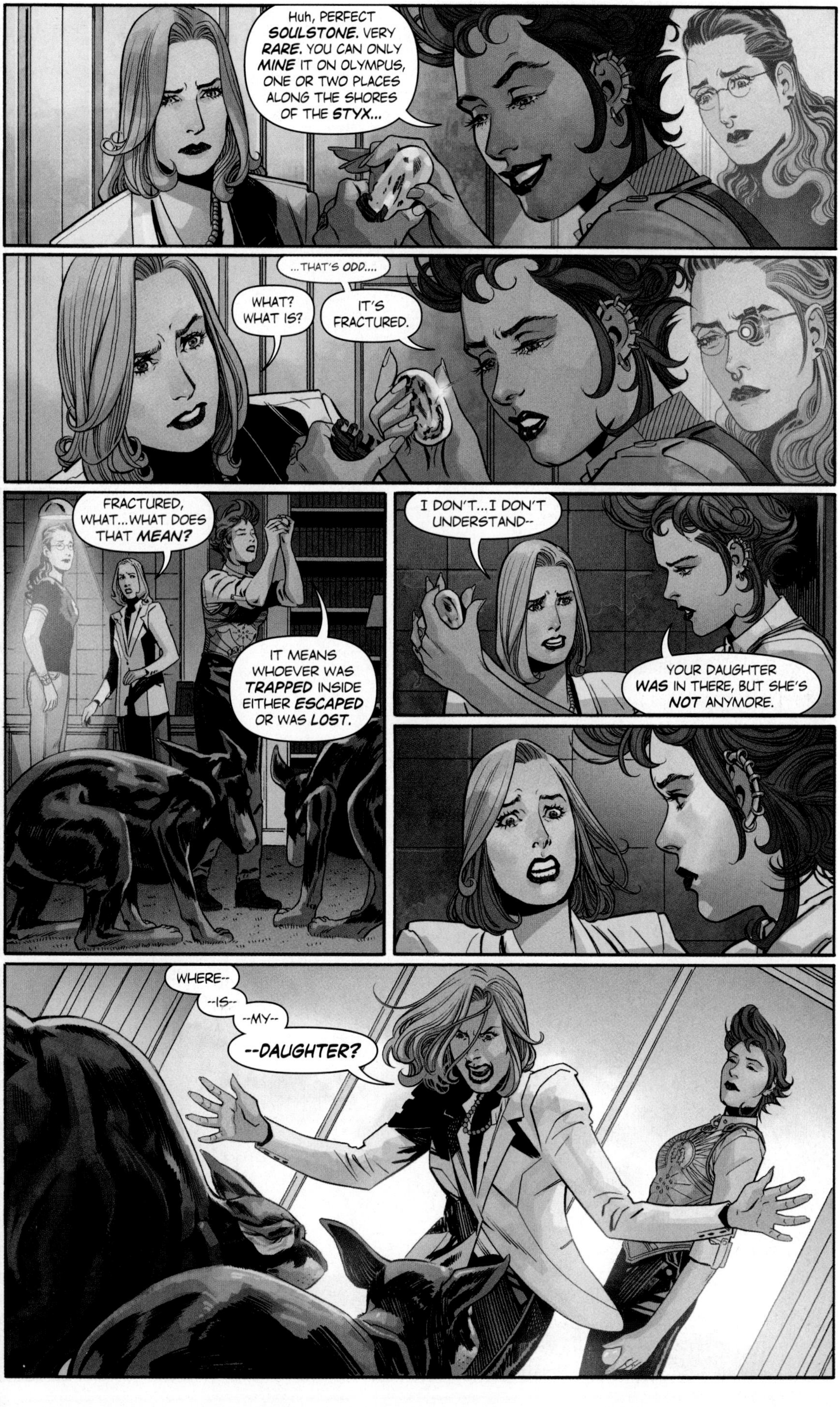
Huh, PERFECT SOULSTONE. VERY RARE. YOU CAN ONLY MINE IT ON OLYMPUS, ONE OR TWO PLACES ALONG THE SHORES OF THE STYX...
...THAT'S ODD....
WHAT? WHAT IS?
IT'S FRACTURED.
FRACTURED, WHAT...WHAT DOES THAT MEAN?
IT MEANS WHOEVER WAS TRAPPED INSIDE EITHER ESCAPED OR WAS LOST.
I DON'T...I DON'T UNDERSTAND--
YOUR DAUGHTER WAS IN THERE, BUT SHE'S NOT ANYMORE.
WHERE--
--IS--
--MY--
--DAUGHTER?

THEY SAY...THEY SAY THEY **LOST** HER, THAT SHE...

...SHE WAS **TAKEN** FROM THEM.

WHO? WHO TOOK HER?

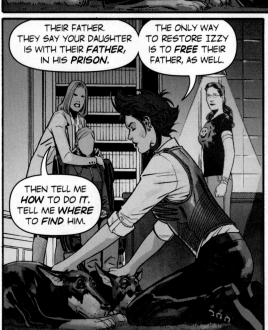

THEIR FATHER. THEY SAY YOUR DAUGHTER IS WITH THEIR **FATHER**, IN HIS **PRISON**.

THE ONLY WAY TO RESTORE IZZY IS TO **FREE** THEIR FATHER, AS WELL.

THEN TELL ME **HOW** TO DO IT. TELL ME **WHERE** TO **FIND** HIM.

ON **THEMYSCIRA**. BUT YOU'LL DO IT **WITHOUT** MY HELP.

I'LL **PAY**--

IT'S **NOT** ABOUT **MONEY**, VERONICA! THEIR FATHER IS **ARES**!

TO **FREE** YOUR DAUGHTER, YOU'RE GOING TO HAVE TO **UNLEASH** THE GOD OF **WAR**!

IF THAT'S WHAT IT TAKES.

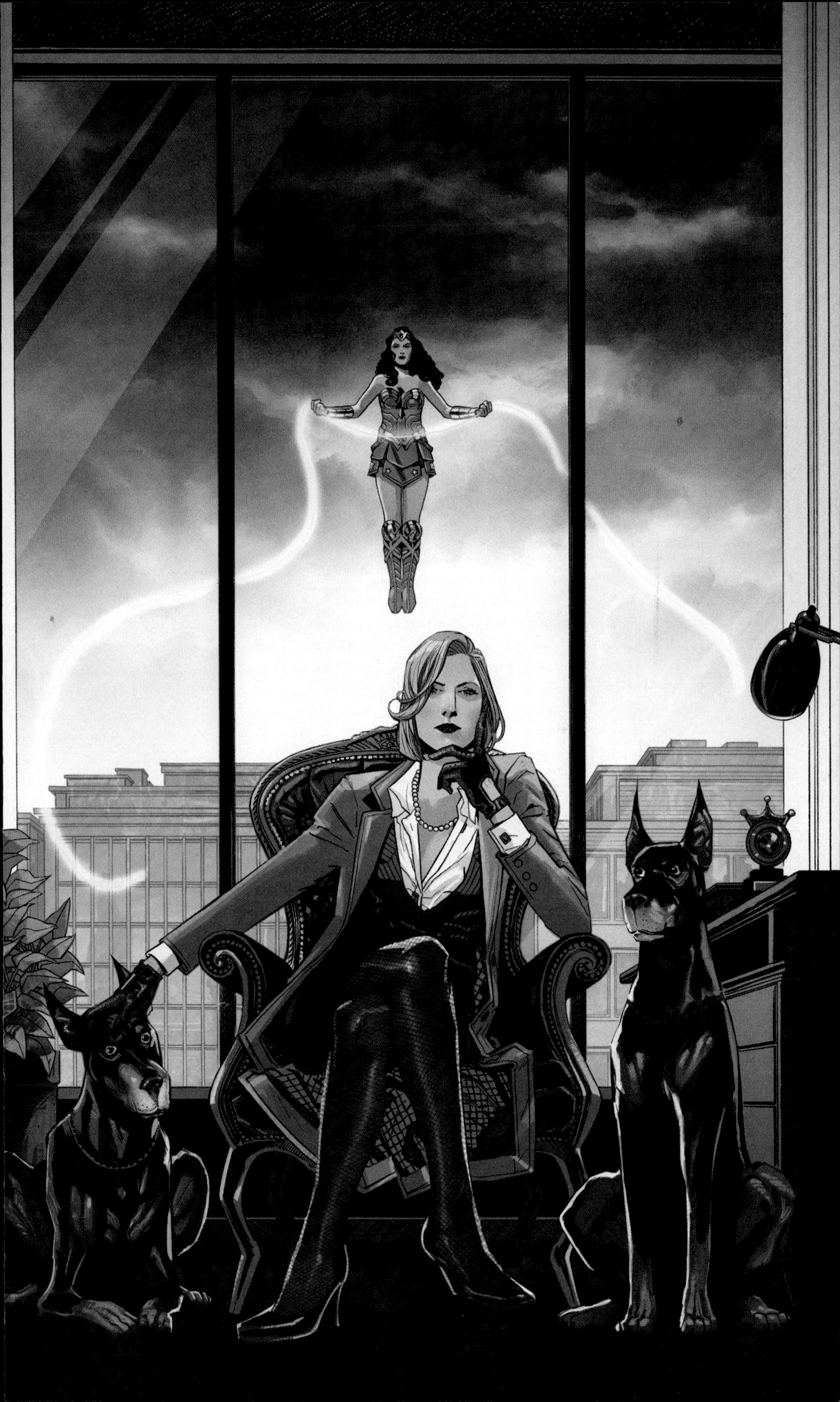

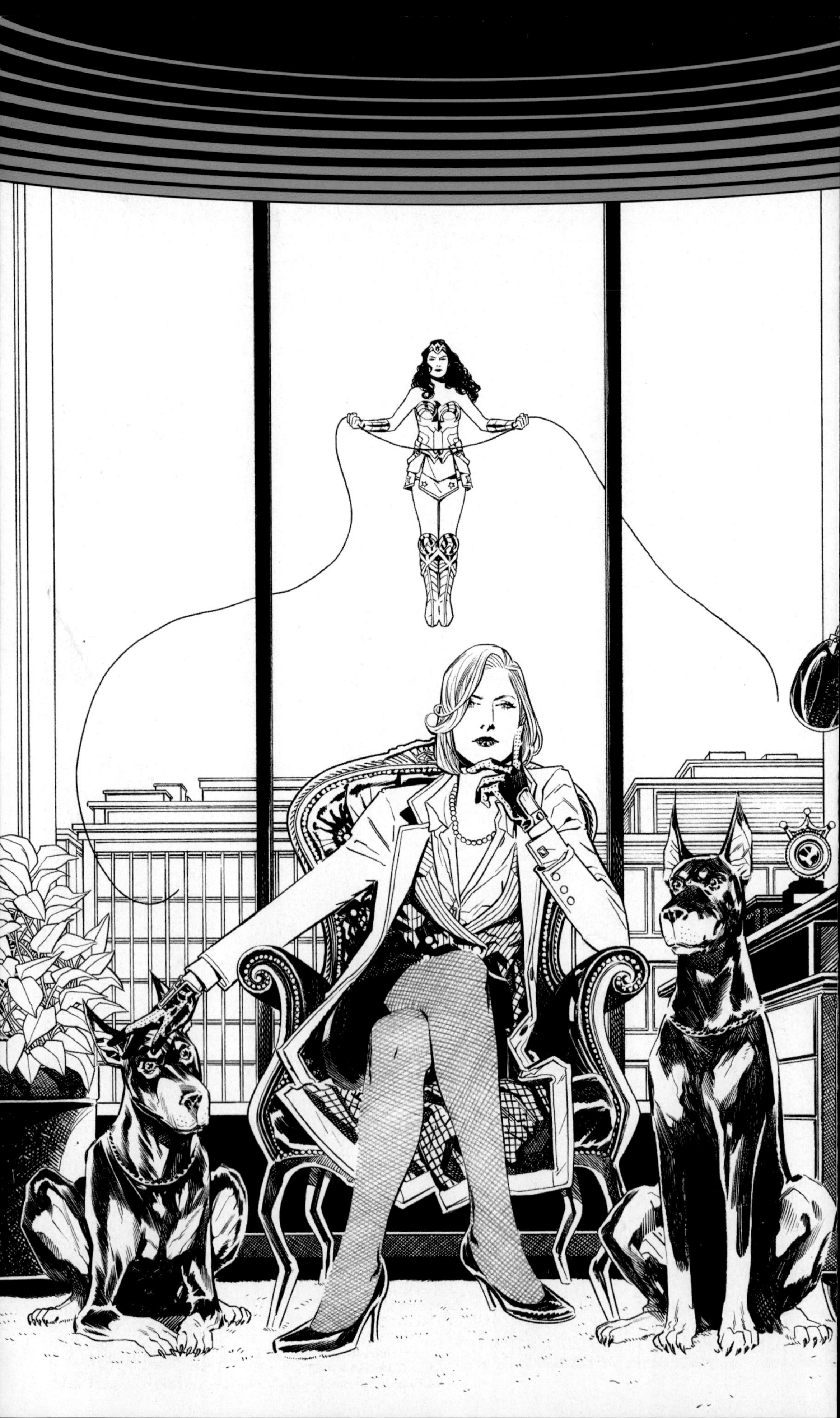

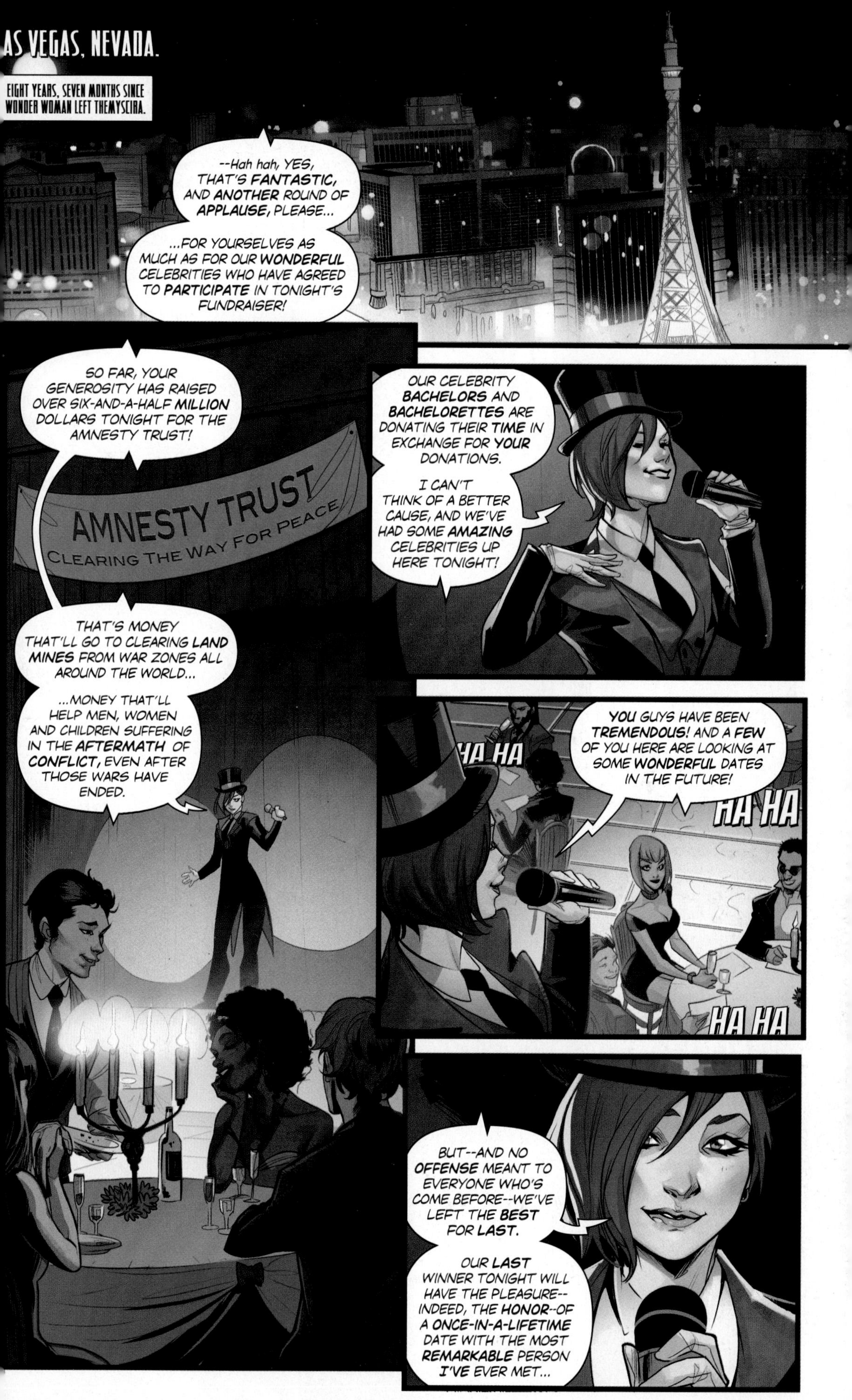

AS VEGAS, NEVADA.
EIGHT YEARS, SEVEN MONTHS SINCE WONDER WOMAN LEFT THEMYSCIRA.
--Hah hah, YES, THAT'S FANTASTIC, AND ANOTHER ROUND OF APPLAUSE, PLEASE...
...FOR YOURSELVES AS MUCH AS FOR OUR WONDERFUL CELEBRITIES WHO HAVE AGREED TO PARTICIPATE IN TONIGHT'S FUNDRAISER!
SO FAR, YOUR GENEROSITY HAS RAISED OVER SIX-AND-A-HALF MILLION DOLLARS TONIGHT FOR THE AMNESTY TRUST!
AMNESTY TRUST
CLEARING THE WAY FOR PEACE
THAT'S MONEY THAT'LL GO TO CLEARING LAND MINES FROM WAR ZONES ALL AROUND THE WORLD...
...MONEY THAT'LL HELP MEN, WOMEN AND CHILDREN SUFFERING IN THE AFTERMATH OF CONFLICT, EVEN AFTER THOSE WARS HAVE ENDED.
OUR CELEBRITY BACHELORS AND BACHELORETTES ARE DONATING THEIR TIME IN EXCHANGE FOR YOUR DONATIONS.
I CAN'T THINK OF A BETTER CAUSE, AND WE'VE HAD SOME AMAZING CELEBRITIES UP HERE TONIGHT!
HA HA
YOU GUYS HAVE BEEN TREMENDOUS! AND A FEW OF YOU HERE ARE LOOKING AT SOME WONDERFUL DATES IN THE FUTURE!
HA HA
HA HA
BUT--AND NO OFFENSE MEANT TO EVERYONE WHO'S COME BEFORE--WE'VE LEFT THE BEST FOR LAST.
OUR LAST WINNER TONIGHT WILL HAVE THE PLEASURE--INDEED, THE HONOR--OF A ONCE-IN-A-LIFETIME DATE WITH THE MOST REMARKABLE PERSON I'VE EVER MET...

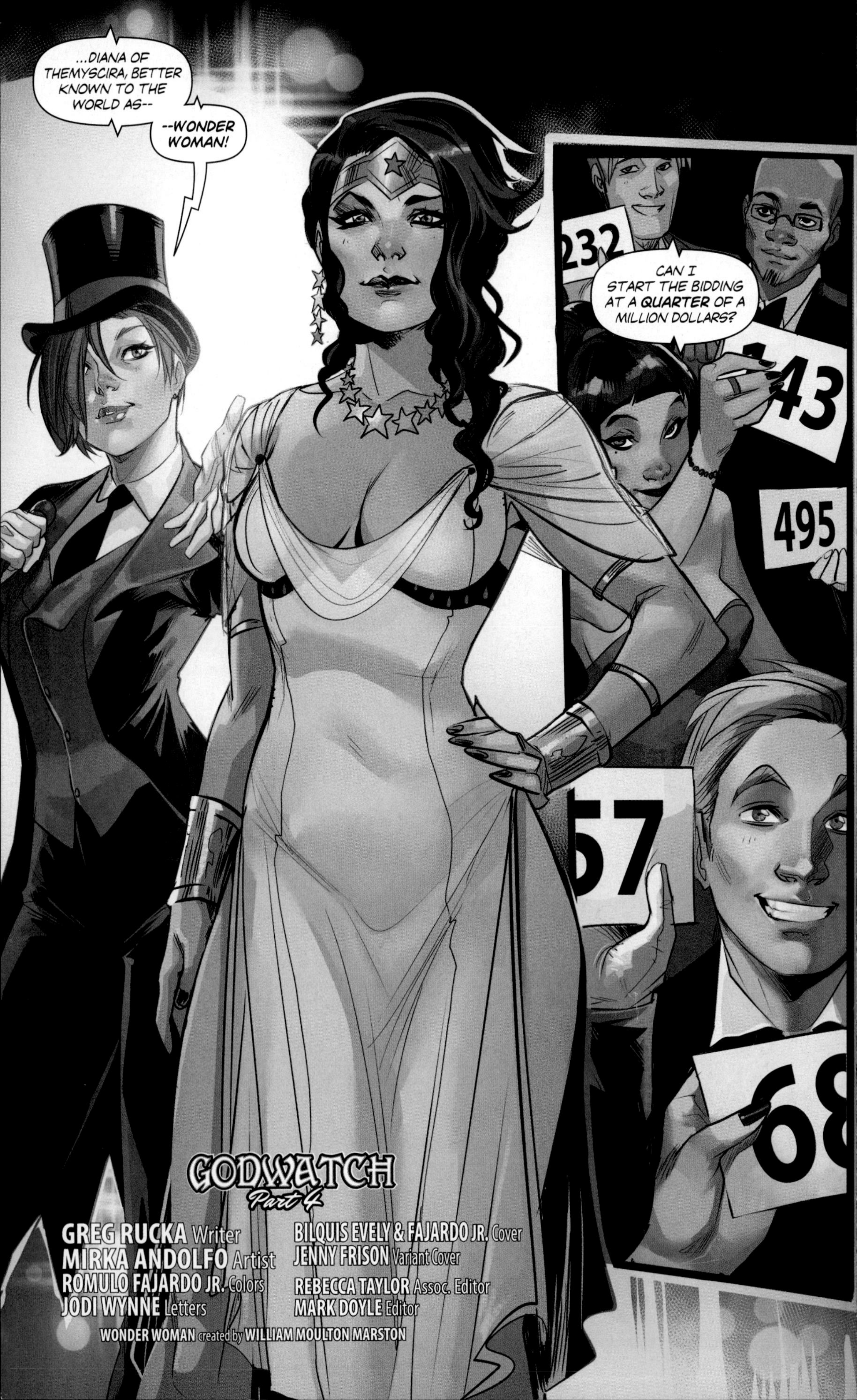
...DIANA OF THEMYSCIRA, BETTER KNOWN TO THE WORLD AS--
--WONDER WOMAN!
232
CAN I START THE BIDDING AT A QUARTER OF A MILLION DOLLARS?
495
GODWATCH
Part 4
GREG RUCKA Writer
MIRKA ANDOLFO Artist
ROMULO FAJARDO JR. Colors
JODI WYNNE Letters
BILQUIS EVELY & FAJARDO JR. Cover
JENNY FRISON Variant Cover
REBECCA TAYLOR Assoc. Editor
MARK DOYLE Editor
WONDER WOMAN created by WILLIAM MOULTON MARSTON

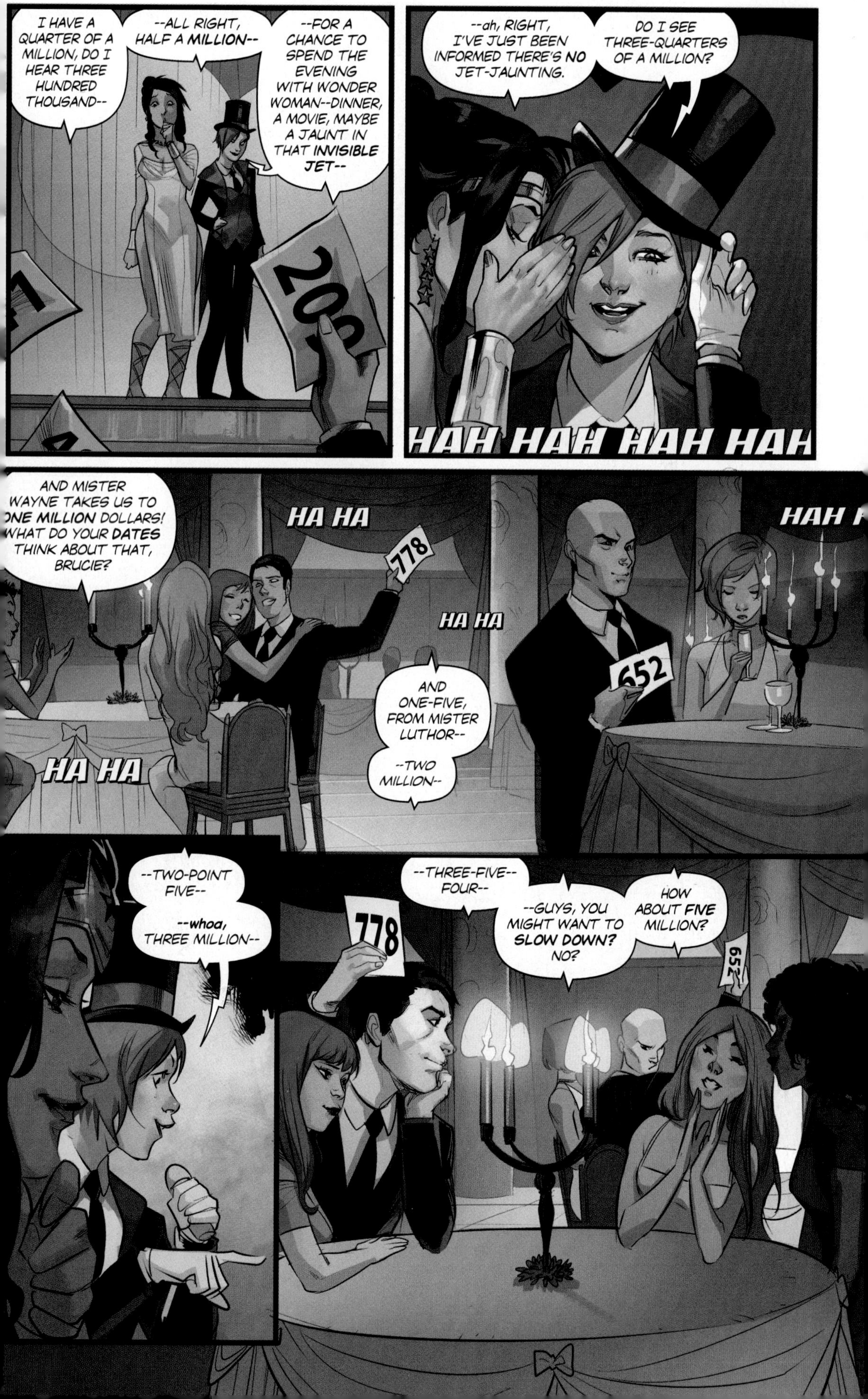
I HAVE A QUARTER OF A MILLION, DO I HEAR THREE HUNDRED THOUSAND--
--ALL RIGHT, HALF A MILLION--
--FOR A CHANCE TO SPEND THE EVENING WITH WONDER WOMAN--DINNER, A MOVIE, MAYBE A JAUNT IN THAT INVISIBLE JET--
200
--ah, RIGHT, I'VE JUST BEEN INFORMED THERE'S NO JET-JAUNTING.
DO I SEE THREE-QUARTERS OF A MILLION?
HAH HAH HAH HAH
AND MISTER WAYNE TAKES US TO ONE MILLION DOLLARS! WHAT DO YOUR DATES THINK ABOUT THAT, BRUCIE?
HA HA
778
HA HA
HA HA
HAH
652
AND ONE-FIVE, FROM MISTER LUTHOR--
--TWO MILLION--
--TWO-POINT FIVE--
--whoa, THREE MILLION--
778
--THREE-FIVE-- FOUR--
--GUYS, YOU MIGHT WANT TO SLOW DOWN? NO?
HOW ABOUT FIVE MILLION?
652

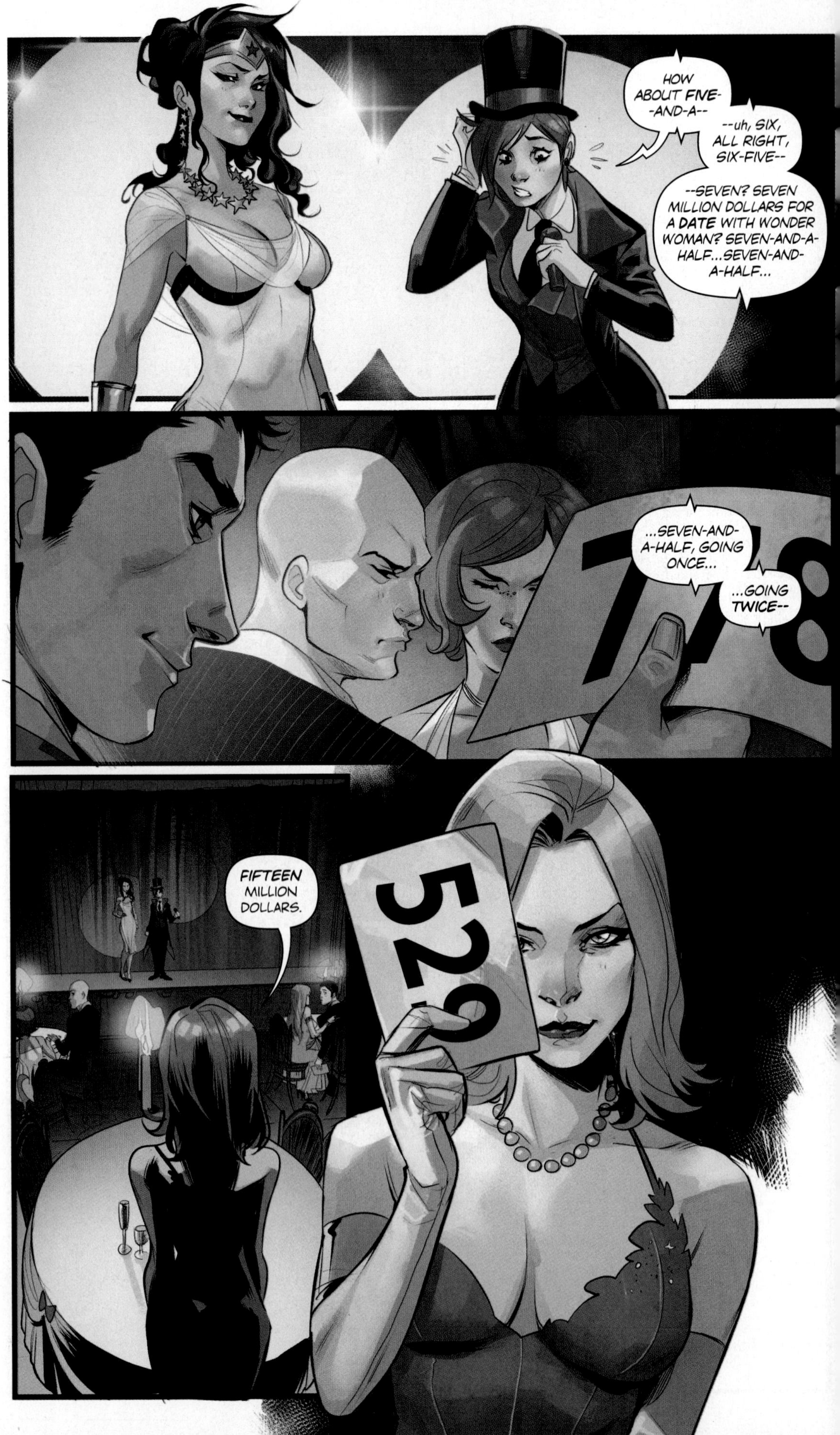
HOW ABOUT FIVE-AND-A--
--uh, SIX, ALL RIGHT, SIX-FIVE--
--SEVEN? SEVEN MILLION DOLLARS FOR A DATE WITH WONDER WOMAN? SEVEN-AND-A-HALF...SEVEN-AND-A-HALF...
...SEVEN-AND-A-HALF, GOING ONCE...
...GOING TWICE--
78
FIFTEEN MILLION DOLLARS.
529

FIFTEEN MILLION DOLLARS!

DONE!

DOCTOR VERONICA CALE WINS THE DREAM DATE WITH WONDER WOMAN!

DOCTOR CALE? IF YOU'D LIKE TO MAKE YOUR WAY BACKSTAGE...

...WHERE WE WILL BE DELIGHTED TO TAKE YOUR CHECK....

BETTER LUCK NEXT TIME, BOYS.

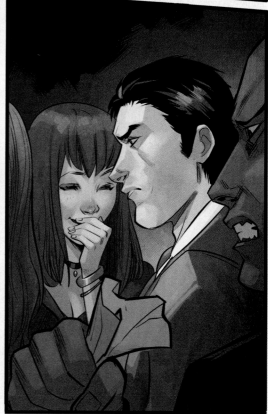

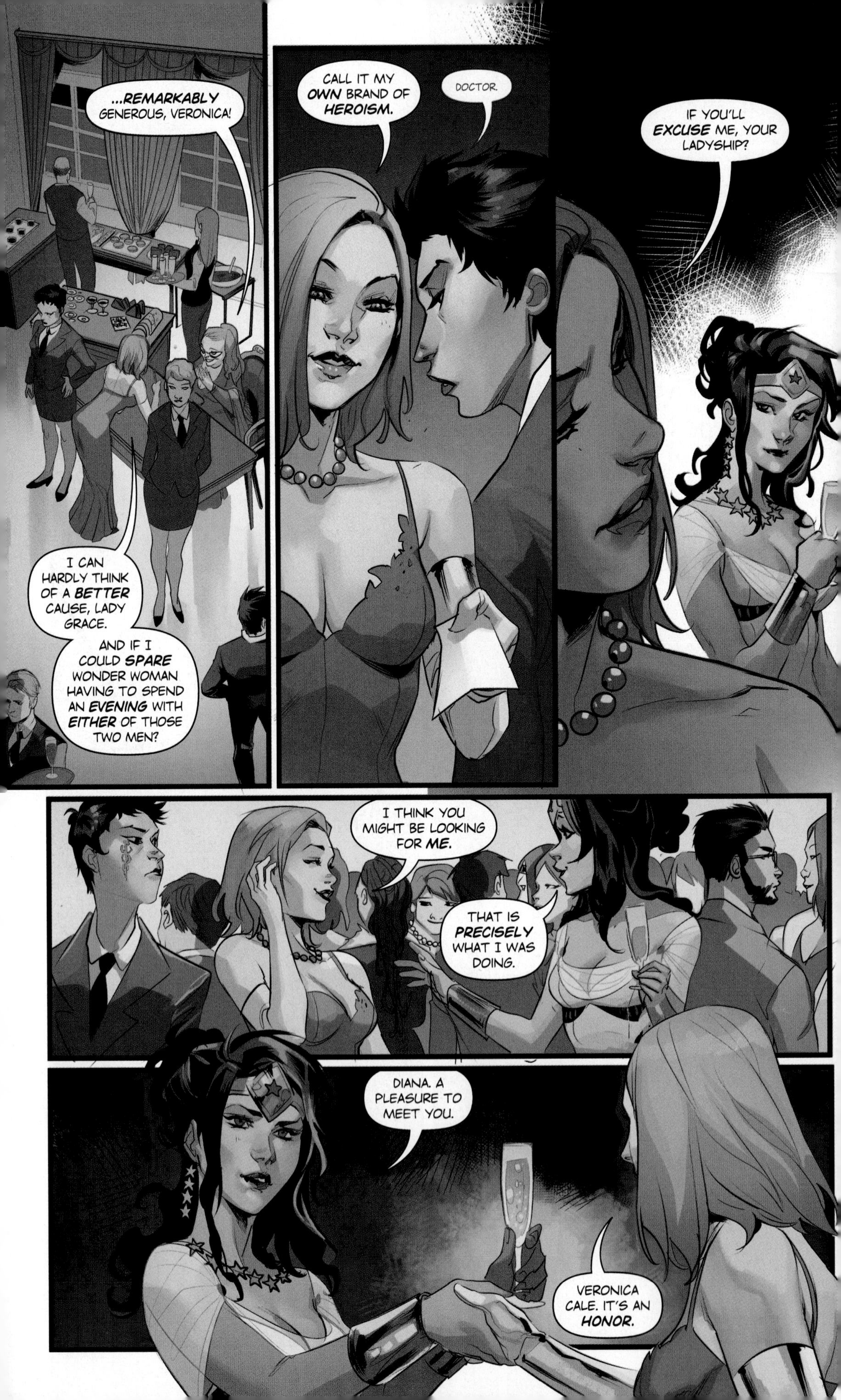
...REMARKABLY GENEROUS, VERONICA!
I CAN HARDLY THINK OF A BETTER CAUSE, LADY GRACE.
AND IF I COULD SPARE WONDER WOMAN HAVING TO SPEND AN EVENING WITH EITHER OF THOSE TWO MEN?
CALL IT MY OWN BRAND OF HEROISM.
DOCTOR.
IF YOU'LL EXCUSE ME, YOUR LADYSHIP?
I THINK YOU MIGHT BE LOOKING FOR ME.
THAT IS PRECISELY WHAT I WAS DOING.
DIANA. A PLEASURE TO MEET YOU.
VERONICA CALE. IT'S AN HONOR.

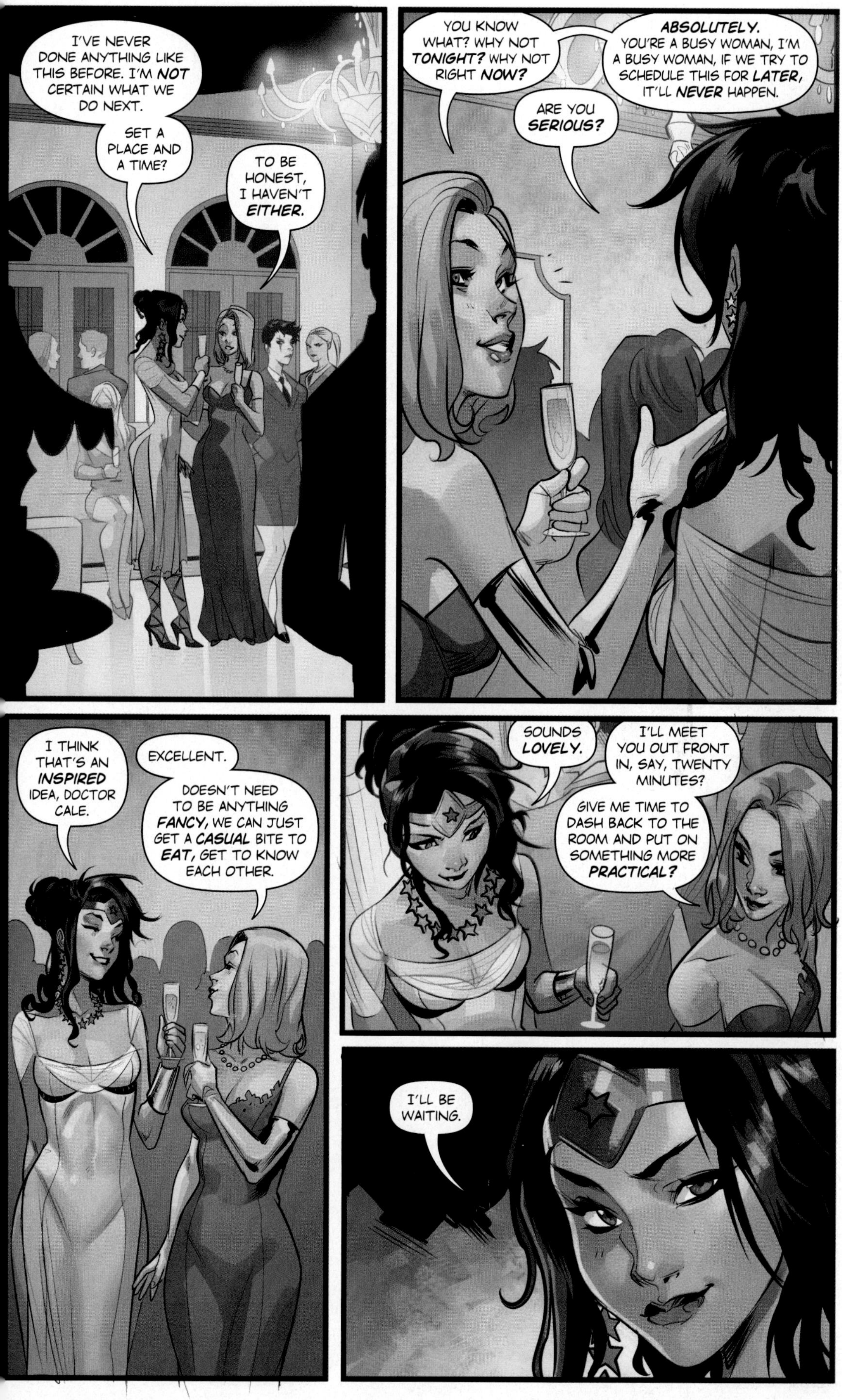
I'VE NEVER DONE ANYTHING LIKE THIS BEFORE. I'M NOT CERTAIN WHAT WE DO NEXT.
SET A PLACE AND A TIME?
TO BE HONEST, I HAVEN'T EITHER.
YOU KNOW WHAT? WHY NOT TONIGHT? WHY NOT RIGHT NOW?
ARE YOU SERIOUS?
ABSOLUTELY. YOU'RE A BUSY WOMAN, I'M A BUSY WOMAN, IF WE TRY TO SCHEDULE THIS FOR LATER, IT'LL NEVER HAPPEN.
I THINK THAT'S AN INSPIRED IDEA, DOCTOR CALE.
EXCELLENT.
DOESN'T NEED TO BE ANYTHING FANCY, WE CAN JUST GET A CASUAL BITE TO EAT, GET TO KNOW EACH OTHER.
SOUNDS LOVELY.
I'LL MEET YOU OUT FRONT IN, SAY, TWENTY MINUTES?
GIVE ME TIME TO DASH BACK TO THE ROOM AND PUT ON SOMETHING MORE PRACTICAL?
I'LL BE WAITING.

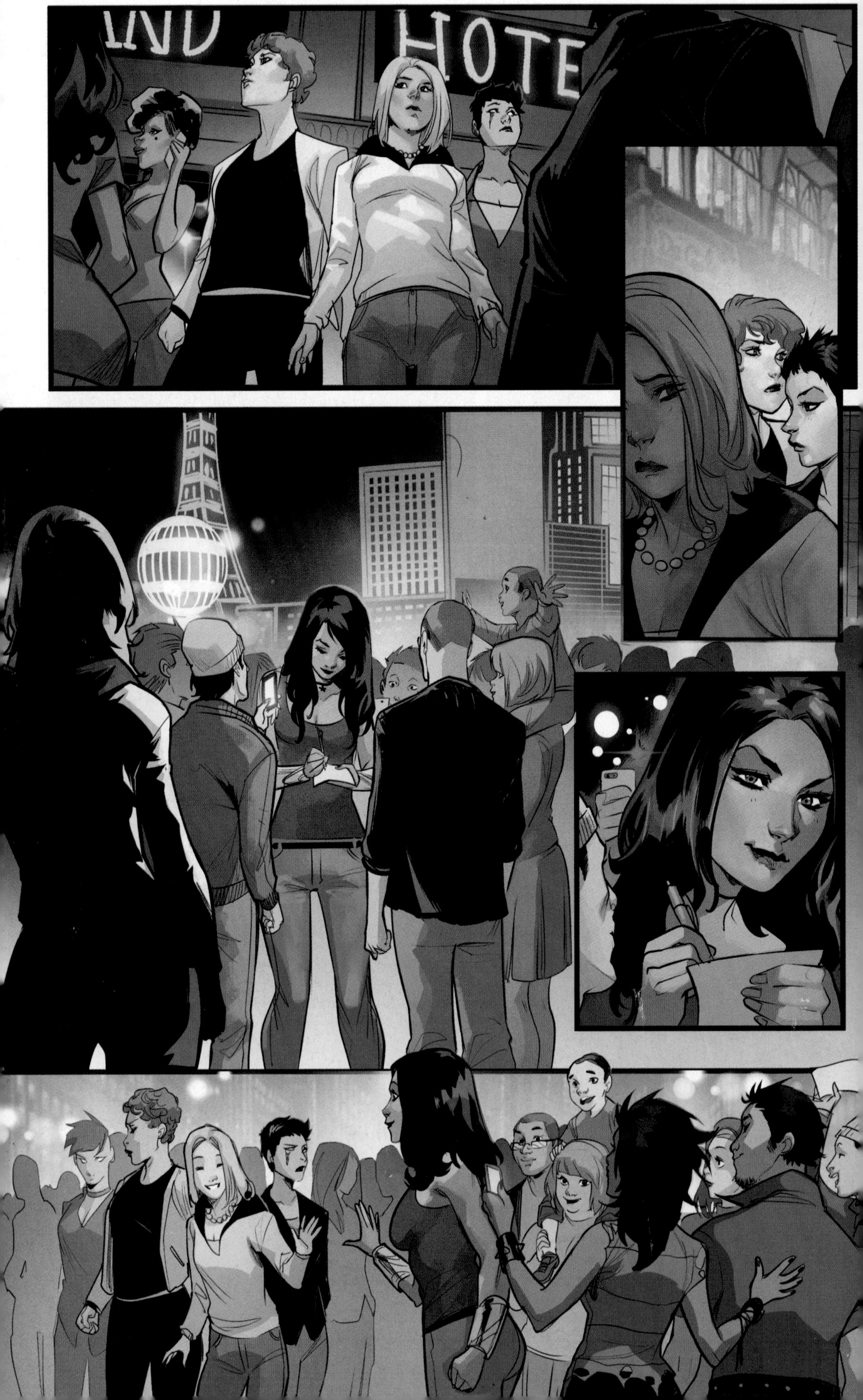
IND
HOTE

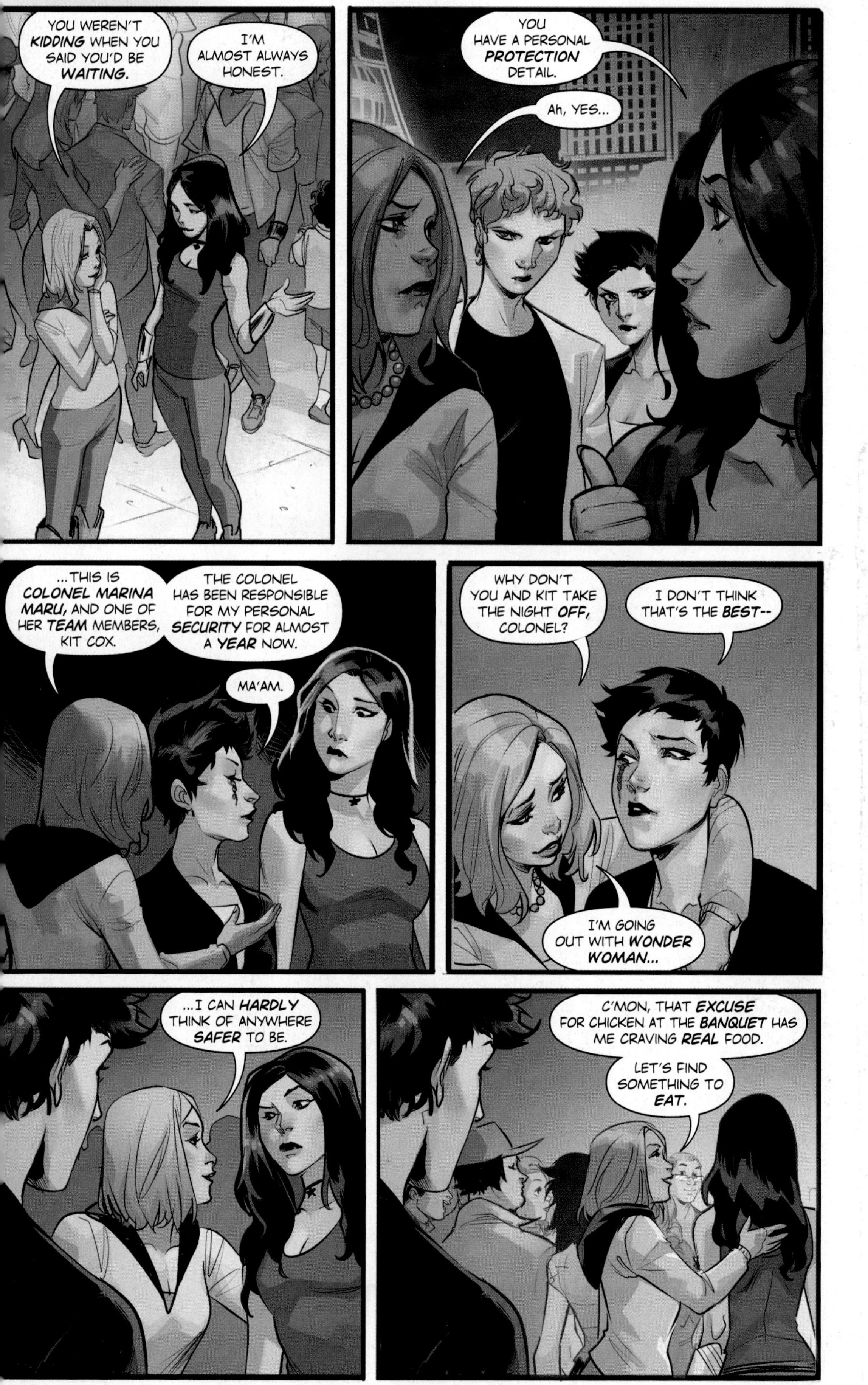

YOU WEREN'T **KIDDING** WHEN YOU SAID YOU'D BE **WAITING.**
I'M ALMOST ALWAYS HONEST.
YOU HAVE A PERSONAL **PROTECTION** DETAIL.
Ah, YES...
...THIS IS **COLONEL MARINA MARU,** AND ONE OF HER **TEAM** MEMBERS, KIT COX.
THE COLONEL HAS BEEN RESPONSIBLE FOR MY PERSONAL **SECURITY** FOR ALMOST A **YEAR** NOW.
MA'AM.
WHY DON'T YOU AND KIT TAKE THE NIGHT **OFF,** COLONEL?
I DON'T THINK THAT'S THE **BEST--**
I'M GOING OUT WITH **WONDER WOMAN...**
...I CAN **HARDLY** THINK OF ANYWHERE **SAFER** TO BE.
C'MON, THAT **EXCUSE** FOR CHICKEN AT THE **BANQUET** HAS ME CRAVING **REAL** FOOD.
LET'S FIND SOMETHING TO **EAT.**

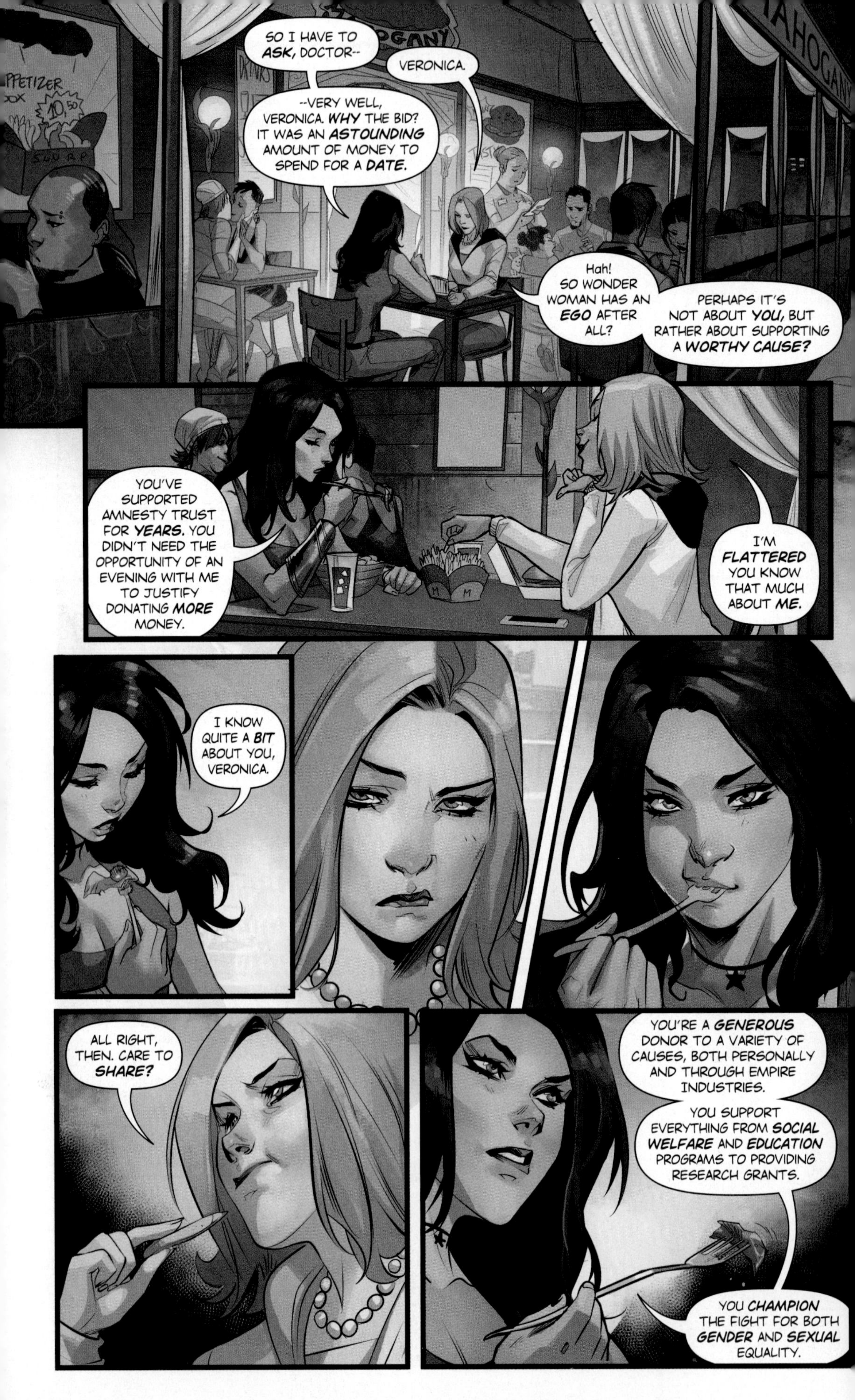

SO I HAVE TO ASK, DOCTOR--
VERONICA.
--VERY WELL, VERONICA. WHY THE BID? IT WAS AN ASTOUNDING AMOUNT OF MONEY TO SPEND FOR A DATE.
Hah! SO WONDER WOMAN HAS AN EGO AFTER ALL?
PERHAPS IT'S NOT ABOUT YOU, BUT RATHER ABOUT SUPPORTING A WORTHY CAUSE?
YOU'VE SUPPORTED AMNESTY TRUST FOR YEARS. YOU DIDN'T NEED THE OPPORTUNITY OF AN EVENING WITH ME TO JUSTIFY DONATING MORE MONEY.
I'M FLATTERED YOU KNOW THAT MUCH ABOUT ME.
I KNOW QUITE A BIT ABOUT YOU, VERONICA.
ALL RIGHT, THEN. CARE TO SHARE?
YOU'RE A GENEROUS DONOR TO A VARIETY OF CAUSES, BOTH PERSONALLY AND THROUGH EMPIRE INDUSTRIES.
YOU SUPPORT EVERYTHING FROM SOCIAL WELFARE AND EDUCATION PROGRAMS TO PROVIDING RESEARCH GRANTS.
YOU CHAMPION THE FIGHT FOR BOTH GENDER AND SEXUAL EQUALITY.

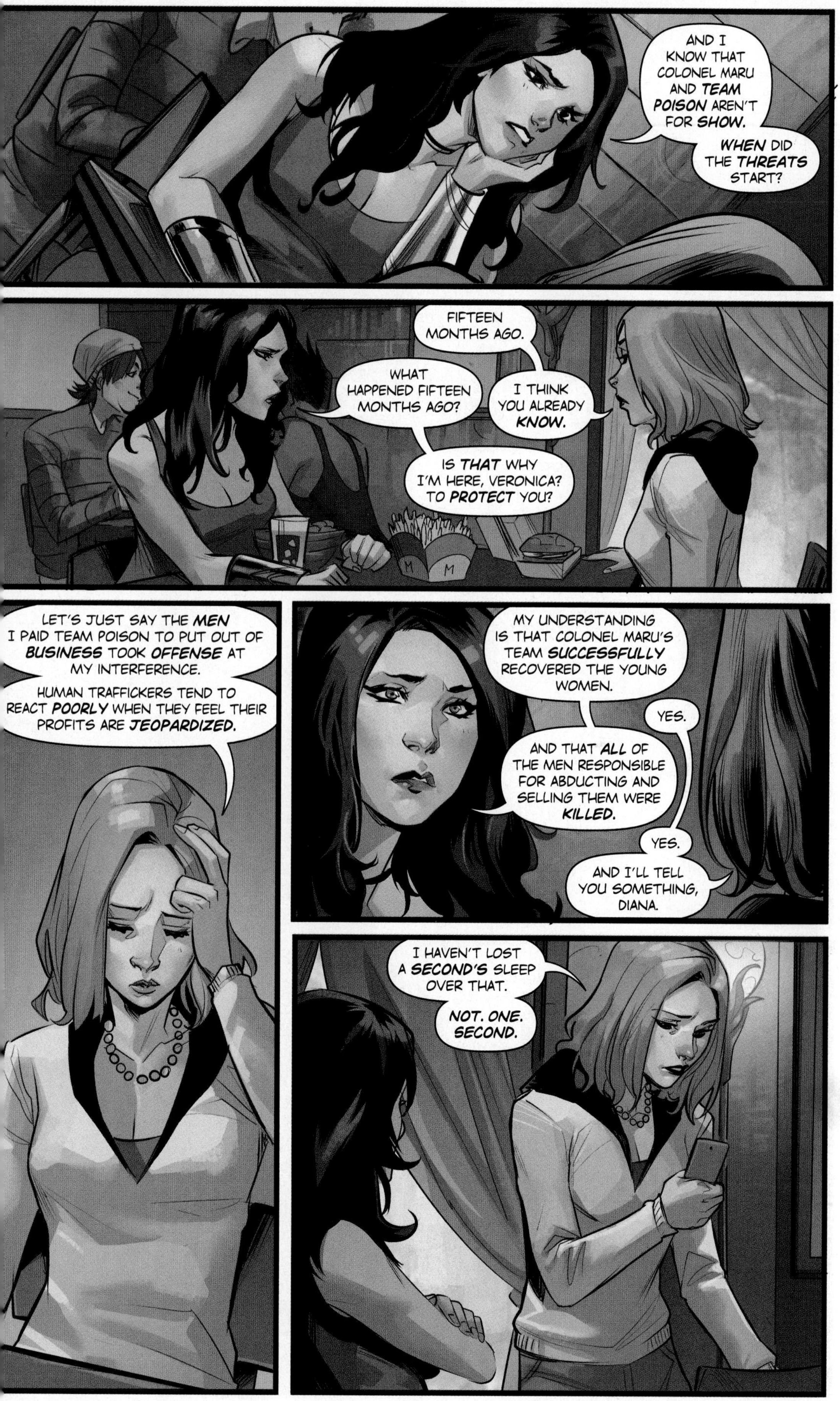
AND I KNOW THAT COLONEL MARU AND TEAM POISON AREN'T FOR SHOW.
WHEN DID THE THREATS START?
FIFTEEN MONTHS AGO.
WHAT HAPPENED FIFTEEN MONTHS AGO?
I THINK YOU ALREADY KNOW.
IS THAT WHY I'M HERE, VERONICA? TO PROTECT YOU?
LET'S JUST SAY THE MEN I PAID TEAM POISON TO PUT OUT OF BUSINESS TOOK OFFENSE AT MY INTERFERENCE.
HUMAN TRAFFICKERS TEND TO REACT POORLY WHEN THEY FEEL THEIR PROFITS ARE JEOPARDIZED.
MY UNDERSTANDING IS THAT COLONEL MARU'S TEAM SUCCESSFULLY RECOVERED THE YOUNG WOMEN.
YES.
AND THAT ALL OF THE MEN RESPONSIBLE FOR ABDUCTING AND SELLING THEM WERE KILLED.
YES.
AND I'LL TELL YOU SOMETHING, DIANA.
I HAVEN'T LOST A SECOND'S SLEEP OVER THAT.
NOT. ONE. SECOND.

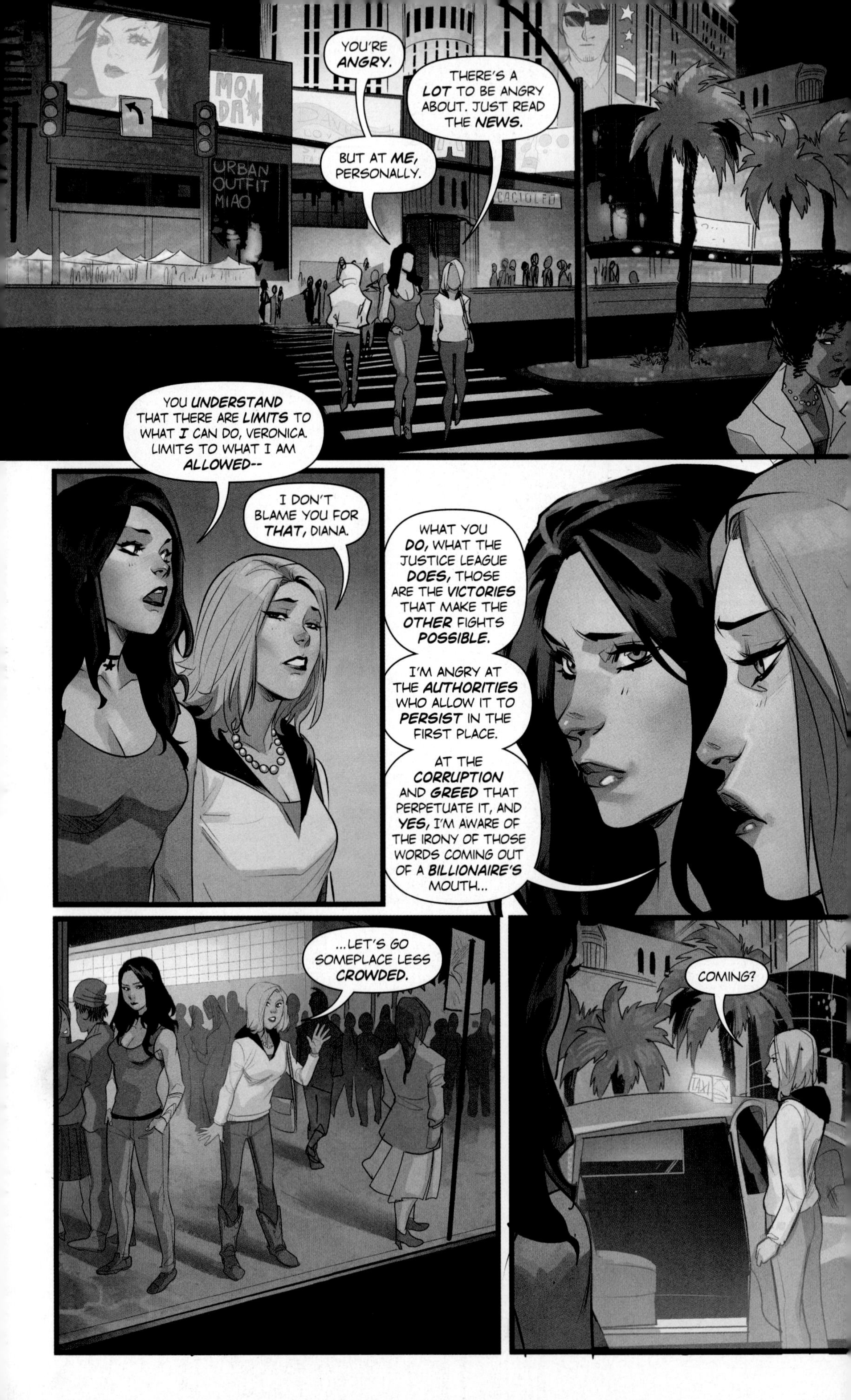
MODA
URBAN OUTFIT MIAO
YOU'RE ANGRY.
THERE'S A LOT TO BE ANGRY ABOUT. JUST READ THE NEWS.
BUT AT ME, PERSONALLY.
YOU UNDERSTAND THAT THERE ARE LIMITS TO WHAT I CAN DO, VERONICA. LIMITS TO WHAT I AM ALLOWED--
I DON'T BLAME YOU FOR THAT, DIANA.
WHAT YOU DO, WHAT THE JUSTICE LEAGUE DOES, THOSE ARE THE VICTORIES THAT MAKE THE OTHER FIGHTS POSSIBLE.
I'M ANGRY AT THE AUTHORITIES WHO ALLOW IT TO PERSIST IN THE FIRST PLACE.
AT THE CORRUPTION AND GREED THAT PERPETUATE IT, AND YES, I'M AWARE OF THE IRONY OF THOSE WORDS COMING OUT OF A BILLIONAIRE'S MOUTH...
...LET'S GO SOMEPLACE LESS CROWDED.
COMING?
TAXI

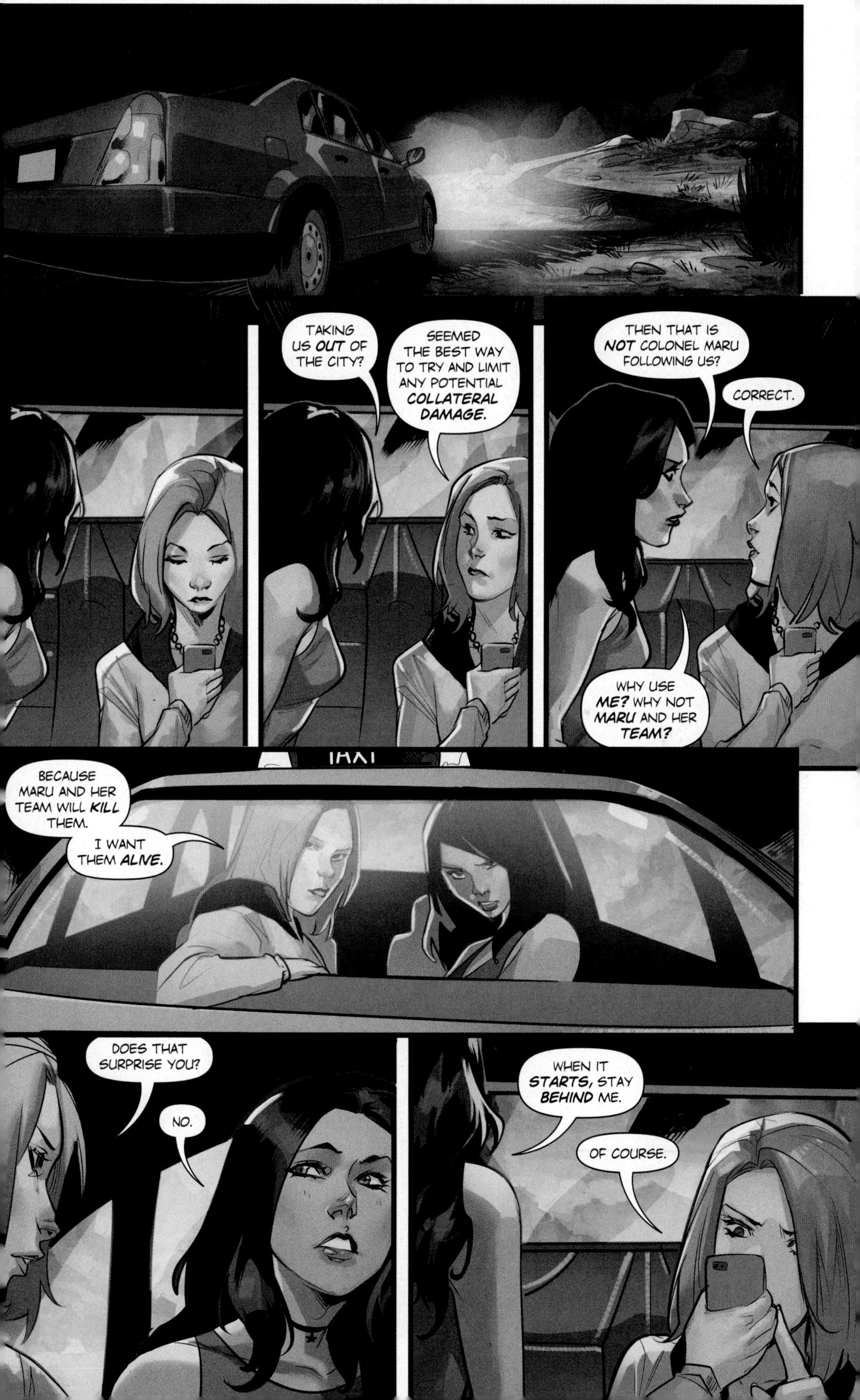
TAKING US OUT OF THE CITY?
SEEMED THE BEST WAY TO TRY AND LIMIT ANY POTENTIAL COLLATERAL DAMAGE.
THEN THAT IS NOT COLONEL MARU FOLLOWING US?
CORRECT.
WHY USE ME? WHY NOT MARU AND HER TEAM?
TAXI
BECAUSE MARU AND HER TEAM WILL KILL THEM.
I WANT THEM ALIVE.
DOES THAT SURPRISE YOU?
NO.
WHEN IT STARTS, STAY BEHIND ME.
OF COURSE.

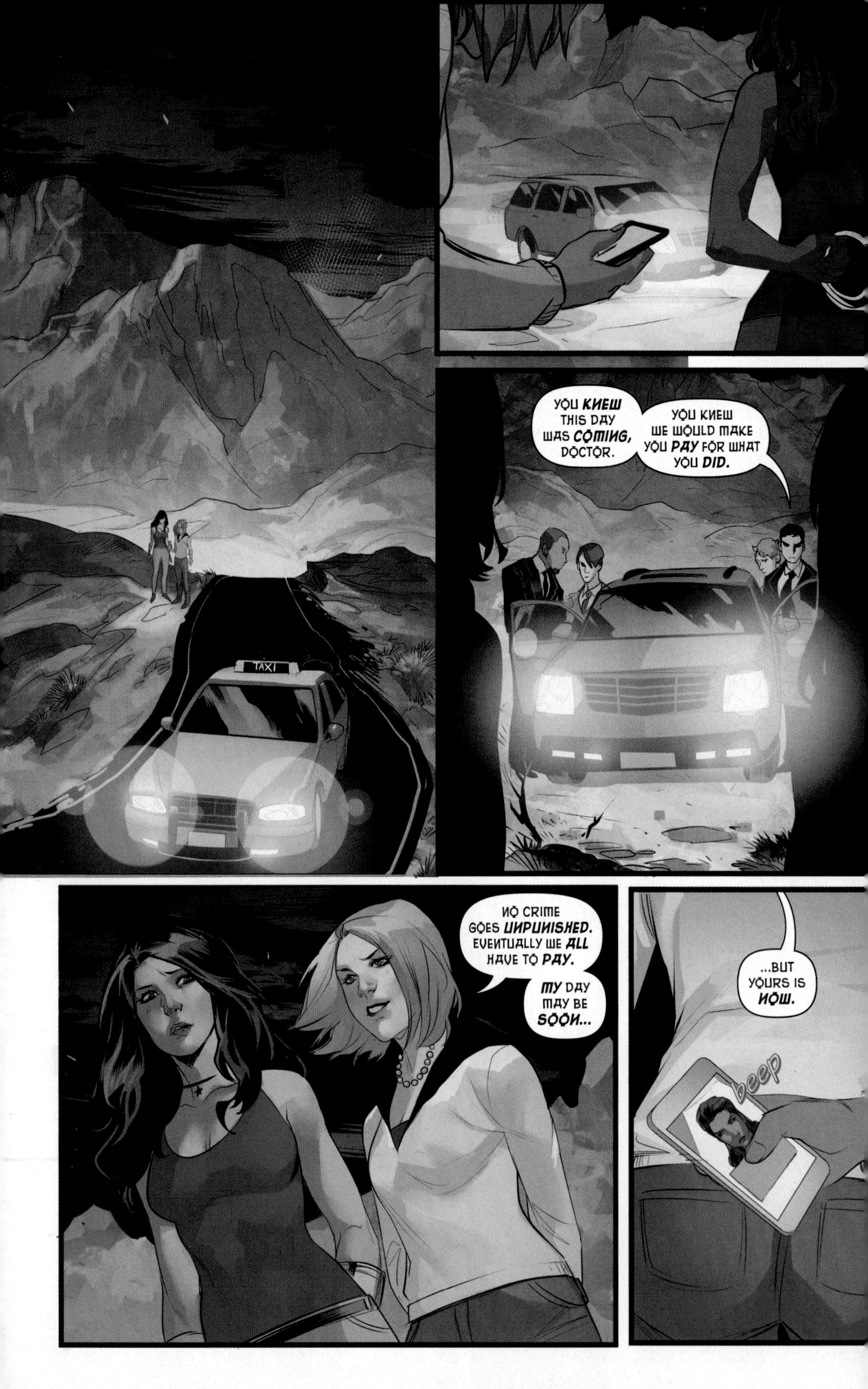
TAXI
YOU KNEW THIS DAY WAS COMING, DOCTOR.
YOU KNEW WE WOULD MAKE YOU PAY FOR WHAT YOU DID.
NO CRIME GOES UNPUNISHED. EVENTUALLY WE ALL HAVE TO PAY.
MY DAY MAY BE SOON...
...BUT YOURS IS NOW.
beep

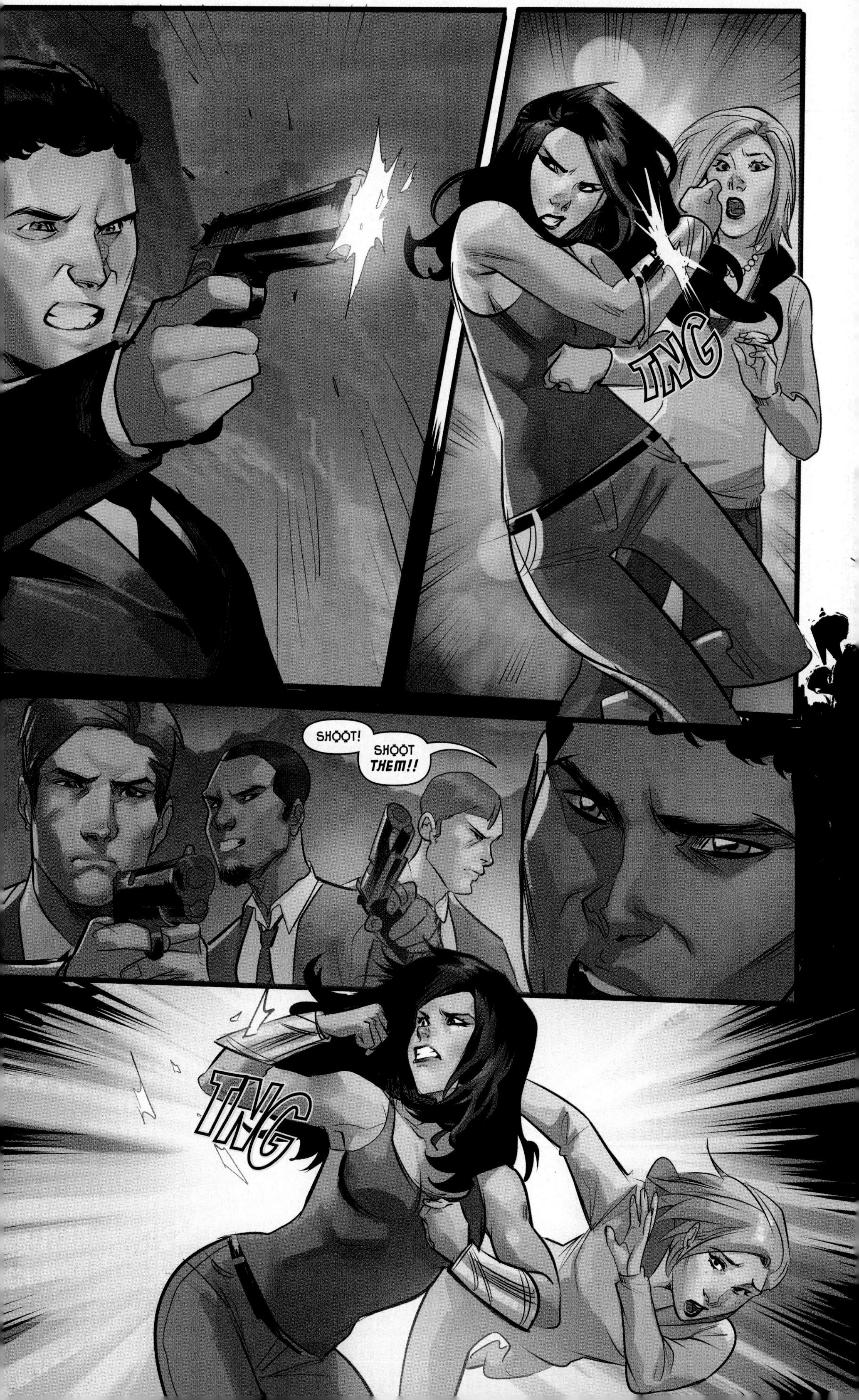
TNG
SHOOT!
SHOOT THEM!!
TNG

RESONANCE
CAPTURED
A

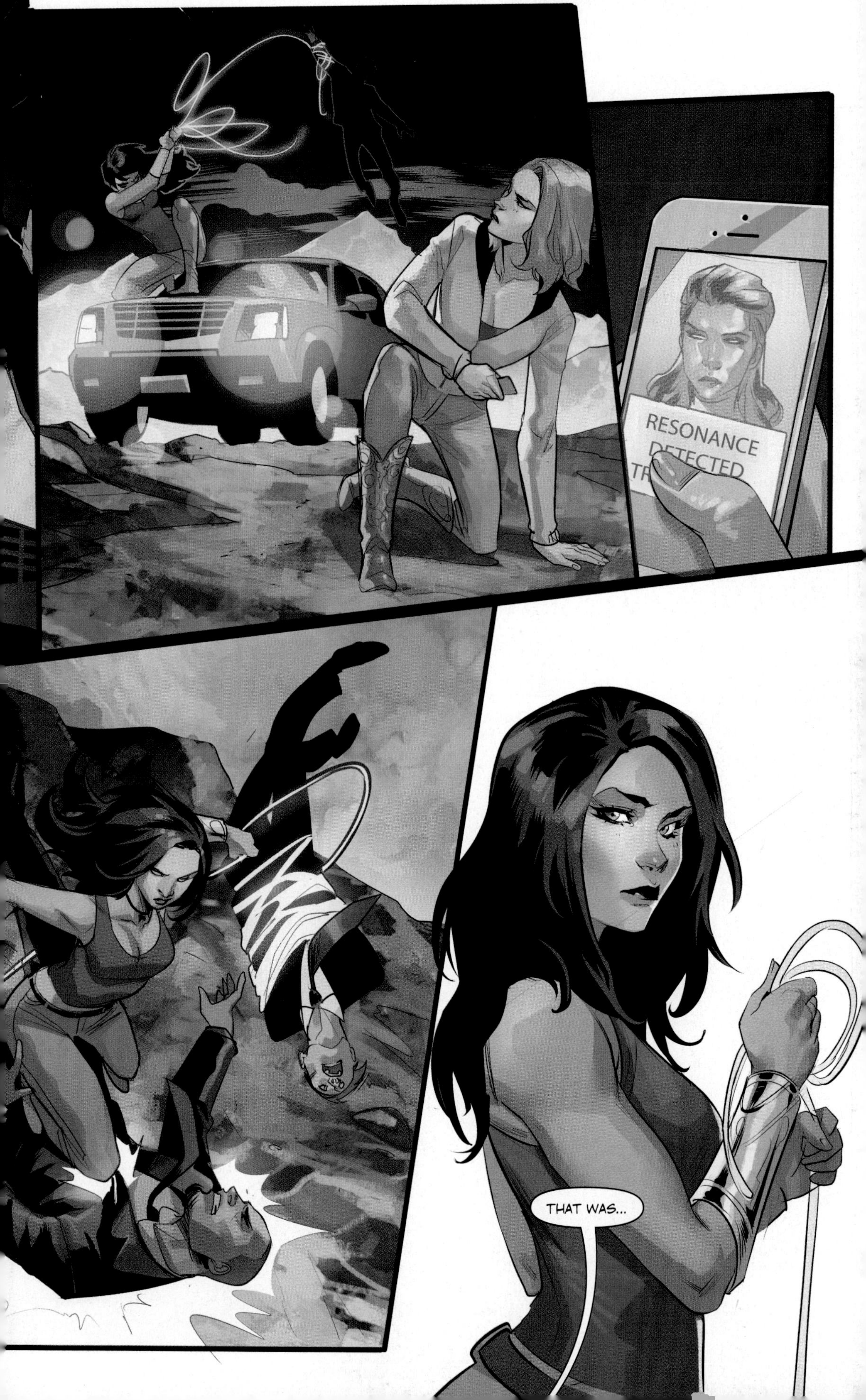
RESONANCE
THAT WAS...

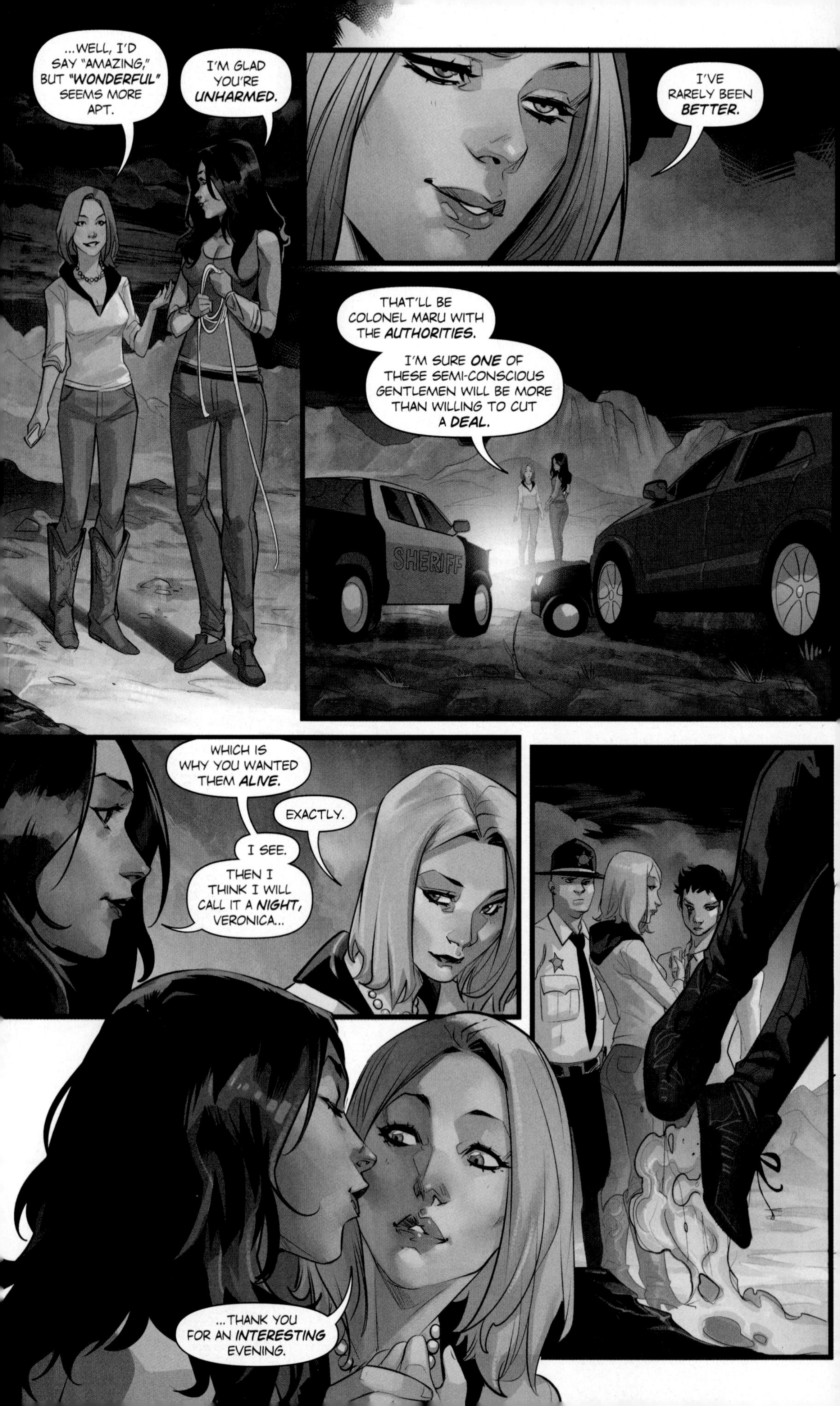

...WELL, I'D SAY "AMAZING," BUT "WONDERFUL" SEEMS MORE APT.
I'M GLAD YOU'RE UNHARMED.
I'VE RARELY BEEN BETTER.
THAT'LL BE COLONEL MARU WITH THE AUTHORITIES.
I'M SURE ONE OF THESE SEMI-CONSCIOUS GENTLEMEN WILL BE MORE THAN WILLING TO CUT A DEAL.
SHERIFF
WHICH IS WHY YOU WANTED THEM ALIVE.
EXACTLY.
I SEE.
THEN I THINK I WILL CALL IT A NIGHT, VERONICA...
...THANK YOU FOR AN INTERESTING EVENING.

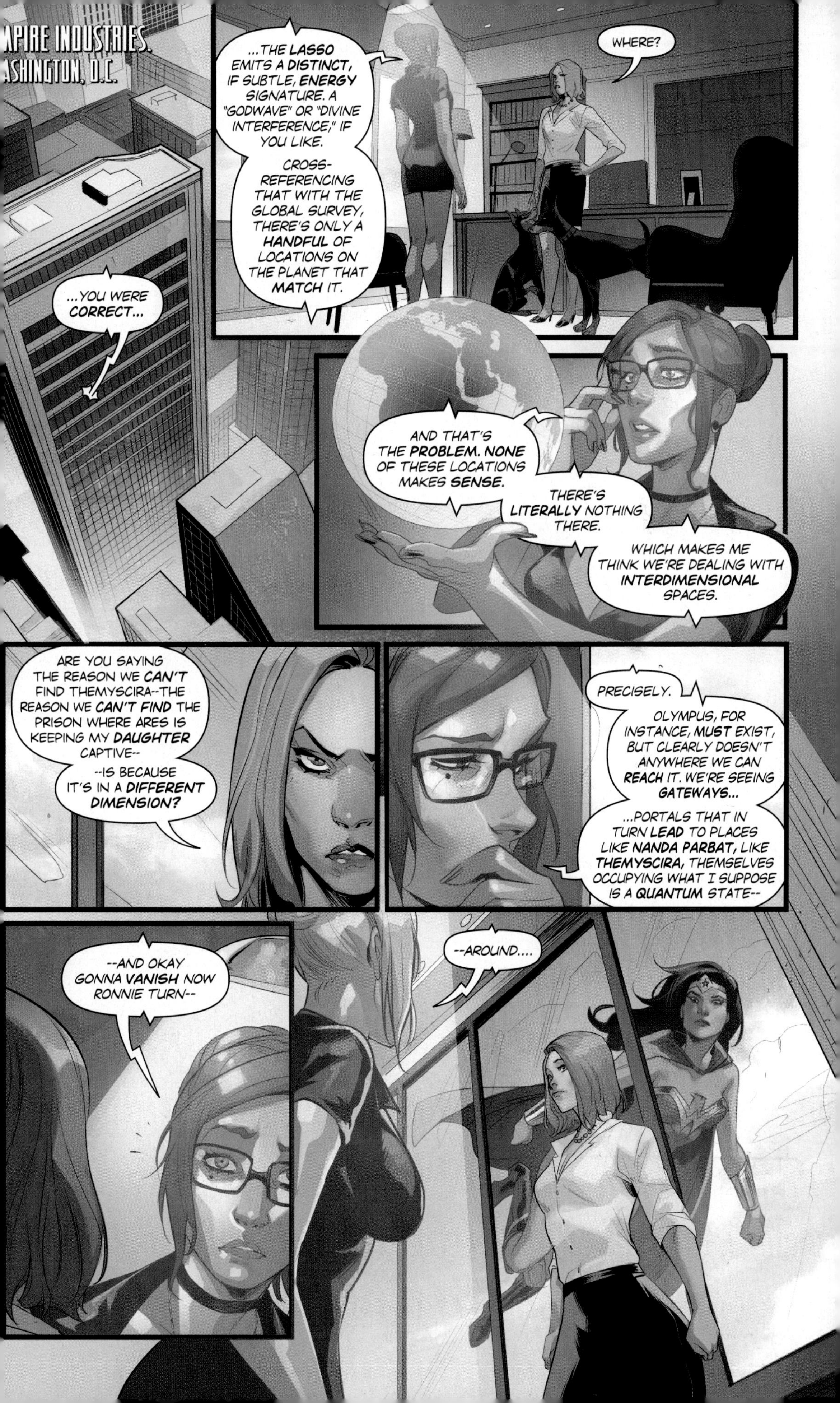

MPIRE INDUSTRIES.
ASHINGTON, D.C.
...YOU WERE CORRECT...
...THE LASSO EMITS A DISTINCT, IF SUBTLE, ENERGY SIGNATURE. A "GODWAVE" OR "DIVINE INTERFERENCE," IF YOU LIKE.
CROSS-REFERENCING THAT WITH THE GLOBAL SURVEY, THERE'S ONLY A HANDFUL OF LOCATIONS ON THE PLANET THAT MATCH IT.
WHERE?
AND THAT'S THE PROBLEM. NONE OF THESE LOCATIONS MAKES SENSE.
THERE'S LITERALLY NOTHING THERE.
WHICH MAKES ME THINK WE'RE DEALING WITH INTERDIMENSIONAL SPACES.
ARE YOU SAYING THE REASON WE CAN'T FIND THEMYSCIRA--THE REASON WE CAN'T FIND THE PRISON WHERE ARES IS KEEPING MY DAUGHTER CAPTIVE--
--IS BECAUSE IT'S IN A DIFFERENT DIMENSION?
PRECISELY.
OLYMPUS, FOR INSTANCE, MUST EXIST, BUT CLEARLY DOESN'T ANYWHERE WE CAN REACH IT. WE'RE SEEING GATEWAYS...
...PORTALS THAT IN TURN LEAD TO PLACES LIKE NANDA PARBAT, LIKE THEMYSCIRA, THEMSELVES OCCUPYING WHAT I SUPPOSE IS A QUANTUM STATE--
--AND OKAY GONNA VANISH NOW RONNIE TURN--
--AROUND....

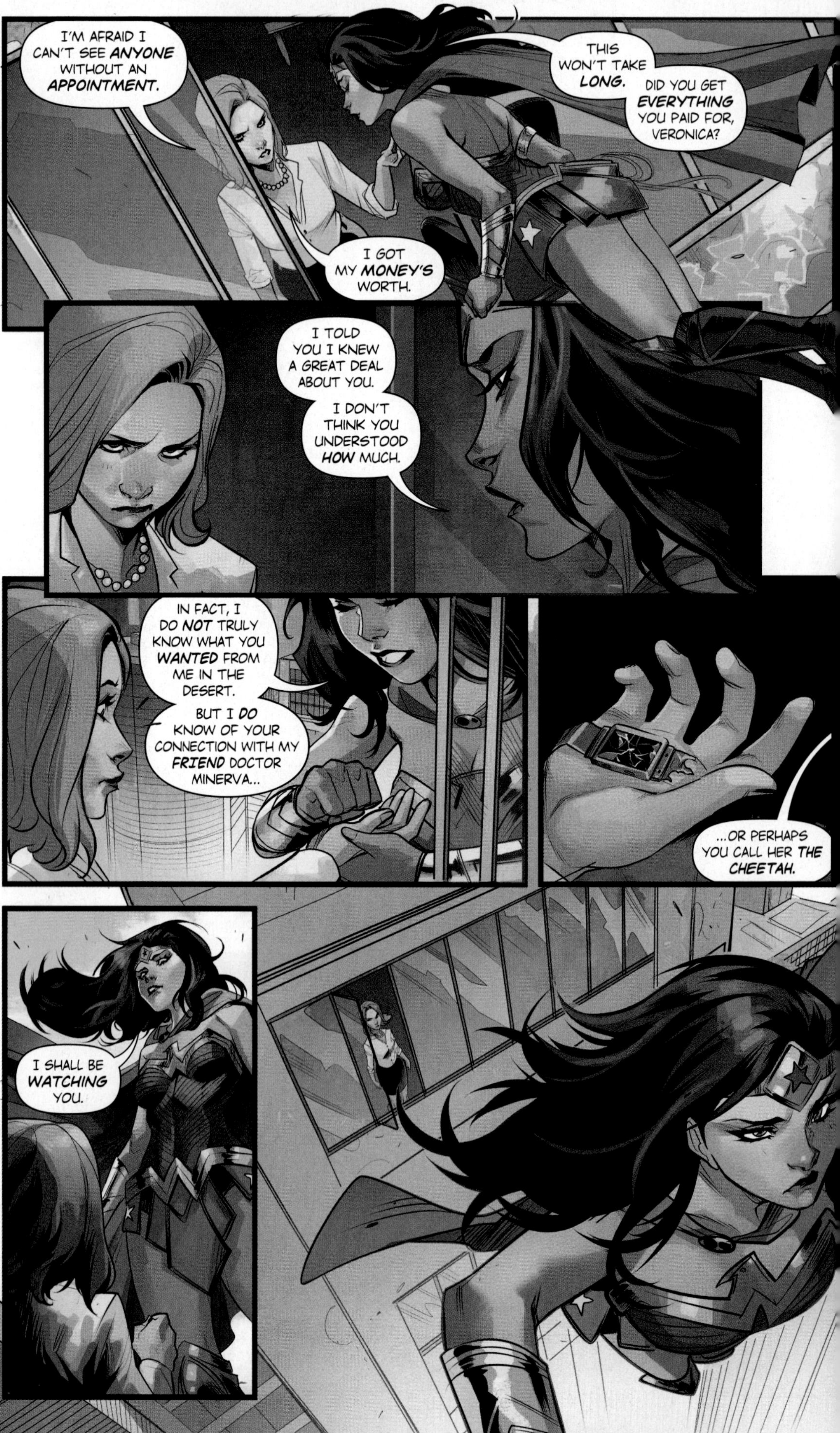
I'M AFRAID I CAN'T SEE ANYONE WITHOUT AN APPOINTMENT.
THIS WON'T TAKE LONG.
DID YOU GET EVERYTHING YOU PAID FOR, VERONICA?
I GOT MY MONEY'S WORTH.
I TOLD YOU I KNEW A GREAT DEAL ABOUT YOU.
I DON'T THINK YOU UNDERSTOOD HOW MUCH.
IN FACT, I DO NOT TRULY KNOW WHAT YOU WANTED FROM ME IN THE DESERT.
BUT I DO KNOW OF YOUR CONNECTION WITH MY FRIEND DOCTOR MINERVA...
...OR PERHAPS YOU CALL HER THE CHEETAH.
I SHALL BE WATCHING YOU.

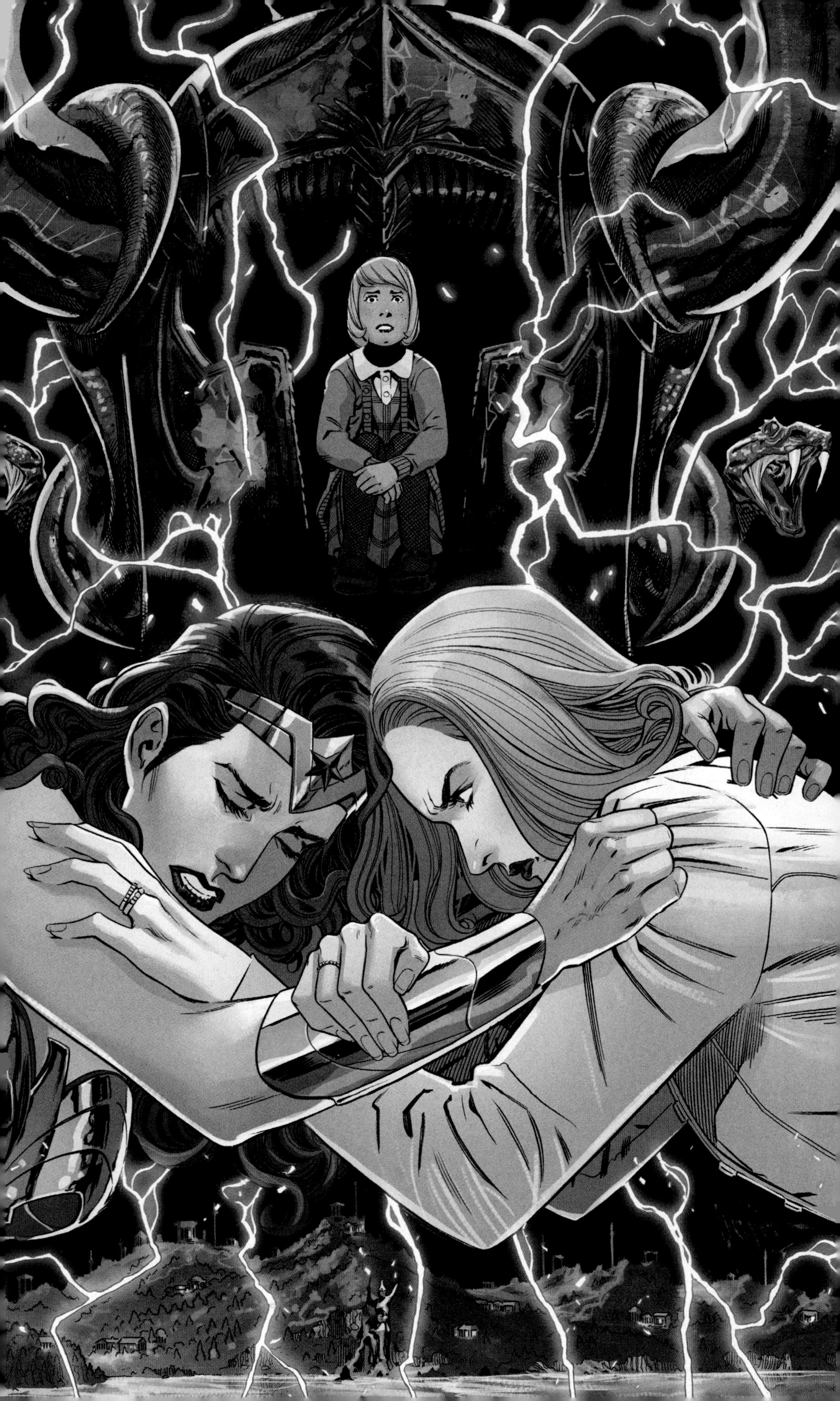

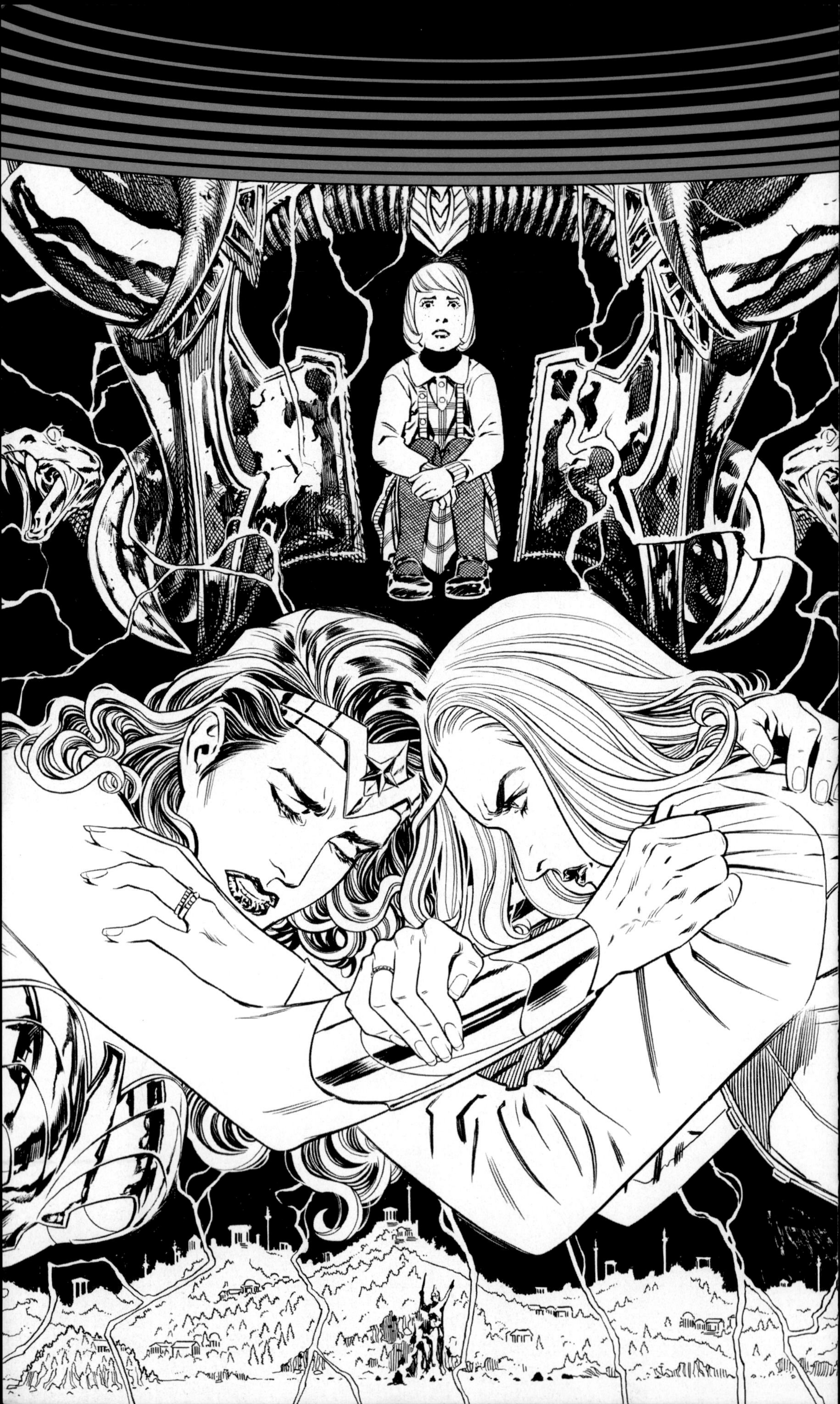

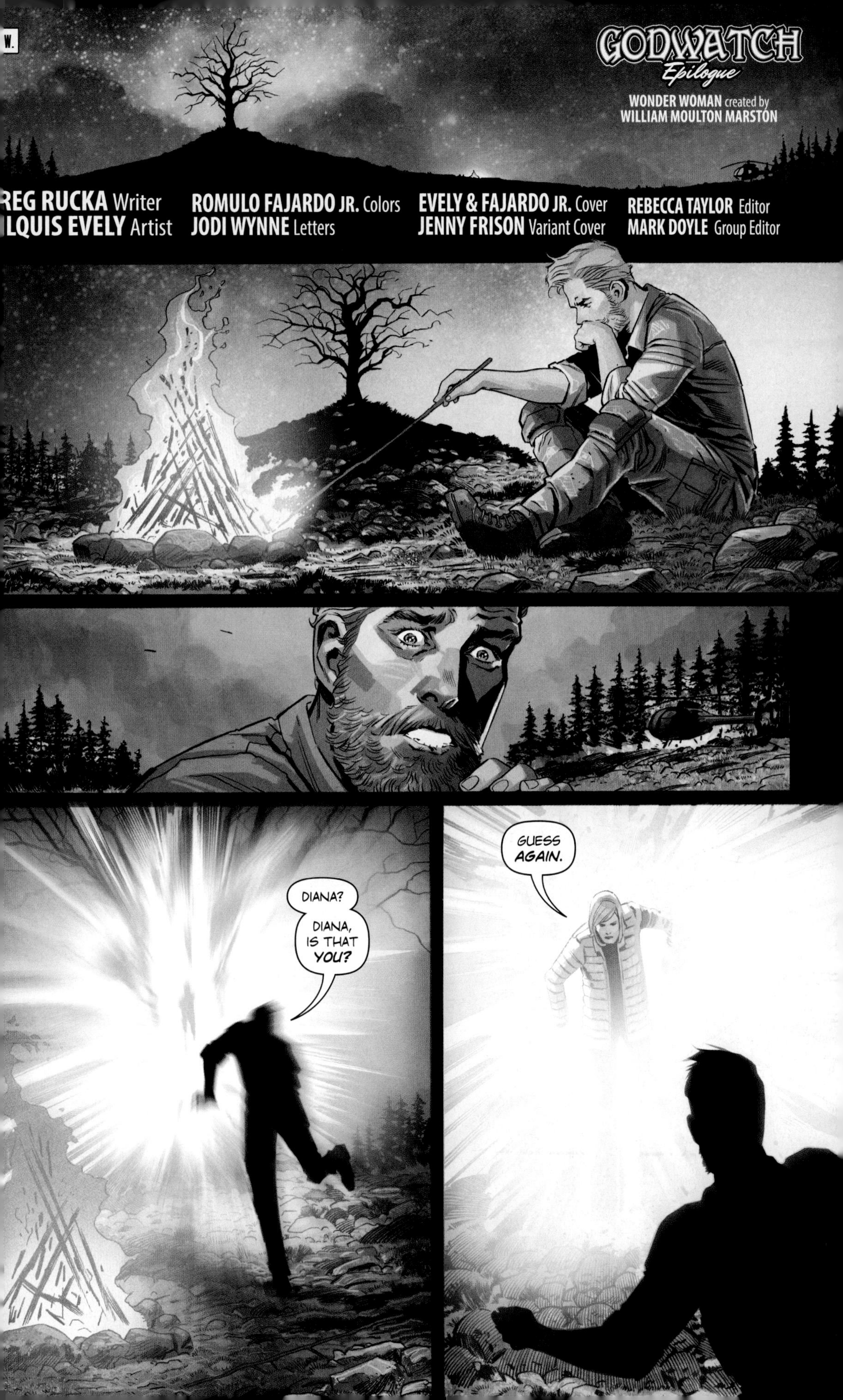
W.
GODWATCH
Epilogue
WONDER WOMAN created by
WILLIAM MOULTON MARSTON
REG RUCKA Writer
LQUIS EVELY Artist
ROMULO FAJARDO JR. Colors
JODI WYNNE Letters
EVELY & FAJARDO JR. Cover
JENNY FRISON Variant Cover
REBECCA TAYLOR Editor
MARK DOYLE Group Editor
DIANA?
DIANA, IS THAT YOU?
GUESS AGAIN.

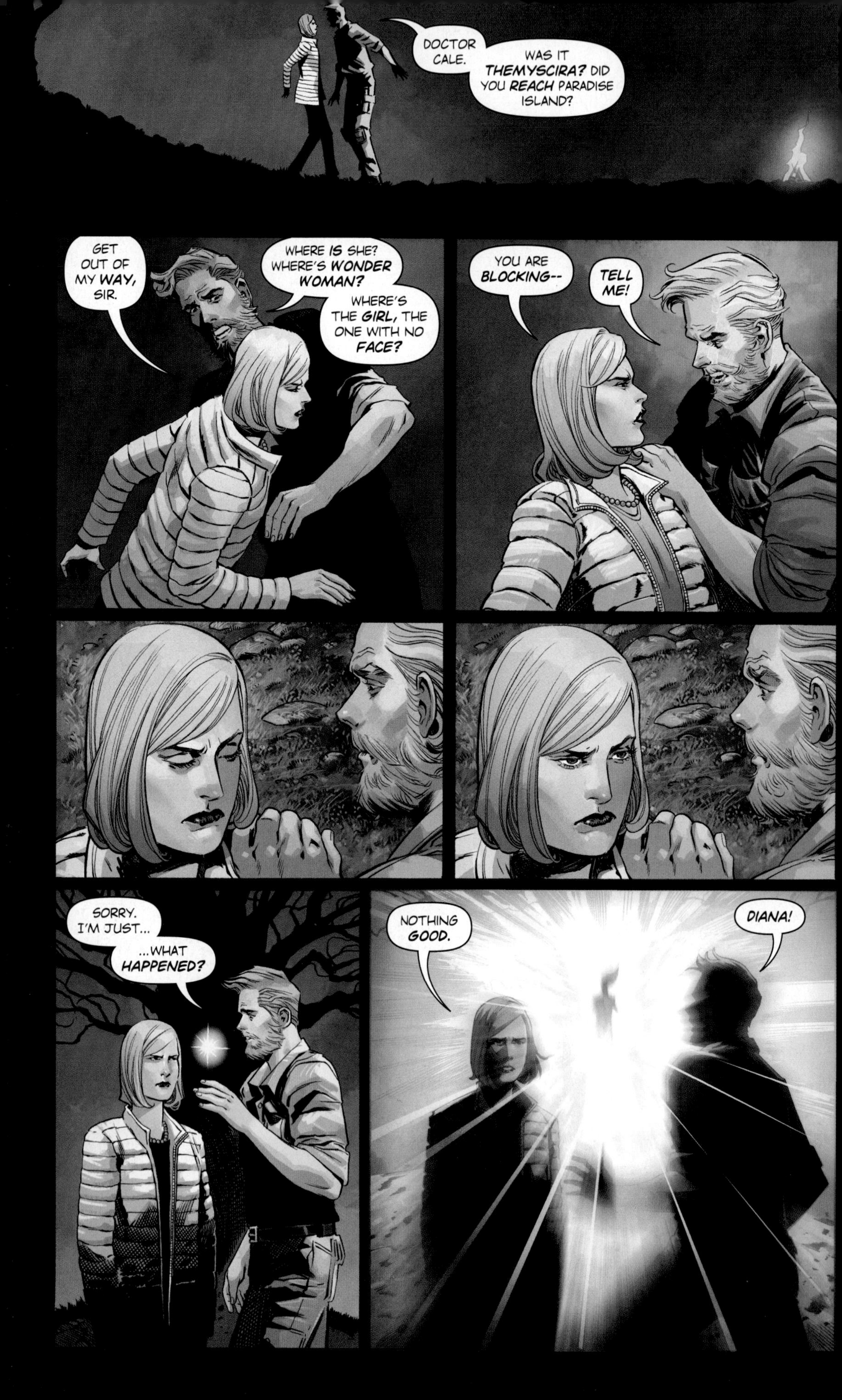

DOCTOR CALE.
WAS IT THEMYSCIRA? DID YOU REACH PARADISE ISLAND?
GET OUT OF MY WAY, SIR.
WHERE IS SHE? WHERE'S WONDER WOMAN?
WHERE'S THE GIRL, THE ONE WITH NO FACE?
YOU ARE BLOCKING--
TELL ME!
SORRY. I'M JUST...
...WHAT HAPPENED?
NOTHING GOOD.
DIANA!

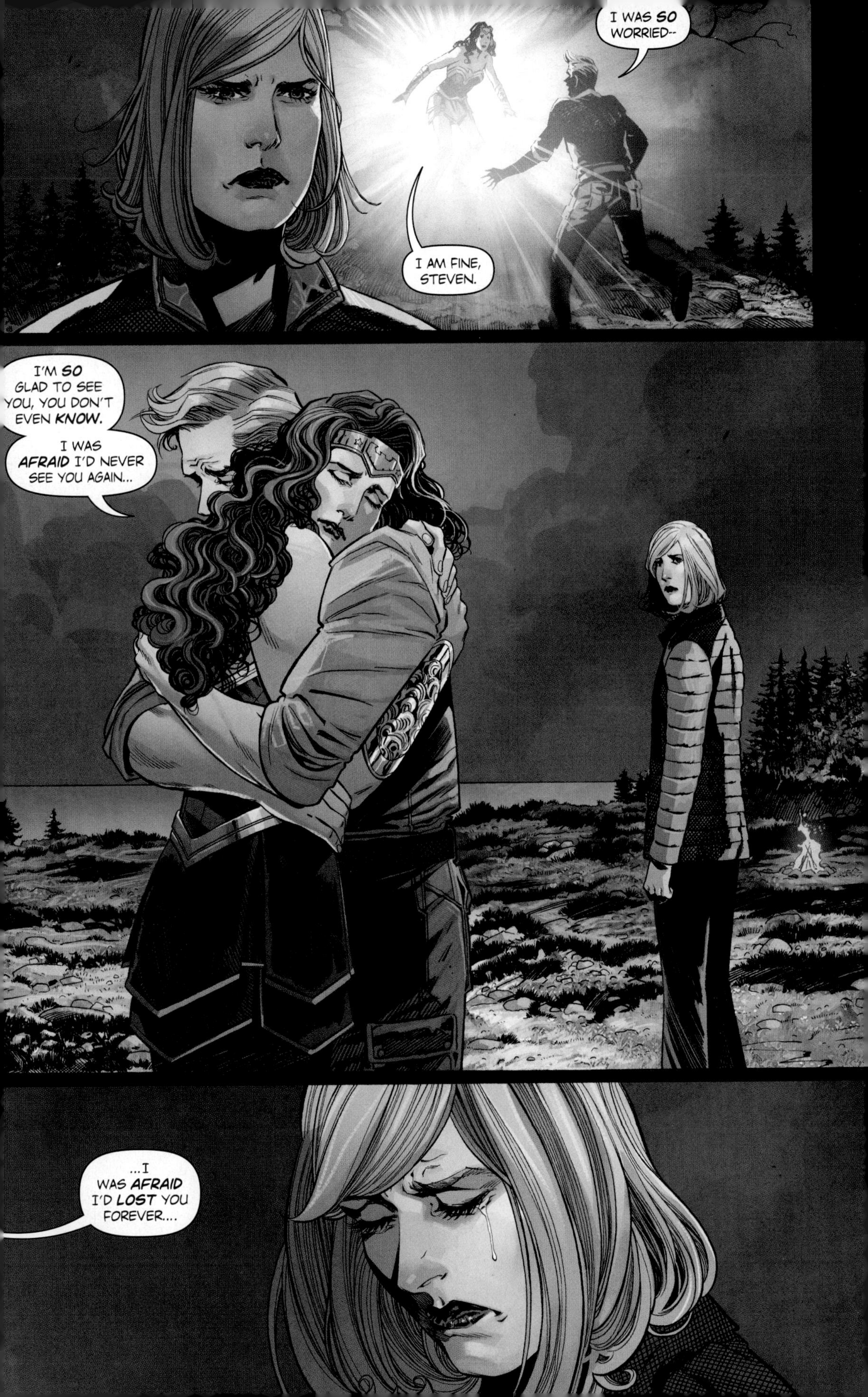
I WAS SO WORRIED--
I AM FINE, STEVEN.
I'M SO GLAD TO SEE YOU, YOU DON'T EVEN KNOW.
I WAS AFRAID I'D NEVER SEE YOU AGAIN...
...I WAS AFRAID I'D LOST YOU FOREVER....

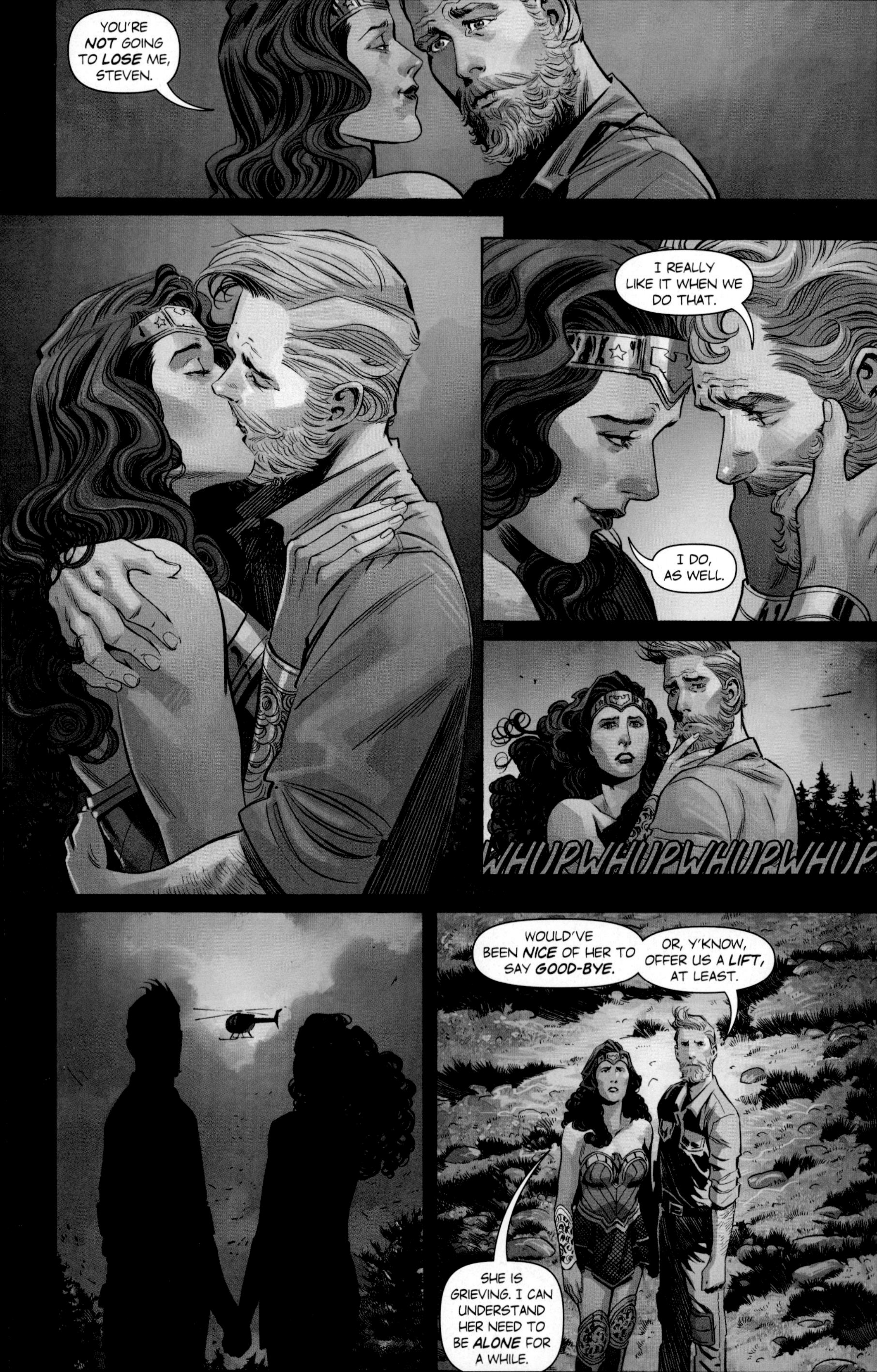
YOU'RE NOT GOING TO LOSE ME, STEVEN.
I REALLY LIKE IT WHEN WE DO THAT.
I DO, AS WELL.
WHUPWHUPWHUPWHUP
WOULD'VE BEEN NICE OF HER TO SAY GOOD-BYE.
OR, Y'KNOW, OFFER US A LIFT, AT LEAST.
SHE IS GRIEVING. I CAN UNDERSTAND HER NEED TO BE ALONE FOR A WHILE.

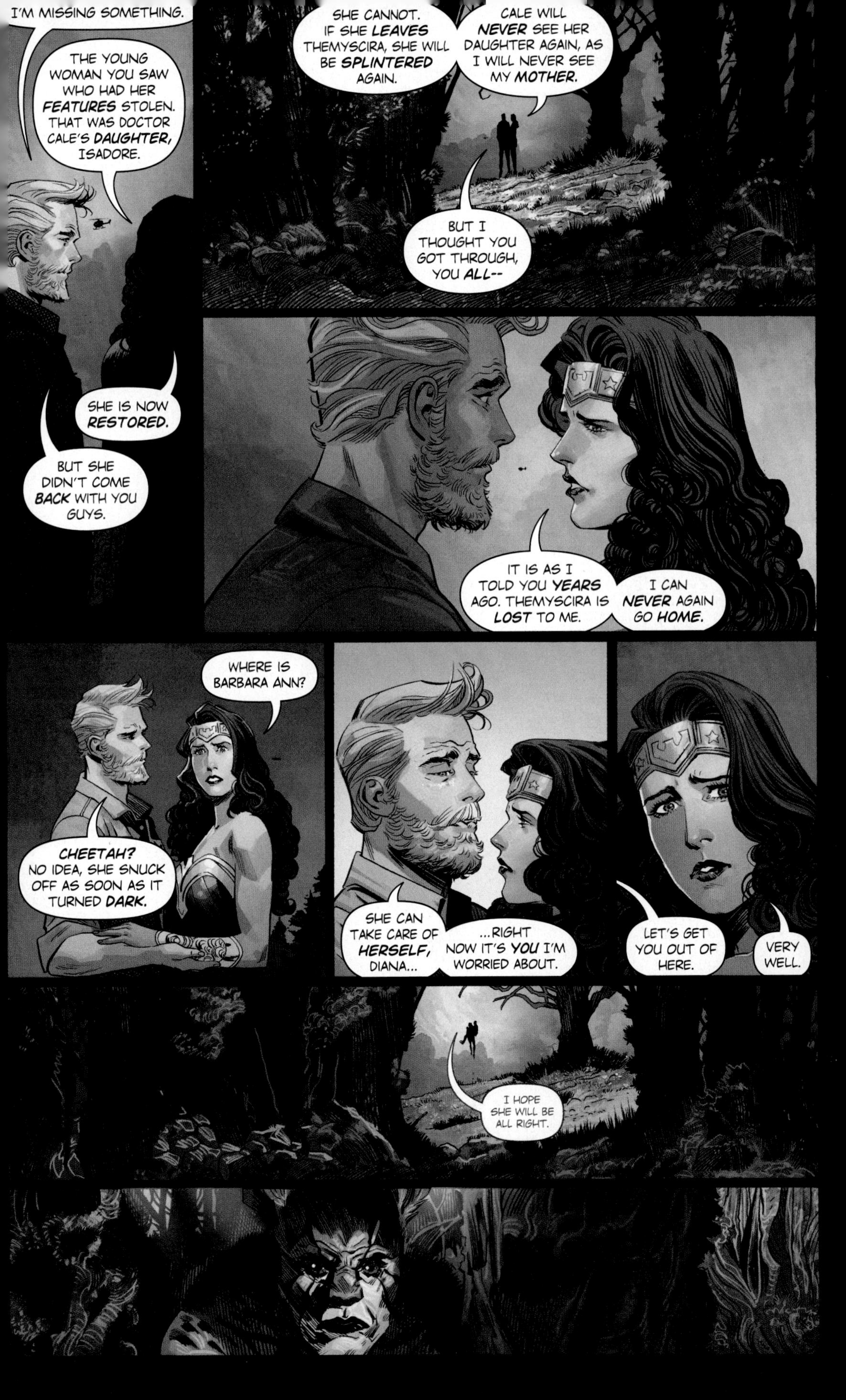
I'M MISSING SOMETHING.
THE YOUNG WOMAN YOU SAW WHO HAD HER FEATURES STOLEN. THAT WAS DOCTOR CALE'S DAUGHTER, ISADORE.
SHE IS NOW RESTORED.
BUT SHE DIDN'T COME BACK WITH YOU GUYS.
SHE CANNOT. IF SHE LEAVES THEMYSCIRA, SHE WILL BE SPLINTERED AGAIN.
CALE WILL NEVER SEE HER DAUGHTER AGAIN, AS I WILL NEVER SEE MY MOTHER.
BUT I THOUGHT YOU GOT THROUGH, YOU ALL--
IT IS AS I TOLD YOU YEARS AGO. THEMYSCIRA IS LOST TO ME.
I CAN NEVER AGAIN GO HOME.
WHERE IS BARBARA ANN?
CHEETAH? NO IDEA, SHE SNUCK OFF AS SOON AS IT TURNED DARK.
SHE CAN TAKE CARE OF HERSELF, DIANA...
...RIGHT NOW IT'S YOU I'M WORRIED ABOUT.
LET'S GET YOU OUT OF HERE.
VERY WELL.
I HOPE SHE WILL BE ALL RIGHT.

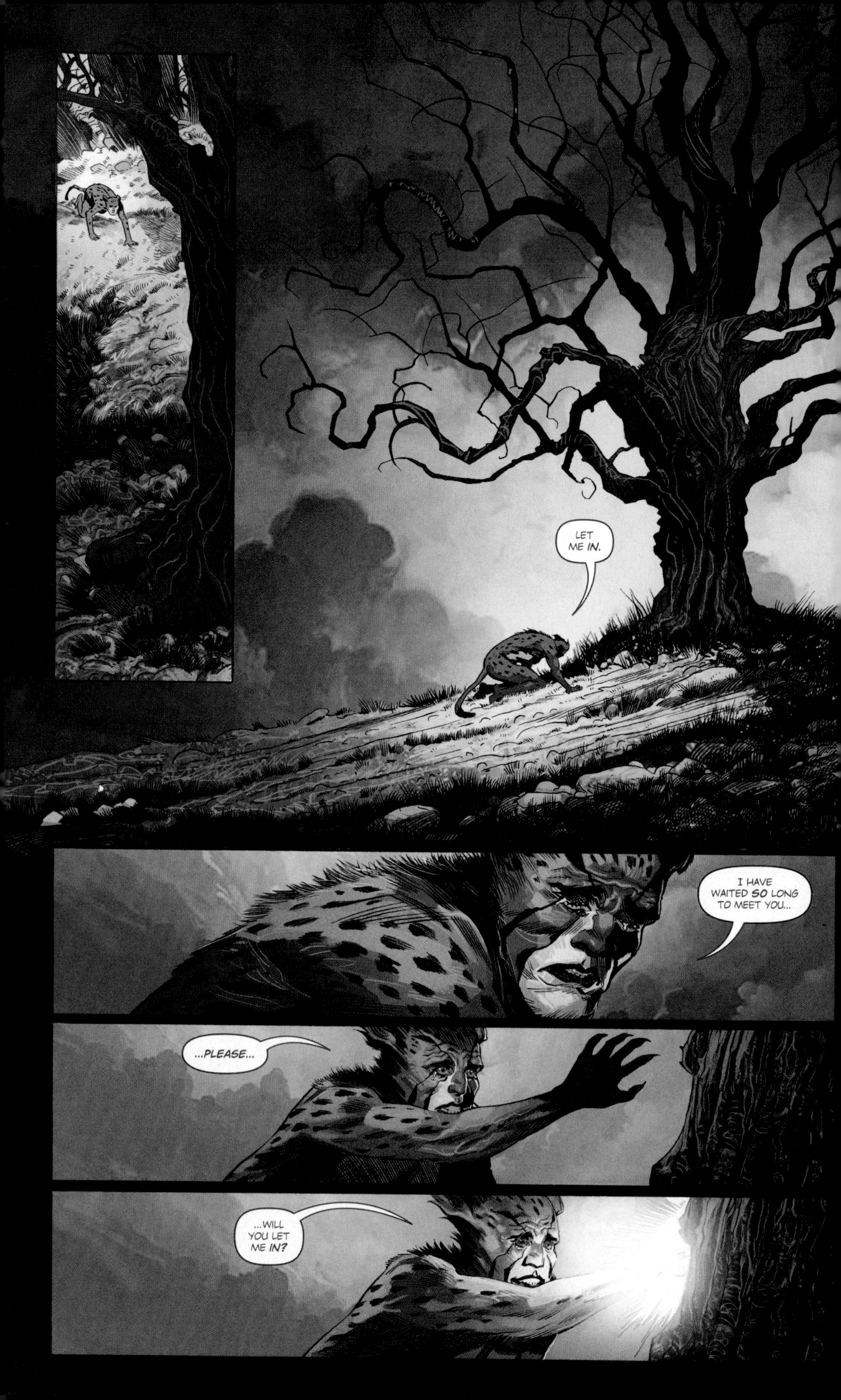
LET ME *IN*.
I HAVE WAITED **SO** LONG TO MEET YOU...
...PLEASE...
...WILL YOU LET ME *IN?*

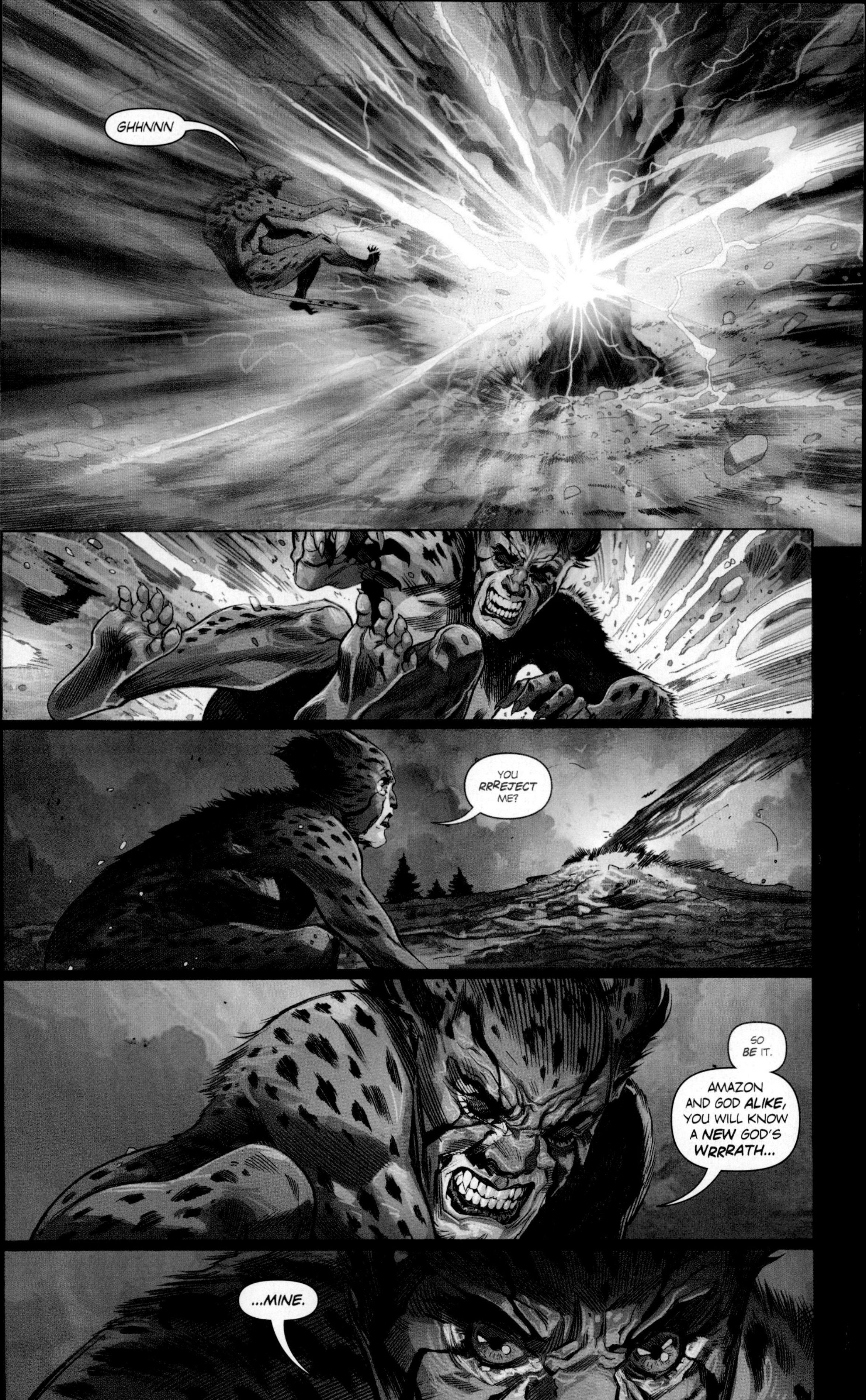
GHHNNN
YOU RRREJECT ME?
SO BE IT.
AMAZON AND GOD ALIKE, YOU WILL KNOW A NEW GOD'S WRRRATH...
...MINE.

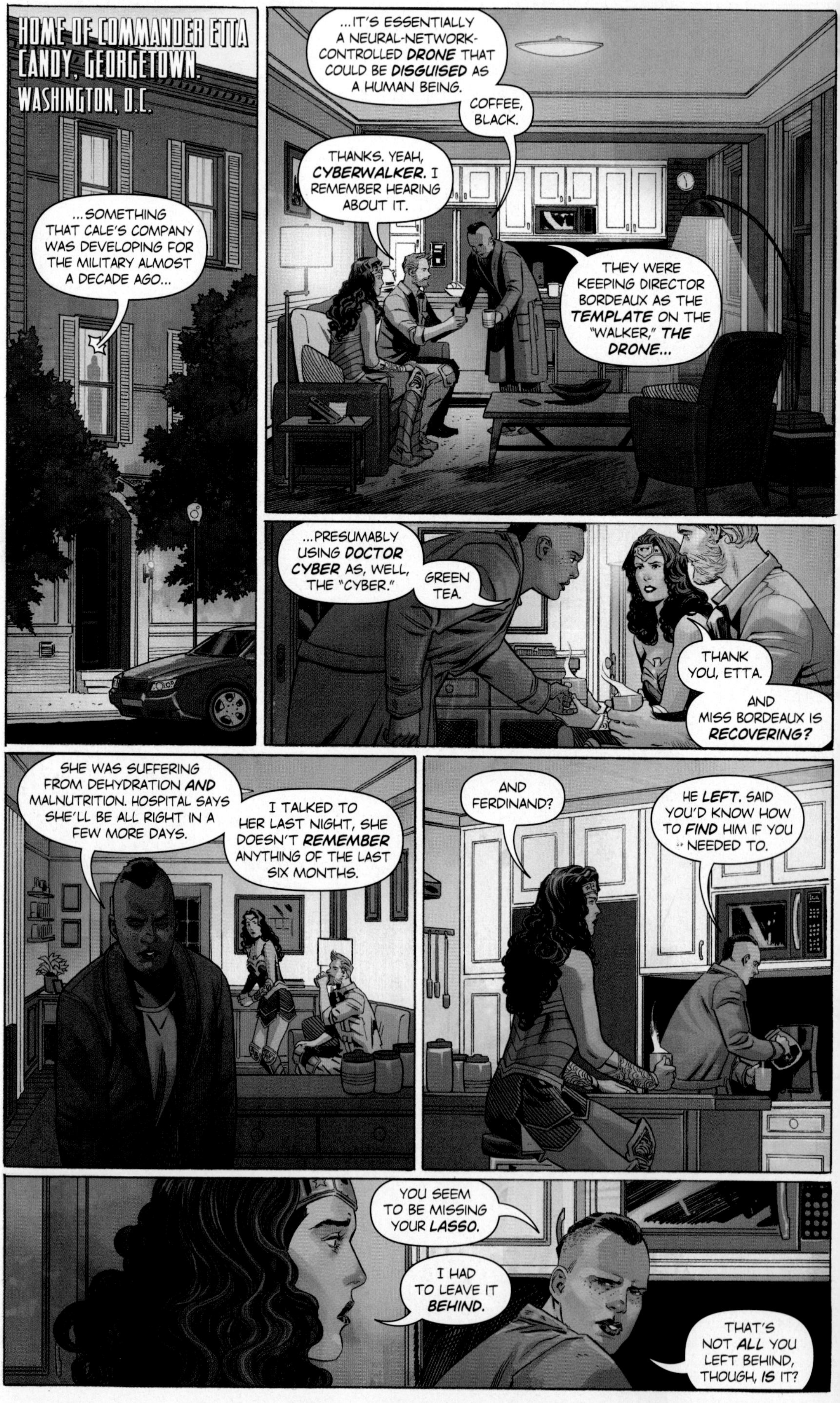

HOME OF COMMANDER ETTA CANDY, GEORGETOWN.
WASHINGTON, D.C.
...SOMETHING THAT CALE'S COMPANY WAS DEVELOPING FOR THE MILITARY ALMOST A DECADE AGO...
...IT'S ESSENTIALLY A NEURAL-NETWORK-CONTROLLED DRONE THAT COULD BE DISGUISED AS A HUMAN BEING.
COFFEE, BLACK.
THANKS. YEAH, CYBERWALKER. I REMEMBER HEARING ABOUT IT.
THEY WERE KEEPING DIRECTOR BORDEAUX AS THE TEMPLATE ON THE "WALKER," THE DRONE...
...PRESUMABLY USING DOCTOR CYBER AS, WELL, THE "CYBER."
GREEN TEA.
THANK YOU, ETTA.
AND MISS BORDEAUX IS RECOVERING?
SHE WAS SUFFERING FROM DEHYDRATION AND MALNUTRITION. HOSPITAL SAYS SHE'LL BE ALL RIGHT IN A FEW MORE DAYS.
I TALKED TO HER LAST NIGHT, SHE DOESN'T REMEMBER ANYTHING OF THE LAST SIX MONTHS.
AND FERDINAND?
HE LEFT. SAID YOU'D KNOW HOW TO FIND HIM IF YOU NEEDED TO.
YOU SEEM TO BE MISSING YOUR LASSO.
I HAD TO LEAVE IT BEHIND.
THAT'S NOT ALL YOU LEFT BEHIND, THOUGH, IS IT?

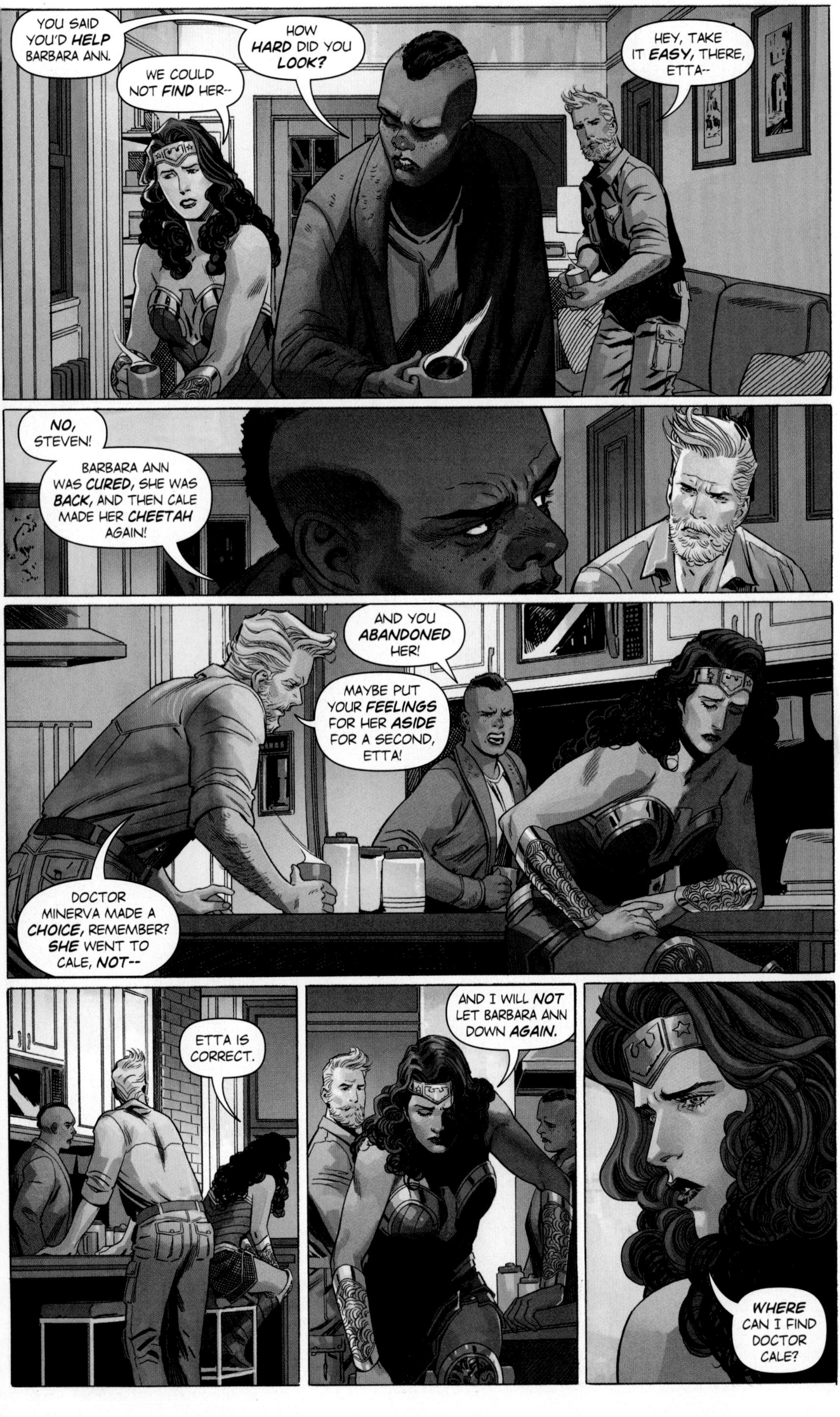

YOU SAID YOU'D HELP BARBARA ANN.
WE COULD NOT FIND HER--
HOW HARD DID YOU LOOK?
HEY, TAKE IT EASY, THERE, ETTA--
NO, STEVEN!
BARBARA ANN WAS CURED, SHE WAS BACK, AND THEN CALE MADE HER CHEETAH AGAIN!
AND YOU ABANDONED HER!
MAYBE PUT YOUR FEELINGS FOR HER ASIDE FOR A SECOND, ETTA!
DOCTOR MINERVA MADE A CHOICE, REMEMBER? SHE WENT TO CALE, NOT--
ETTA IS CORRECT.
AND I WILL NOT LET BARBARA ANN DOWN AGAIN.
WHERE CAN I FIND DOCTOR CALE?

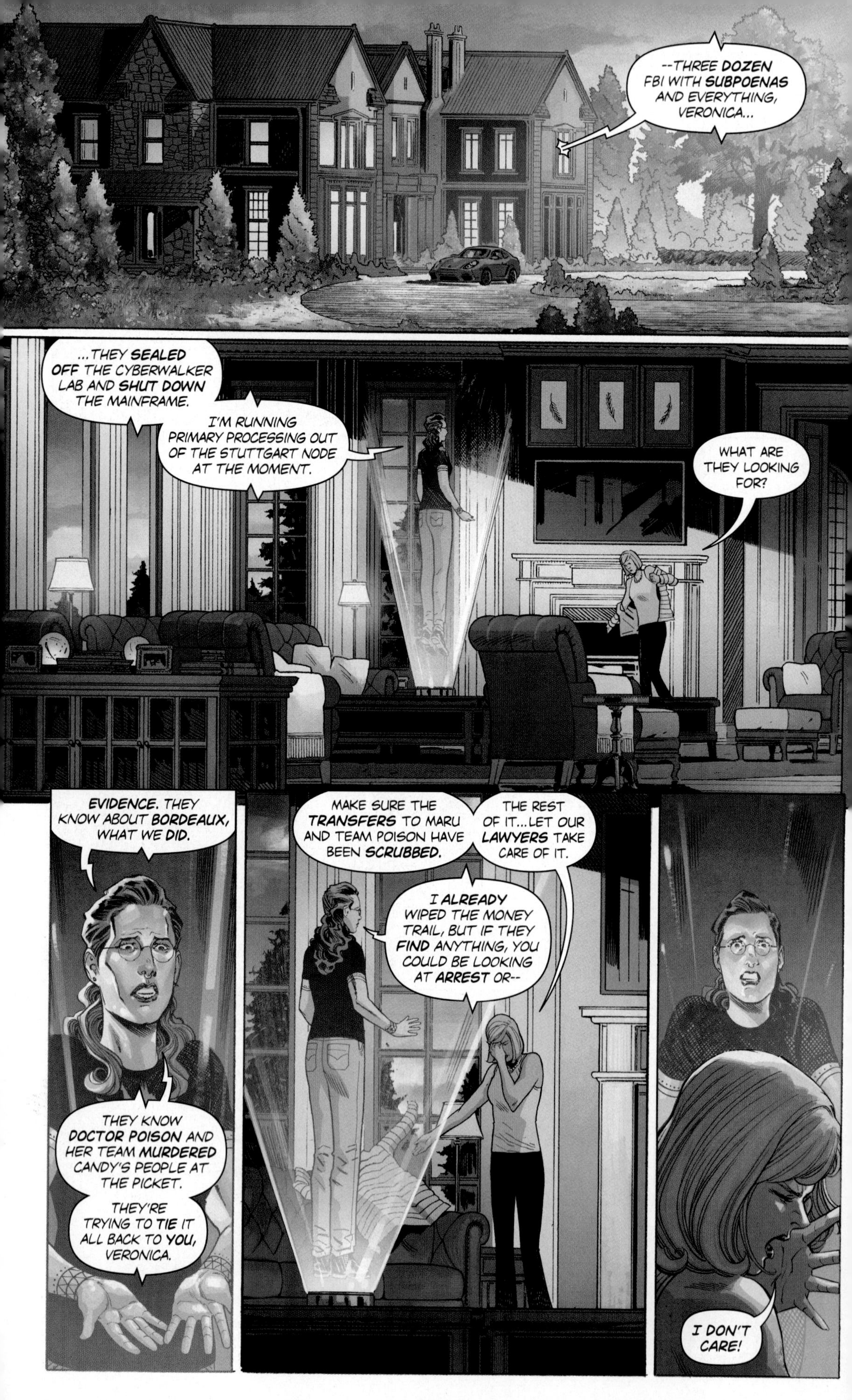
--THREE DOZEN FBI WITH SUBPOENAS AND EVERYTHING, VERONICA...
...THEY SEALED OFF THE CYBERWALKER LAB AND SHUT DOWN THE MAINFRAME.
I'M RUNNING PRIMARY PROCESSING OUT OF THE STUTTGART NODE AT THE MOMENT.
WHAT ARE THEY LOOKING FOR?
EVIDENCE. THEY KNOW ABOUT BORDEAUX, WHAT WE DID.
THEY KNOW DOCTOR POISON AND HER TEAM MURDERED CANDY'S PEOPLE AT THE PICKET.
THEY'RE TRYING TO TIE IT ALL BACK TO YOU, VERONICA.
MAKE SURE THE TRANSFERS TO MARU AND TEAM POISON HAVE BEEN SCRUBBED.
THE REST OF IT...LET OUR LAWYERS TAKE CARE OF IT.
I ALREADY WIPED THE MONEY TRAIL, BUT IF THEY FIND ANYTHING, YOU COULD BE LOOKING AT ARREST OR--
I DON'T CARE!

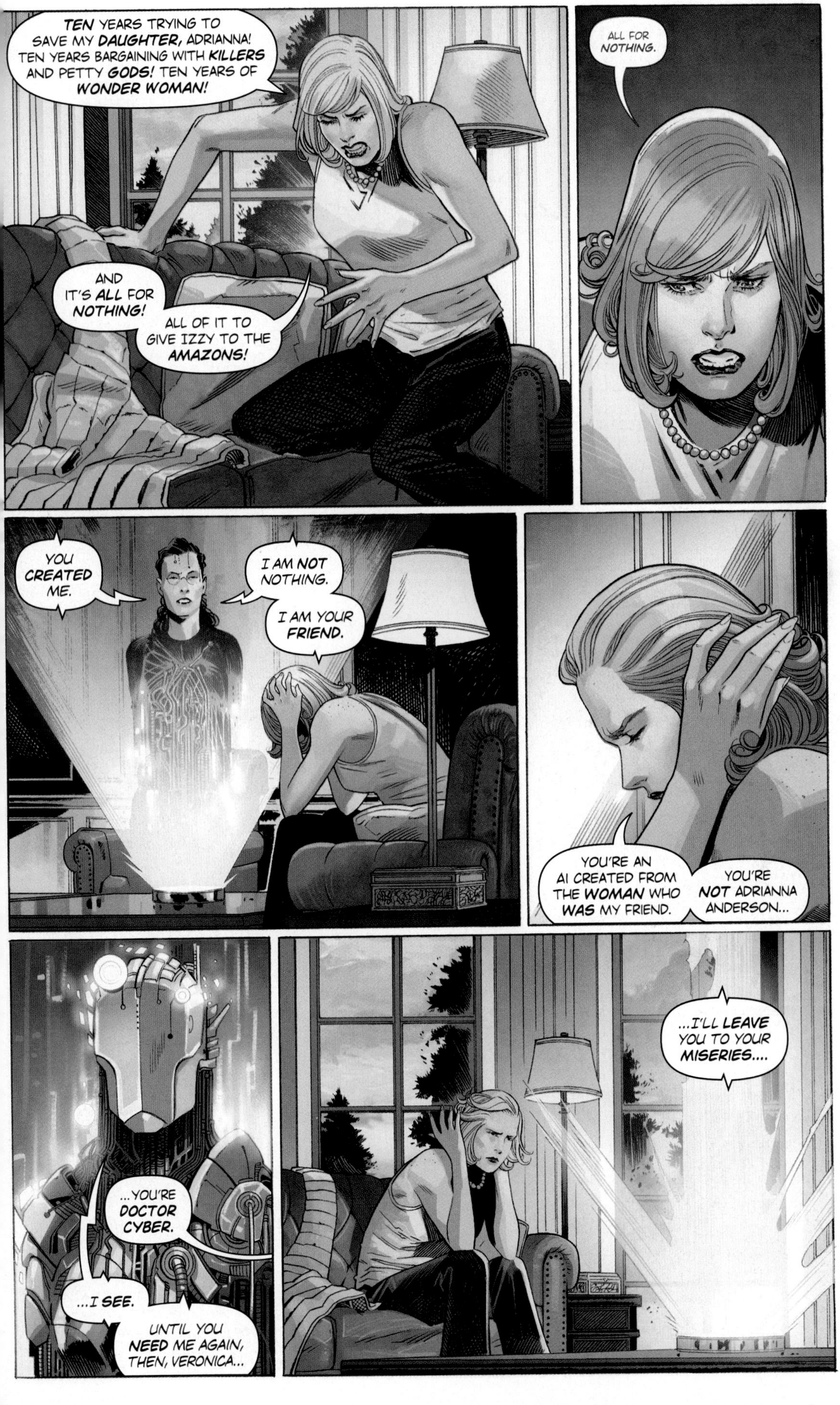
TEN YEARS TRYING TO SAVE MY DAUGHTER, ADRIANNA! TEN YEARS BARGAINING WITH KILLERS AND PETTY GODS! TEN YEARS OF WONDER WOMAN!
AND IT'S ALL FOR NOTHING!
ALL OF IT TO GIVE IZZY TO THE AMAZONS!
ALL FOR NOTHING.
YOU CREATED ME.
I AM NOT NOTHING.
I AM YOUR FRIEND.
YOU'RE NOT ADRIANNA ANDERSON...
YOU'RE AN AI CREATED FROM THE WOMAN WHO WAS MY FRIEND.
...YOU'RE DOCTOR CYBER.
...I SEE.
UNTIL YOU NEED ME AGAIN, THEN, VERONICA...
...I'LL LEAVE YOU TO YOUR MISERIES....

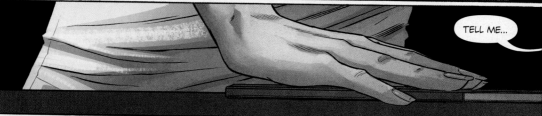

TELL ME...

...DOES IT HURRRT? ALL YOU'VE DONE, ALL THE LIES AND BETRRRAYALS...

...ALL FORRR YOURRR DAUGHTERRR...

...IS IT KILLING YOU INSIDE, VERRRONICA?

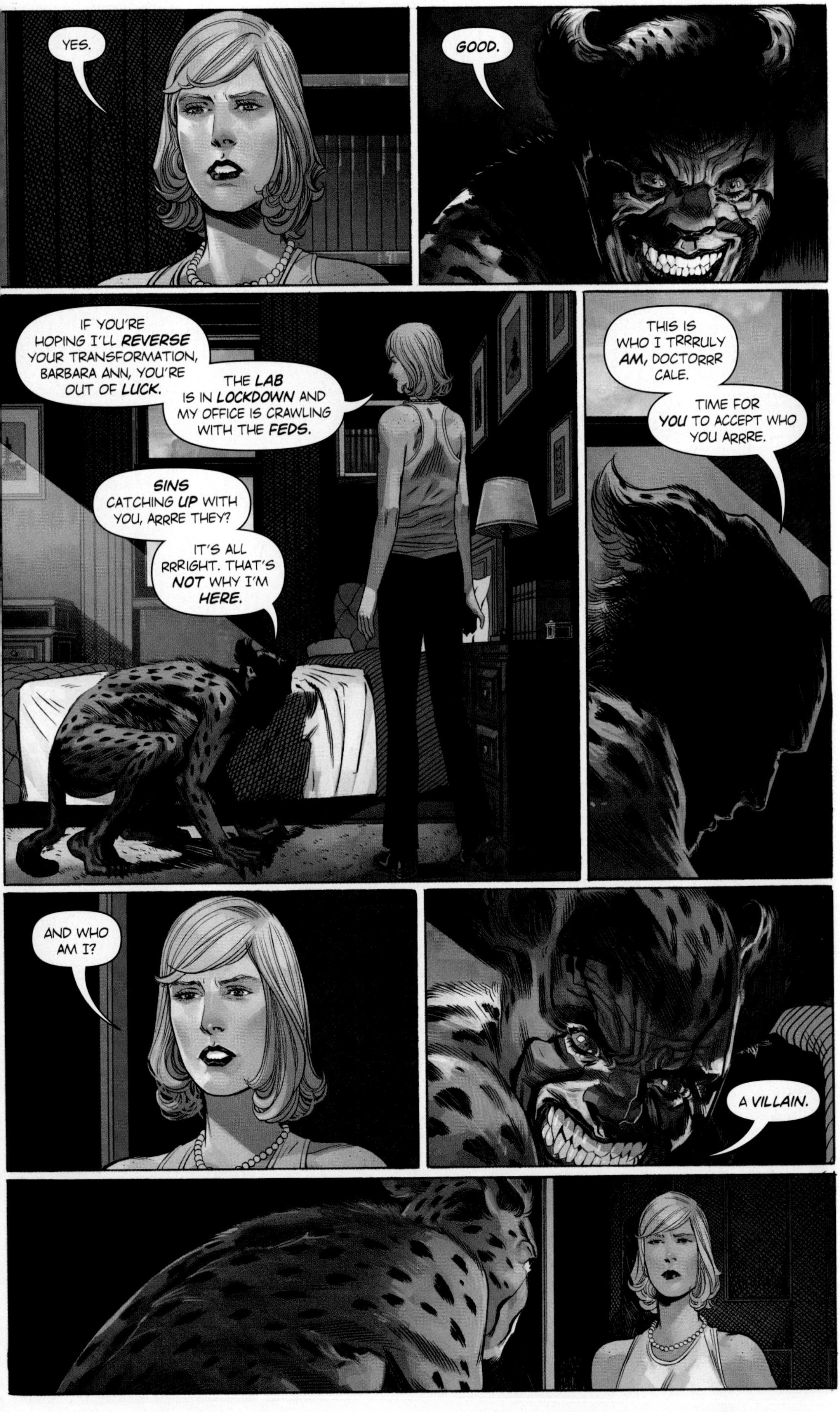
YES.
GOOD.
IF YOU'RE HOPING I'LL REVERSE YOUR TRANSFORMATION, BARBARA ANN, YOU'RE OUT OF LUCK.
THE LAB IS IN LOCKDOWN AND MY OFFICE IS CRAWLING WITH THE FEDS.
SINS CATCHING UP WITH YOU, ARRRE THEY?
IT'S ALL RRRIGHT. THAT'S NOT WHY I'M HERE.
THIS IS WHO I TRRRULY AM, DOCTORRR CALE.
TIME FOR YOU TO ACCEPT WHO YOU ARRRE.
AND WHO AM I?
A VILLAIN.

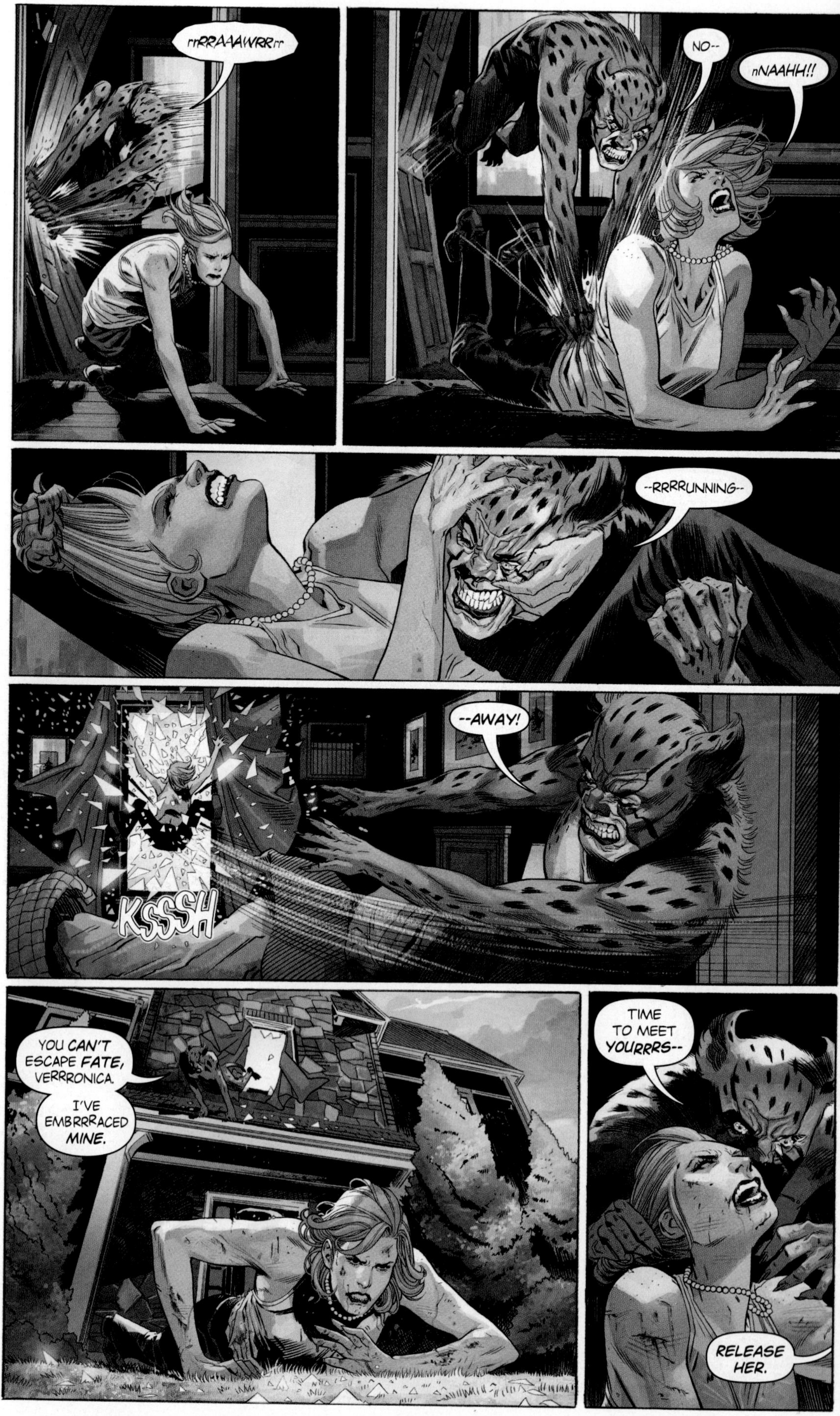

rrRRAAAWRRrr
NO--
nNAAHH!!
--RRRRUNNING--
--AWAY!
KSSSH
YOU CAN'T ESCAPE FATE, VERRONICA.
I'VE EMBRRRACED MINE.
TIME TO MEET YOURRRS--
RELEASE HER.

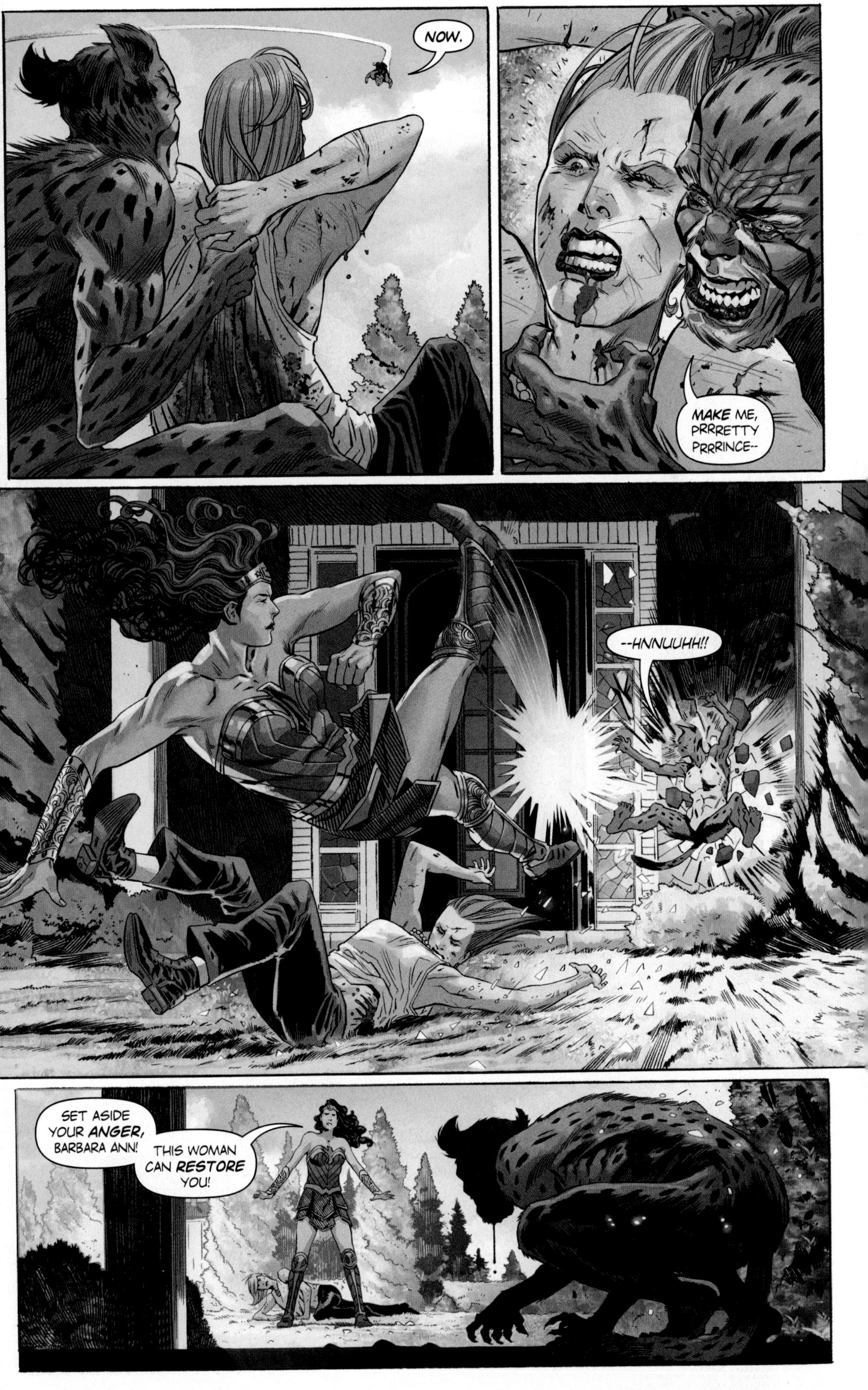
NOW.
MAKE ME, PRRRETTY PRRRINCE--
--HNNUUHH!!
SET ASIDE YOUR ANGER, BARBARA ANN!
THIS WOMAN CAN RESTORE YOU!

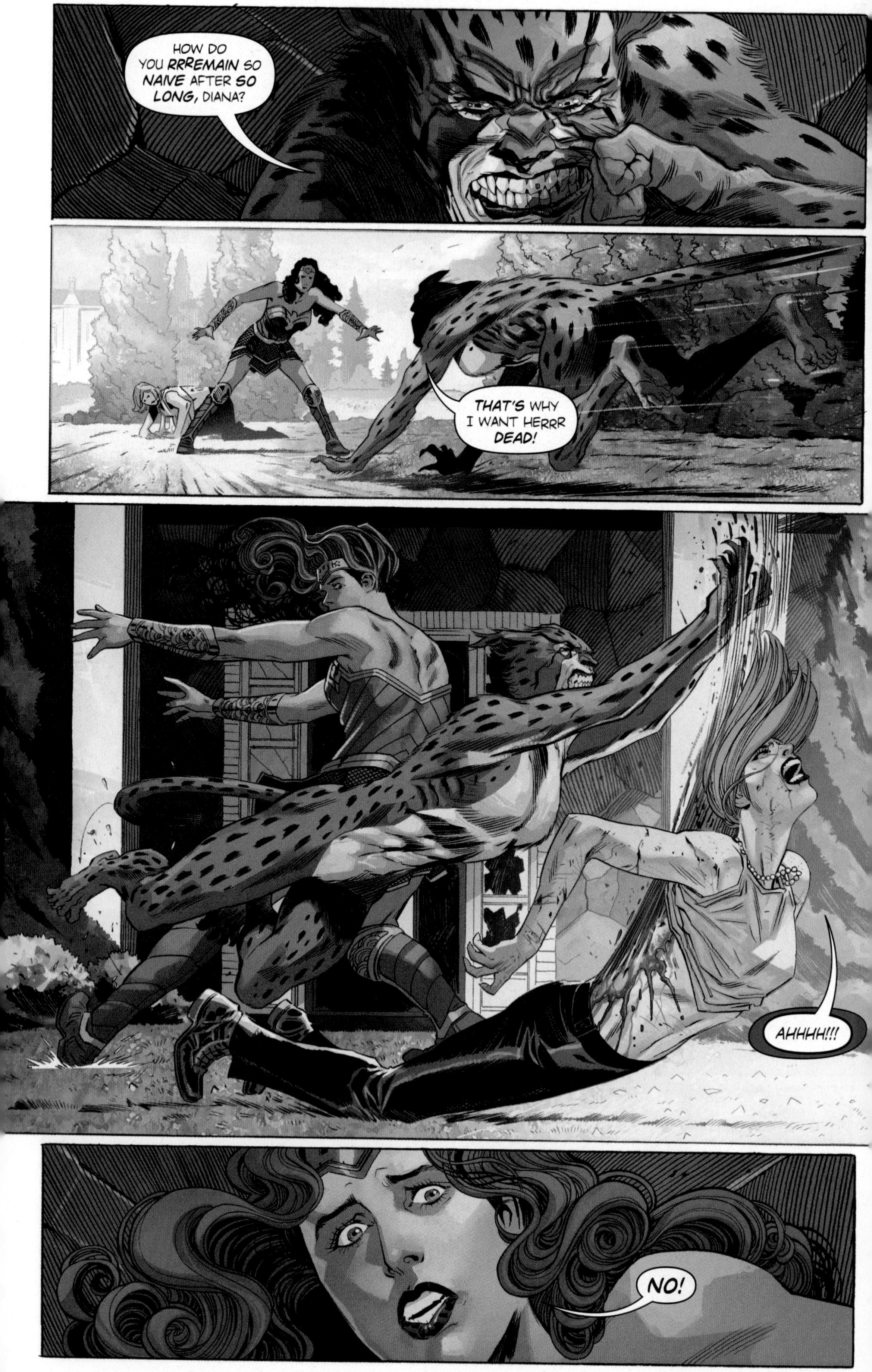
HOW DO YOU RRREMAIN SO NAIVE AFTER SO LONG, DIANA?
THAT'S WHY I WANT HERRR DEAD!
AHHHH!!!
NO!

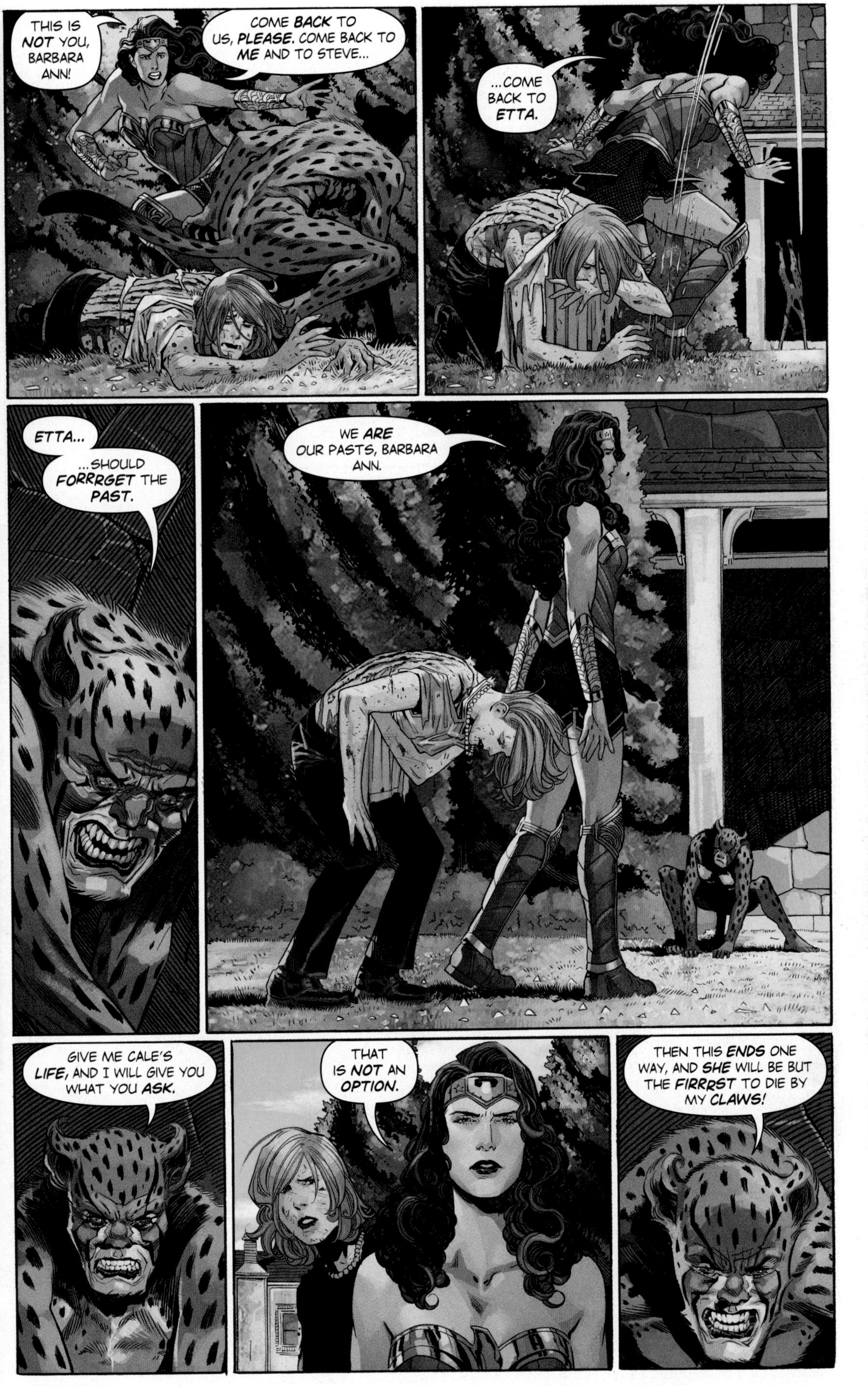
THIS IS NOT YOU, BARBARA ANN!
COME BACK TO US, PLEASE. COME BACK TO ME AND TO STEVE...
...COME BACK TO ETTA.
ETTA...
...SHOULD FORRRGET THE PAST.
WE ARE OUR PASTS, BARBARA ANN.
GIVE ME CALE'S LIFE, AND I WILL GIVE YOU WHAT YOU ASK.
THAT IS NOT AN OPTION.
THEN THIS ENDS ONE WAY, AND SHE WILL BE BUT THE FIRRRST TO DIE BY MY CLAWS!

RRRARRWW'L

HUSH, MY FRIEND...

kkHkk khhh

...HUSH...
...AND SLEEP....

hhk hhkk kk

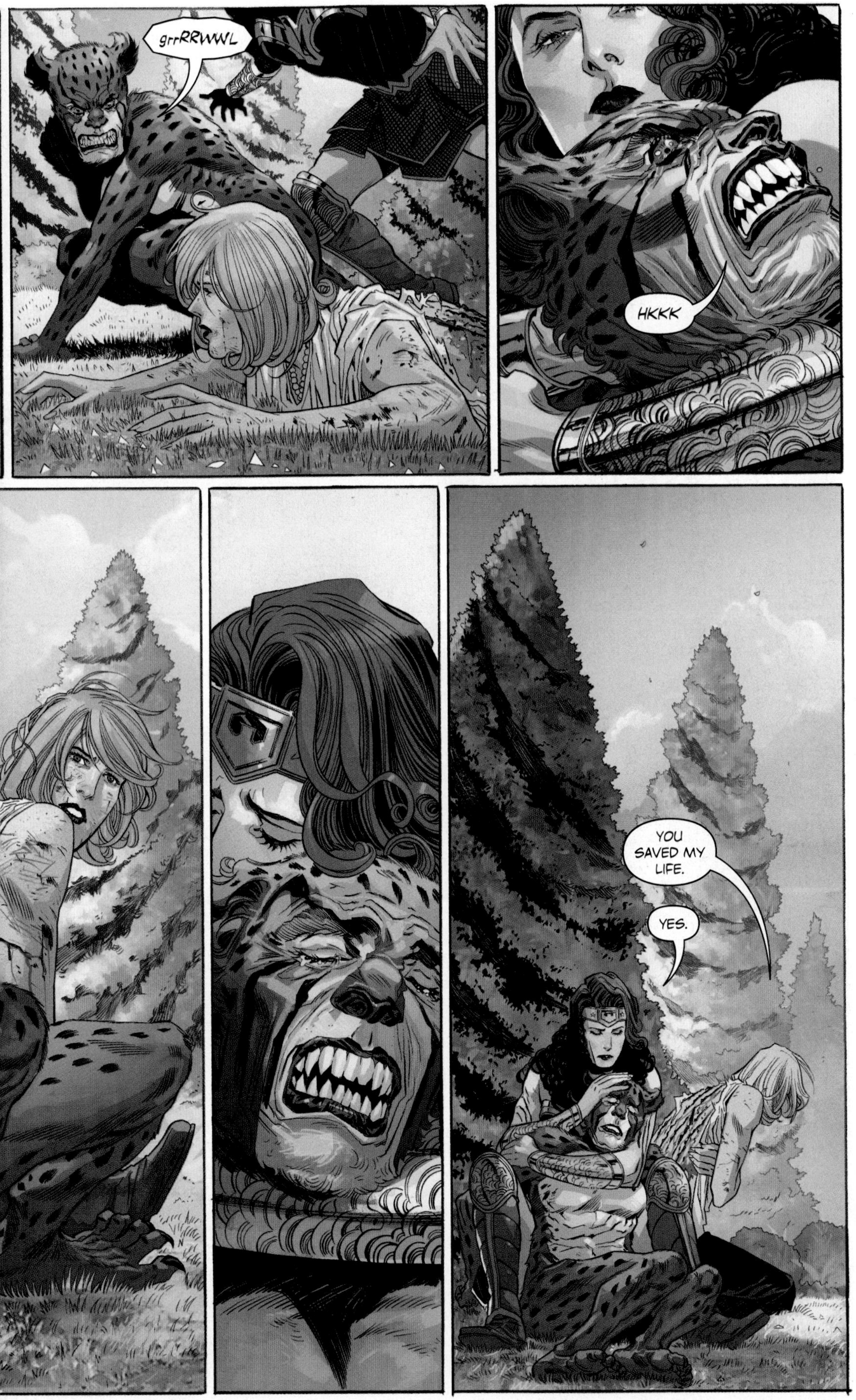
grrRRWWL
HKKK
YOU SAVED MY LIFE.
YES.

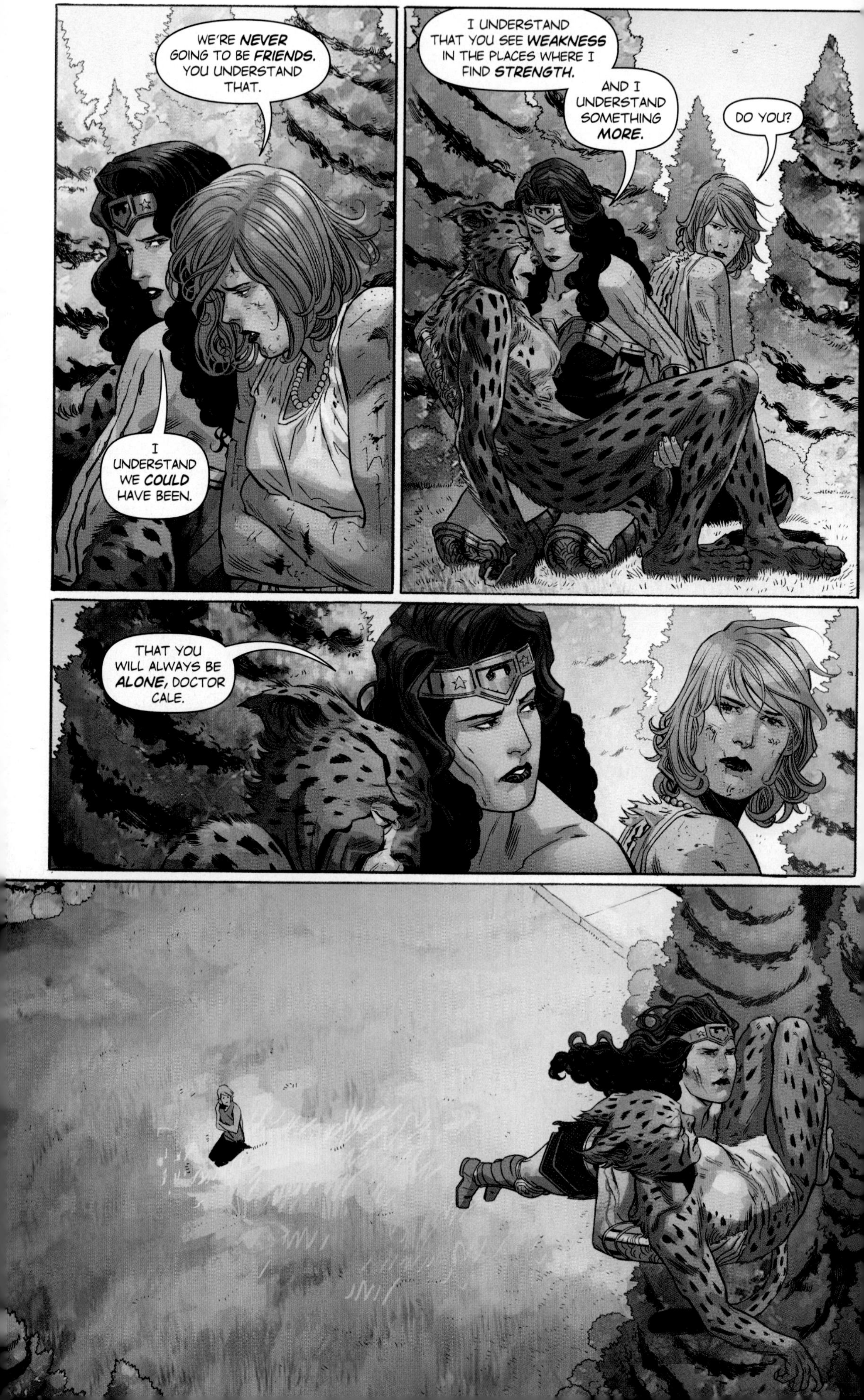
WE'RE **NEVER** GOING TO BE **FRIENDS.** YOU UNDERSTAND THAT.
I UNDERSTAND WE **COULD** HAVE BEEN.
I UNDERSTAND THAT YOU SEE **WEAKNESS** IN THE PLACES WHERE I FIND **STRENGTH.**
AND I UNDERSTAND SOMETHING **MORE.**
DO YOU?
THAT YOU WILL ALWAYS BE **ALONE,** DOCTOR CALE.

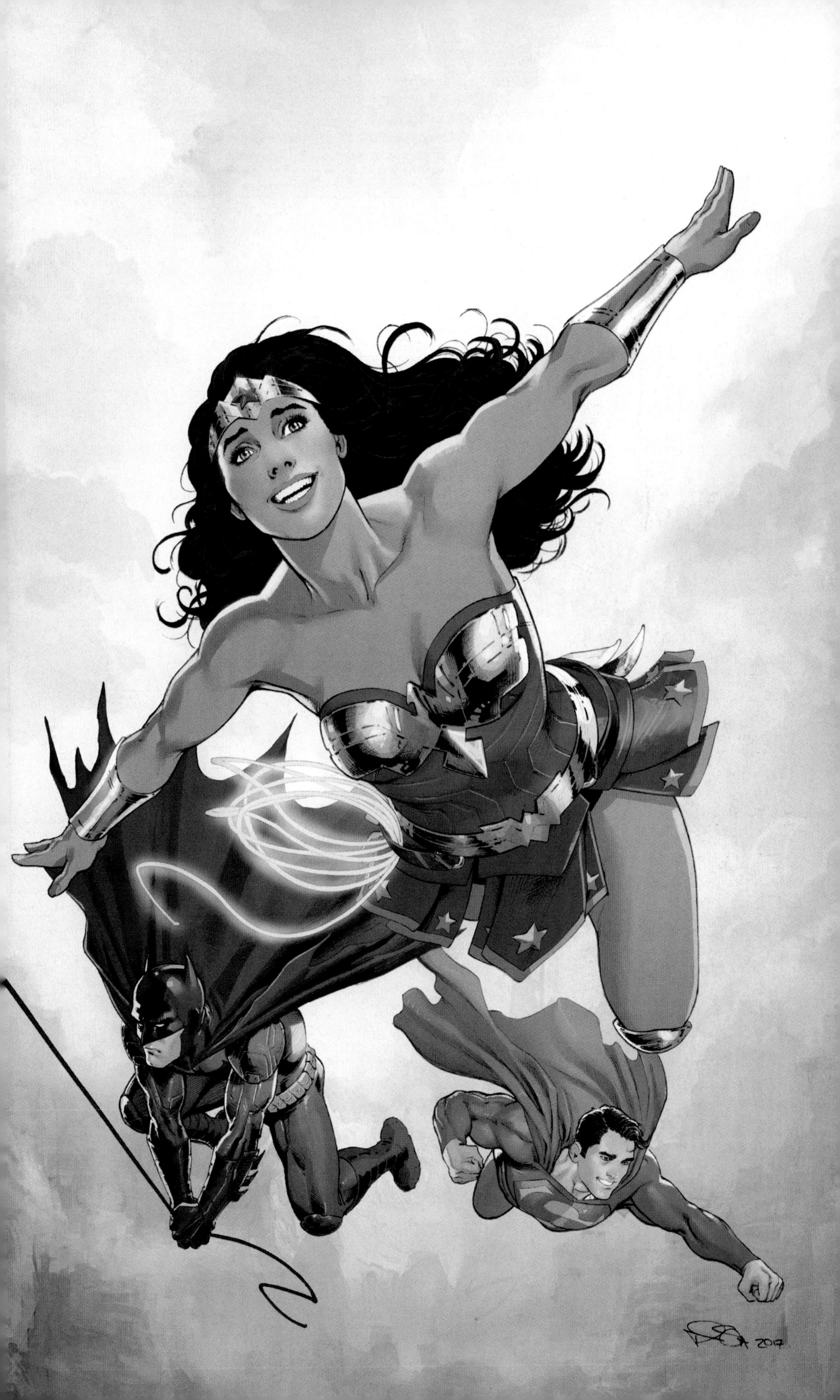

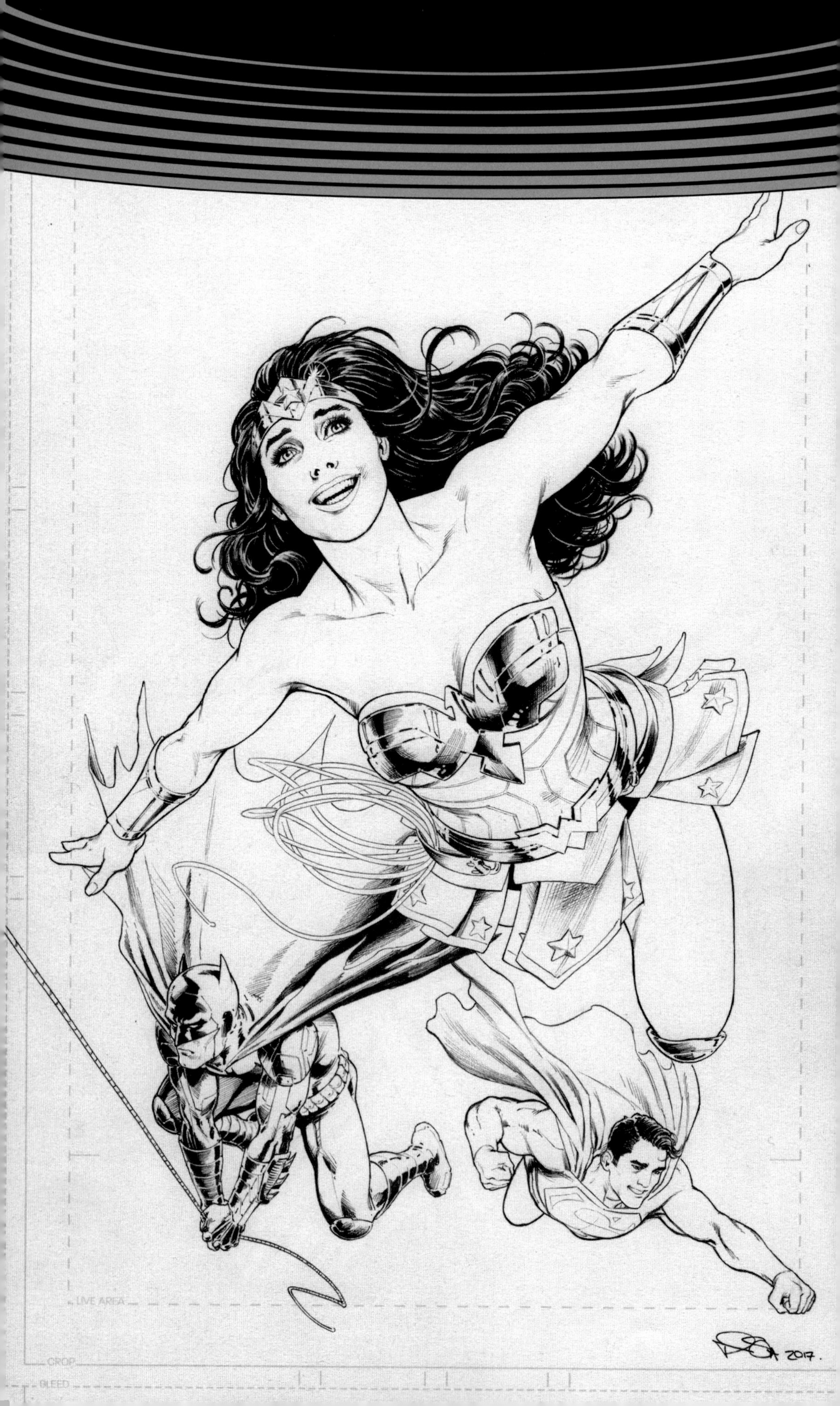
LIVE AREA
2017.
CROP
BLEED

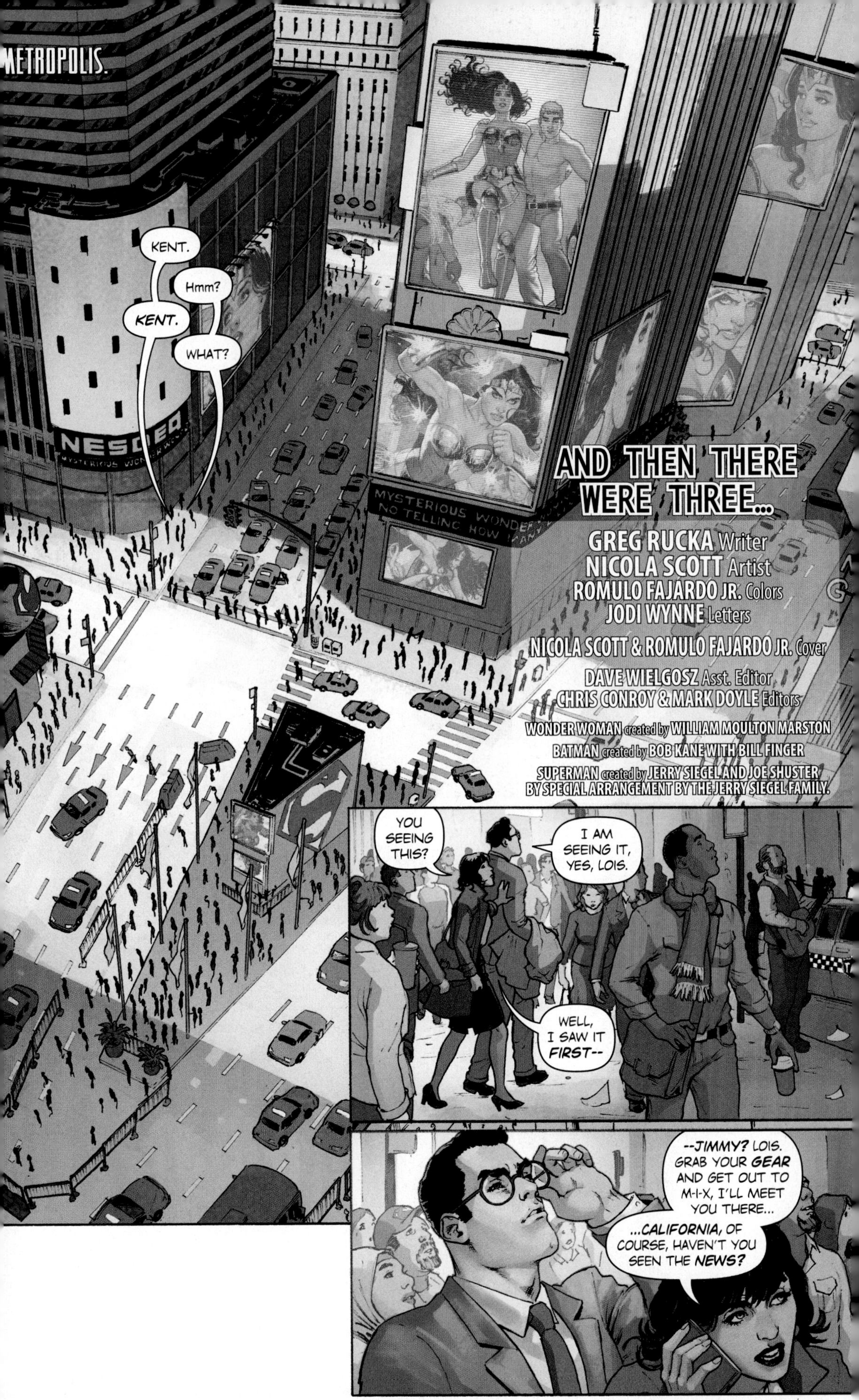
METROPOLIS.
KENT.
Hmm?
KENT.
WHAT?
NESDEQ
MYSTERIOUS WONDER WO
MYSTERIOUS WONDER
NO TELLING HOW MANY
AND THEN THERE WERE THREE...
GREG RUCKA Writer
NICOLA SCOTT Artist
ROMULO FAJARDO JR. Colors
JODI WYNNE Letters
NICOLA SCOTT & ROMULO FAJARDO JR. Cover
DAVE WIELGOSZ Asst. Editor
CHRIS CONROY & MARK DOYLE Editors
WONDER WOMAN created by WILLIAM MOULTON MARSTON
BATMAN created by BOB KANE WITH BILL FINGER
SUPERMAN created by JERRY SIEGEL AND JOE SHUSTER
BY SPECIAL ARRANGEMENT BY THE JERRY SIEGEL FAMILY.
YOU SEEING THIS?
I AM SEEING IT, YES, LOIS.
WELL, I SAW IT FIRST--
--JIMMY? LOIS. GRAB YOUR GEAR AND GET OUT TO M-I-X, I'LL MEET YOU THERE...
...CALIFORNIA, OF COURSE, HAVEN'T YOU SEEN THE NEWS?

ANOTHER SUCCESSFUL *FORAY* INTO THE DEPTHS OF THE CRIMINAL *UNDERWORLD*, I SEE...

...I TRUST IT WAS *WORSE* FOR *THEM* THAN IT WAS FOR *YOU*, SIR?

I AM *BATHED* IN YOUR *WARMTH* AS ALWAYS, ALFRED.

IF IT'S NOT TOO MUCH *TROUBLE*, MIGHT I BOTHER YOU FOR THE *FIRST AID KIT?*

AND HERE I WAS JUST *LAMENTING* THAT IT HAD BEEN A WHOLE TWENTY-FOUR *HOURS* SINCE I LAST RAN *STITCHES* THROUGH YOUR *FLESH*, MASTER BRUCE.

YOU KNOW ME. ANYTHING TO KEEP YOU *HAPPY*.

AND ON *THAT* NOTE...

...A LITTLE *MYSTERY* TO HOLD YOUR *ATTENTION* WHILE I COMMENCE WITH MY EVENING'S *NEEDLEWORK*.

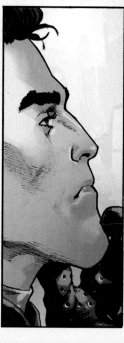

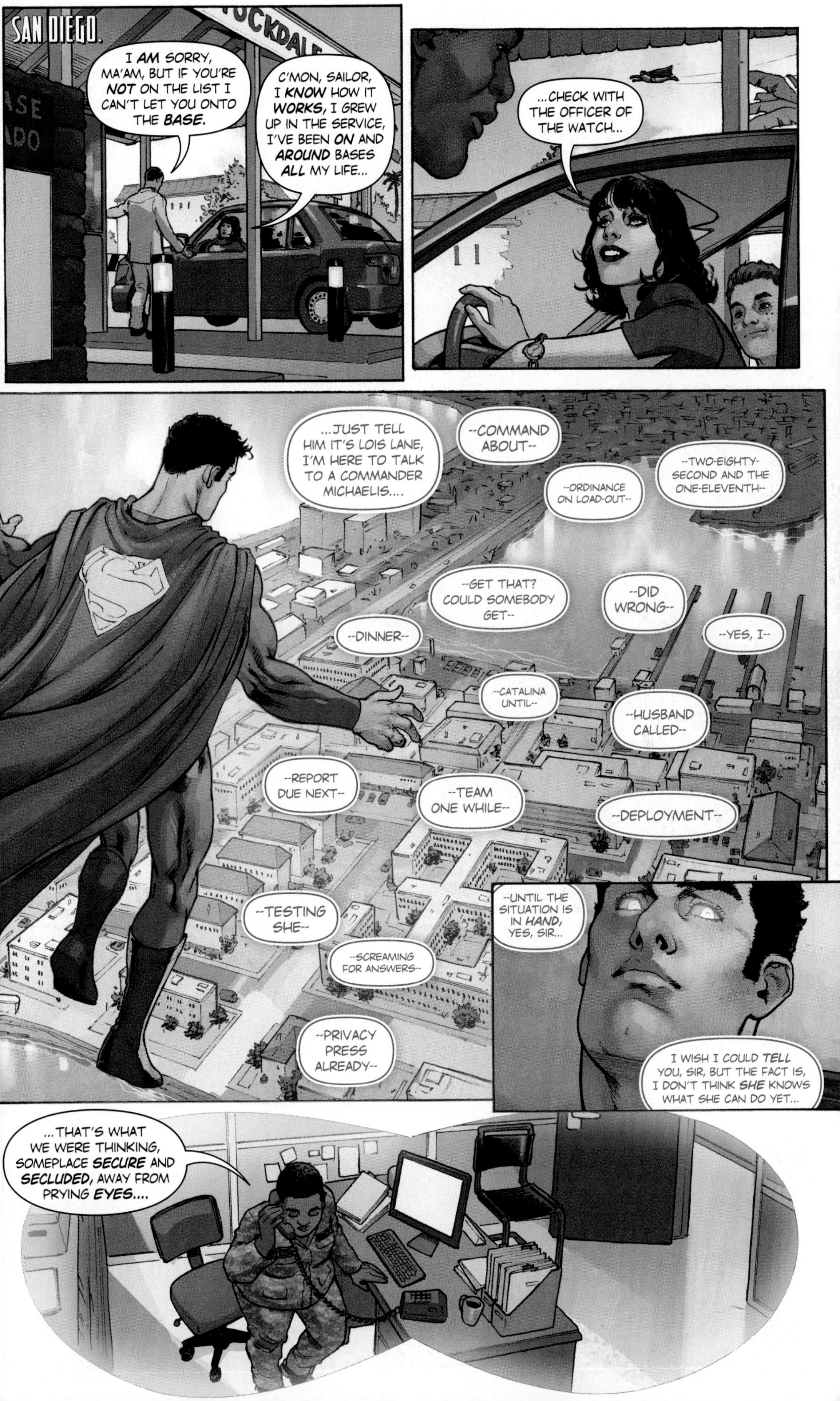
SAN DIEGO.
I AM SORRY, MA'AM, BUT IF YOU'RE NOT ON THE LIST I CAN'T LET YOU ONTO THE BASE.
C'MON, SAILOR, I KNOW HOW IT WORKS, I GREW UP IN THE SERVICE, I'VE BEEN ON AND AROUND BASES ALL MY LIFE...
...CHECK WITH THE OFFICER OF THE WATCH...
...JUST TELL HIM IT'S LOIS LANE, I'M HERE TO TALK TO A COMMANDER MICHAELIS....
--COMMAND ABOUT--
--ORDINANCE ON LOAD-OUT--
--TWO-EIGHTY-SECOND AND THE ONE-ELEVENTH--
--GET THAT? COULD SOMEBODY GET--
--DID WRONG--
--DINNER--
--YES, I--
--CATALINA UNTIL--
--HUSBAND CALLED--
--REPORT DUE NEXT--
--TEAM ONE WHILE--
--DEPLOYMENT--
--TESTING SHE--
--SCREAMING FOR ANSWERS--
--PRIVACY PRESS ALREADY--
--UNTIL THE SITUATION IS IN HAND, YES, SIR...
I WISH I COULD TELL YOU, SIR, BUT THE FACT IS, I DON'T THINK SHE KNOWS WHAT SHE CAN DO YET...
...THAT'S WHAT WE WERE THINKING, SOMEPLACE SECURE AND SECLUDED, AWAY FROM PRYING EYES....

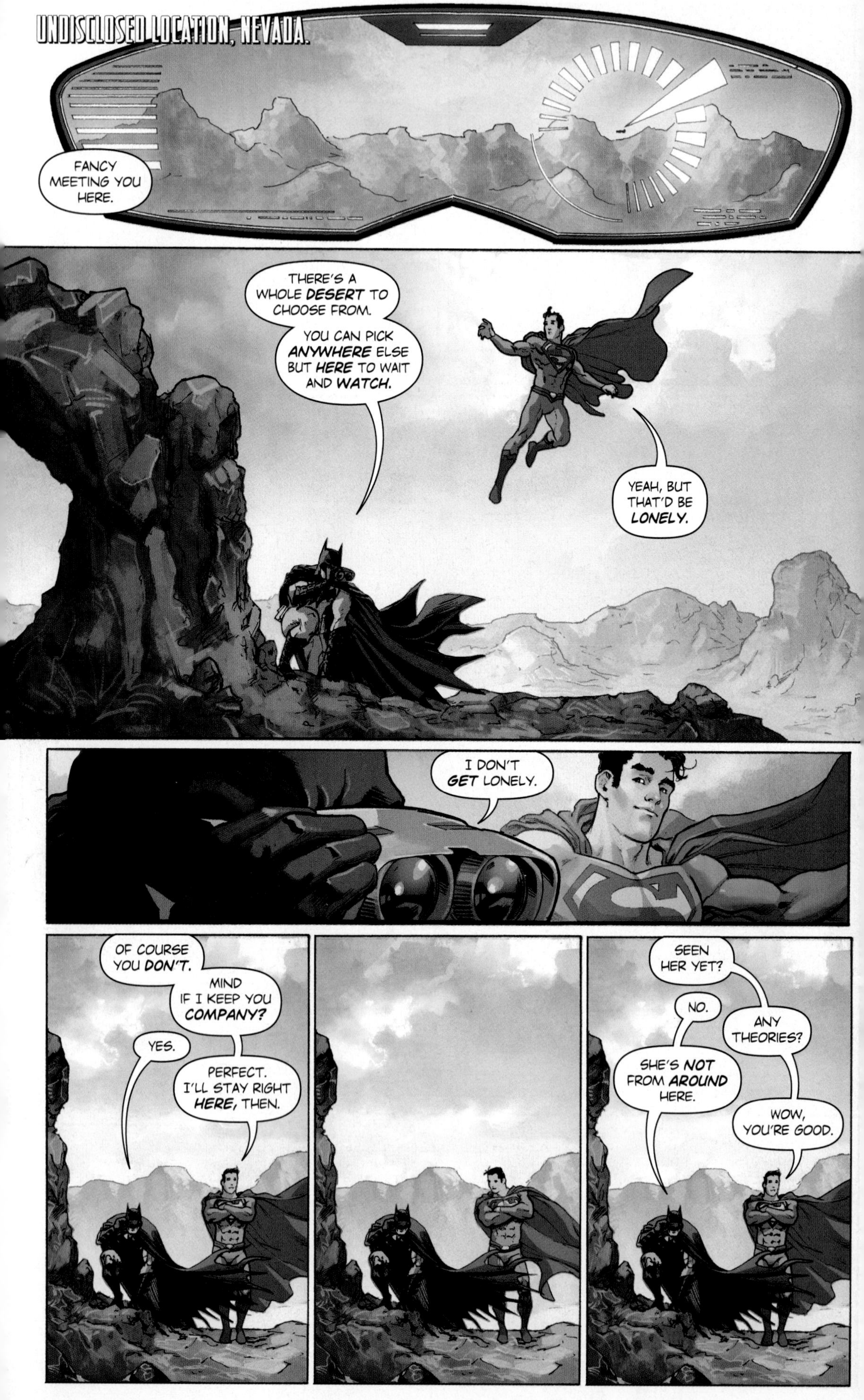

UNDISCLOSED LOCATION, NEVADA.
FANCY MEETING YOU HERE.
THERE'S A WHOLE DESERT TO CHOOSE FROM.
YOU CAN PICK ANYWHERE ELSE BUT HERE TO WAIT AND WATCH.
YEAH, BUT THAT'D BE LONELY.
I DON'T GET LONELY.
OF COURSE YOU DON'T.
MIND IF I KEEP YOU COMPANY?
YES.
PERFECT. I'LL STAY RIGHT HERE, THEN.
SEEN HER YET?
NO.
ANY THEORIES?
SHE'S NOT FROM AROUND HERE.
WOW, YOU'RE GOOD.

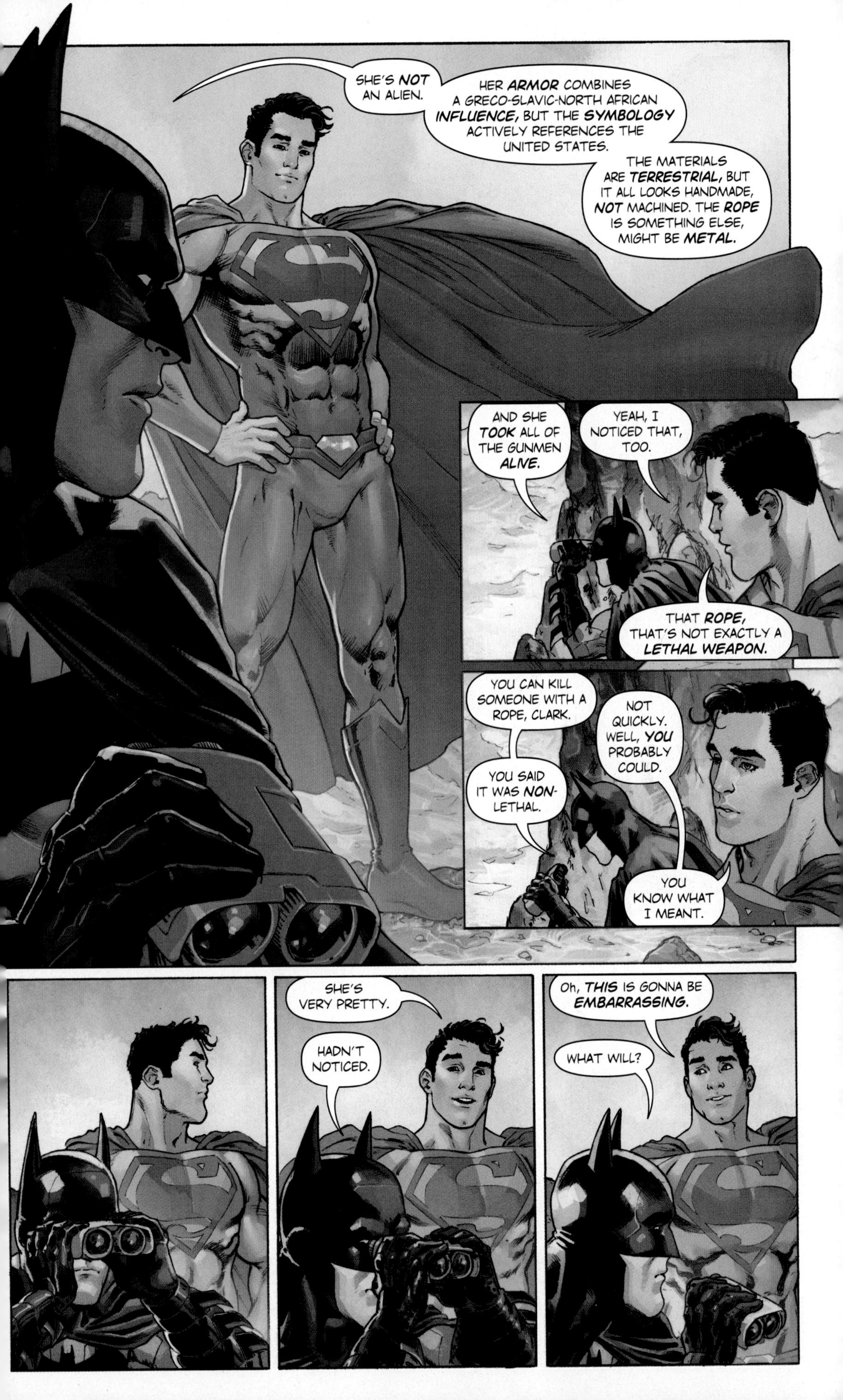
SHE'S NOT AN ALIEN.
HER ARMOR COMBINES A GRECO-SLAVIC-NORTH AFRICAN INFLUENCE, BUT THE SYMBOLOGY ACTIVELY REFERENCES THE UNITED STATES.
THE MATERIALS ARE TERRESTRIAL, BUT IT ALL LOOKS HANDMADE, NOT MACHINED. THE ROPE IS SOMETHING ELSE, MIGHT BE METAL.
AND SHE TOOK ALL OF THE GUNMEN ALIVE.
YEAH, I NOTICED THAT, TOO.
THAT ROPE, THAT'S NOT EXACTLY A LETHAL WEAPON.
YOU CAN KILL SOMEONE WITH A ROPE, CLARK.
NOT QUICKLY. WELL, YOU PROBABLY COULD.
YOU SAID IT WAS NON-LETHAL.
YOU KNOW WHAT I MEANT.
SHE'S VERY PRETTY.
HADN'T NOTICED.
Oh, THIS IS GONNA BE EMBARRASSING.
WHAT WILL?

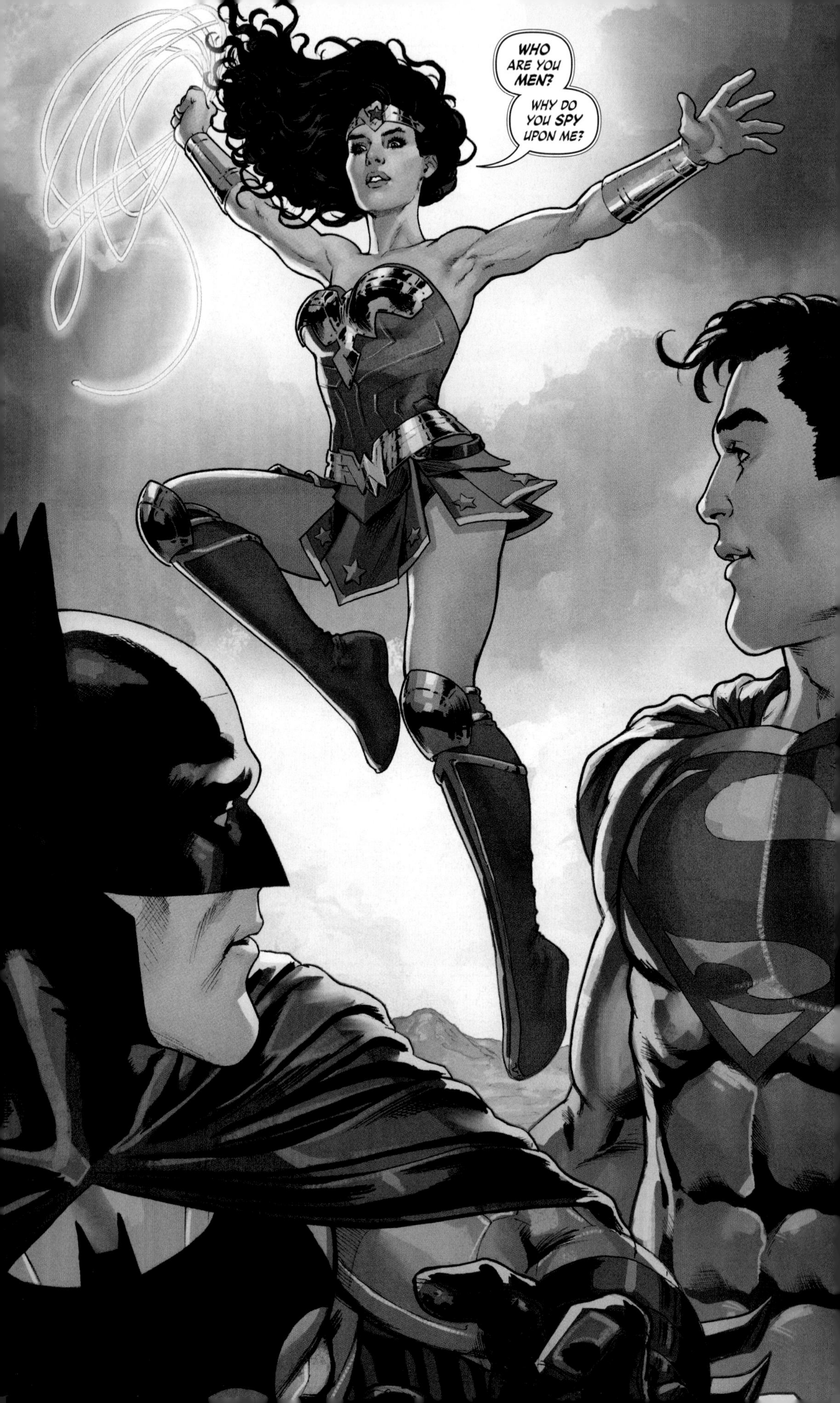
WHO ARE YOU MEN?
WHY DO YOU SPY UPON ME?

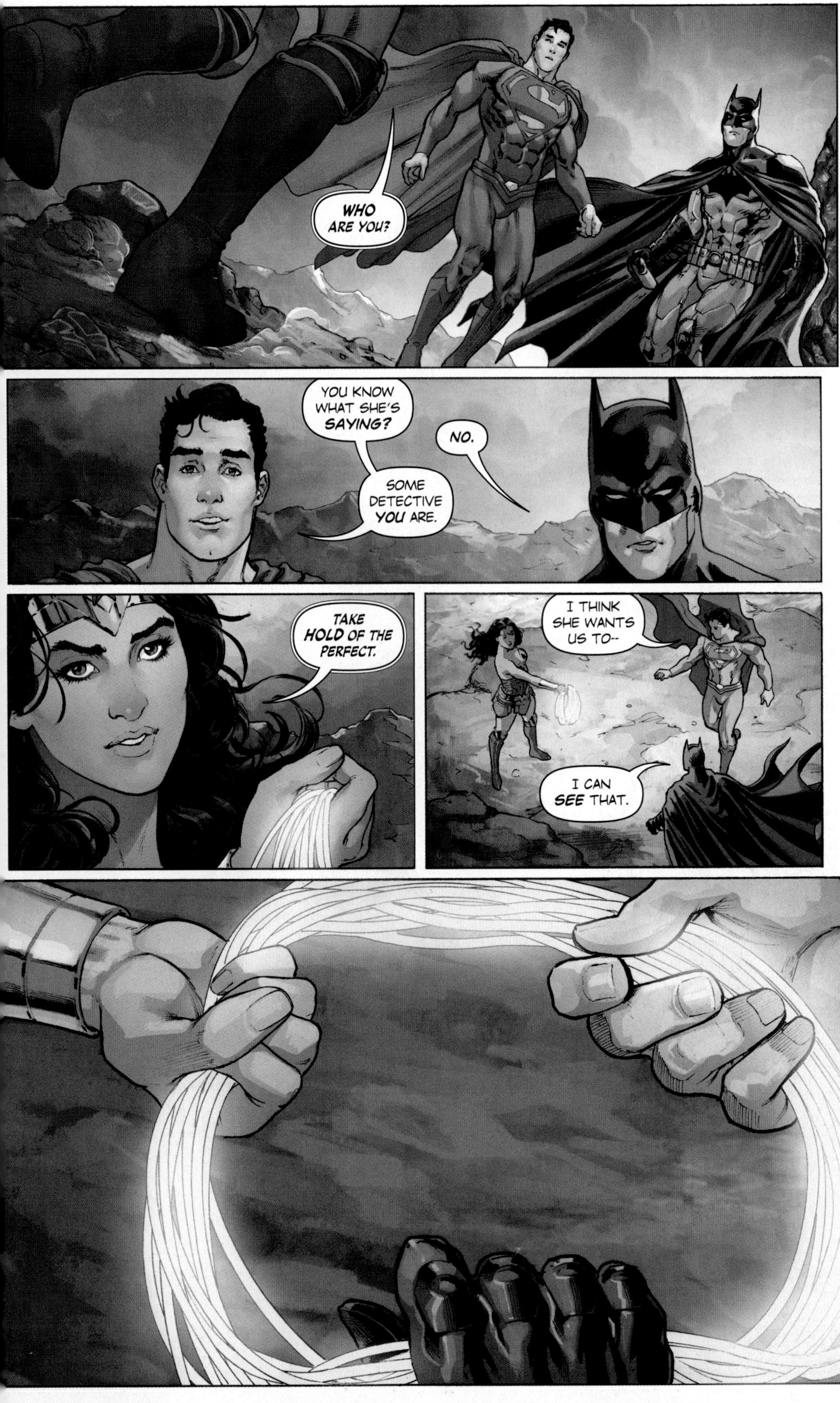
WHO ARE YOU?
YOU KNOW WHAT SHE'S SAYING?
NO.
SOME DETECTIVE YOU ARE.
TAKE HOLD OF THE PERFECT.
I THINK SHE WANTS US TO--
I CAN SEE THAT.

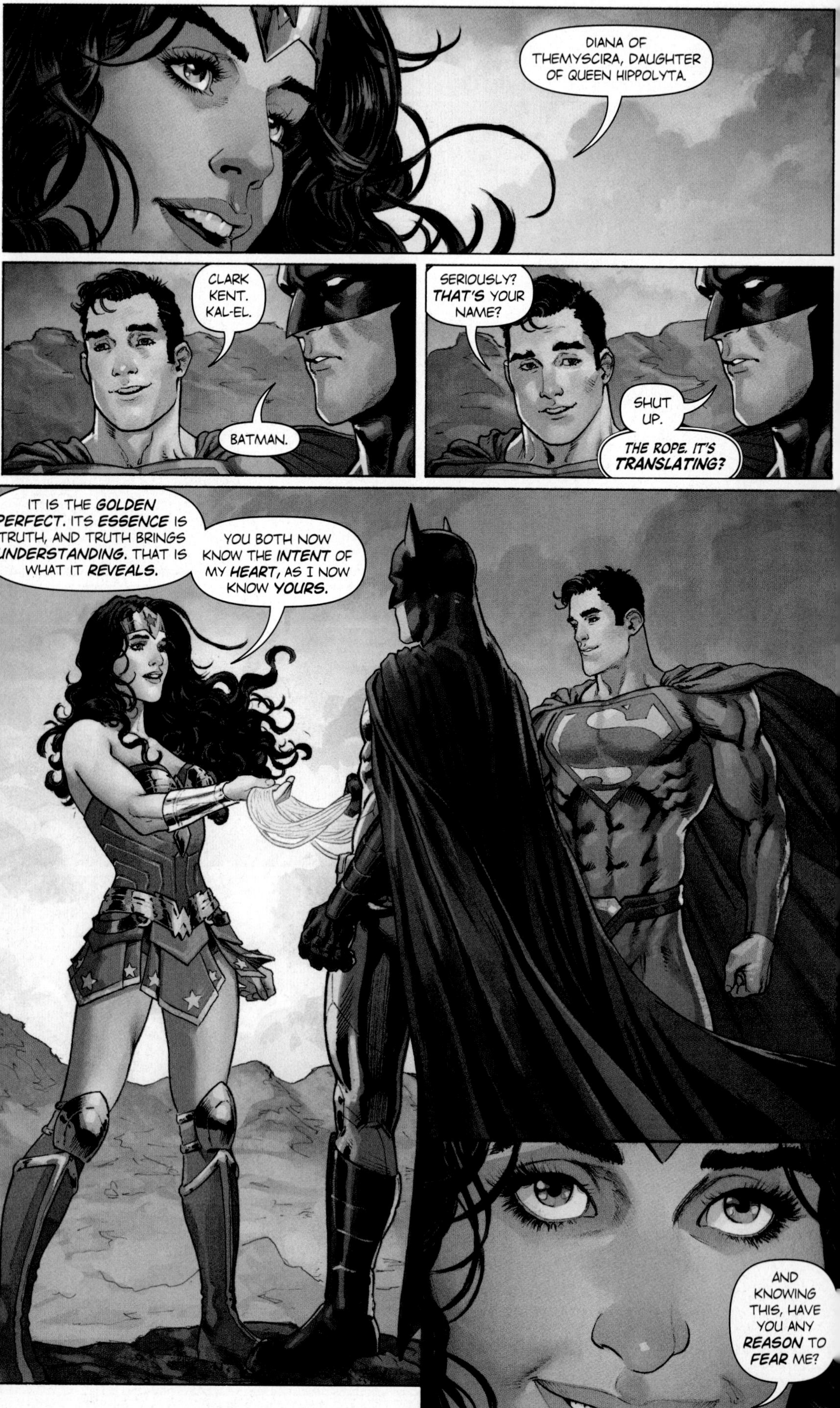
DIANA OF THEMYSCIRA, DAUGHTER OF QUEEN HIPPOLYTA.
CLARK KENT. KAL-EL.
BATMAN.
SERIOUSLY? **THAT'S** YOUR NAME?
SHUT UP.
THE ROPE. IT'S TRANSLATING?
IT IS THE **GOLDEN PERFECT.** ITS **ESSENCE** IS TRUTH, AND TRUTH BRINGS **UNDERSTANDING.** THAT IS WHAT IT **REVEALS.**
YOU BOTH NOW KNOW THE **INTENT** OF MY **HEART,** AS I NOW KNOW **YOURS.**
AND KNOWING THIS, HAVE YOU ANY **REASON** TO **FEAR** ME?

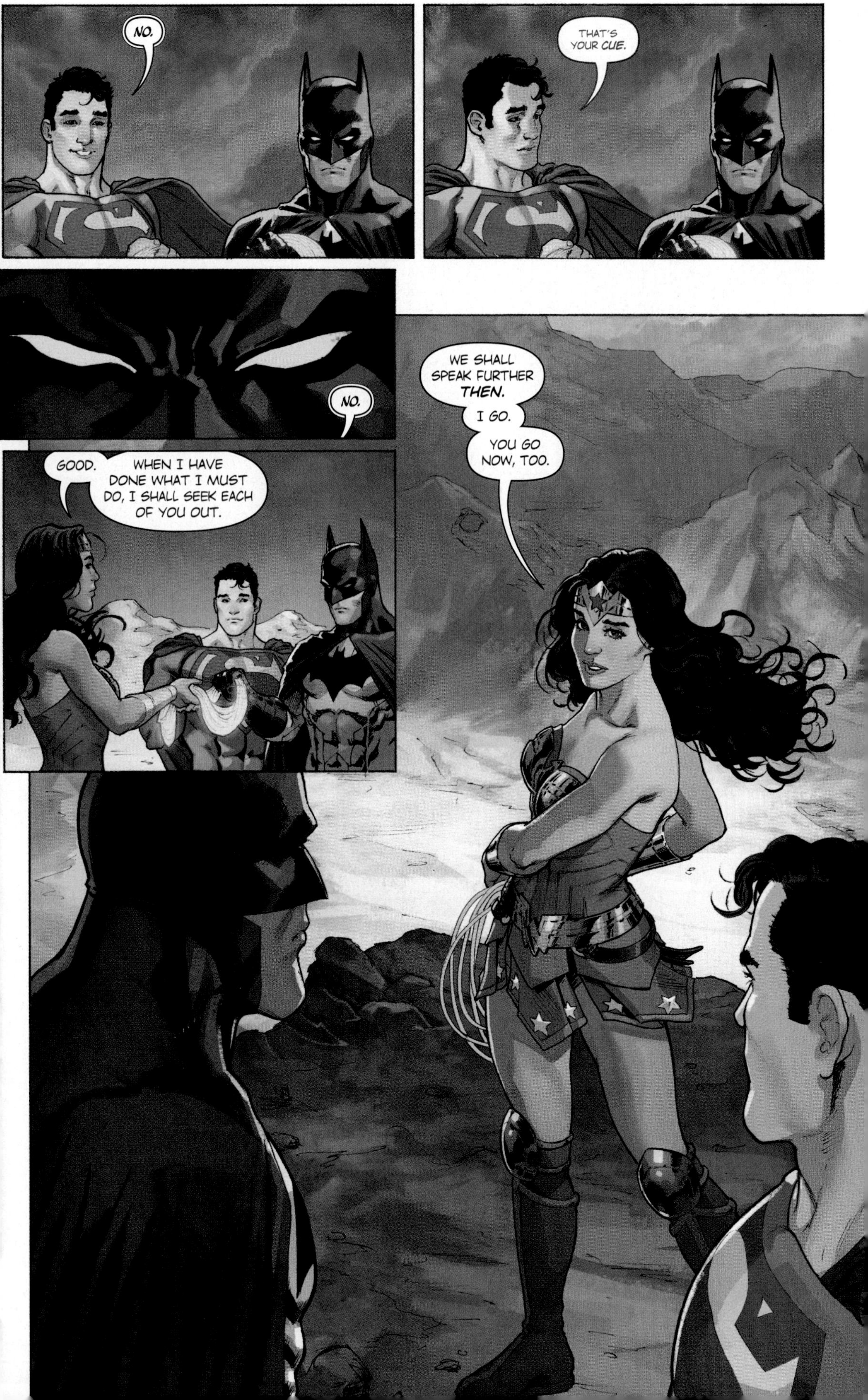
NO.
THAT'S YOUR CUE.
NO.
GOOD.
WHEN I HAVE DONE WHAT I MUST DO, I SHALL SEEK EACH OF YOU OUT.
WE SHALL SPEAK FURTHER THEN.
I GO.
YOU GO NOW, TOO.

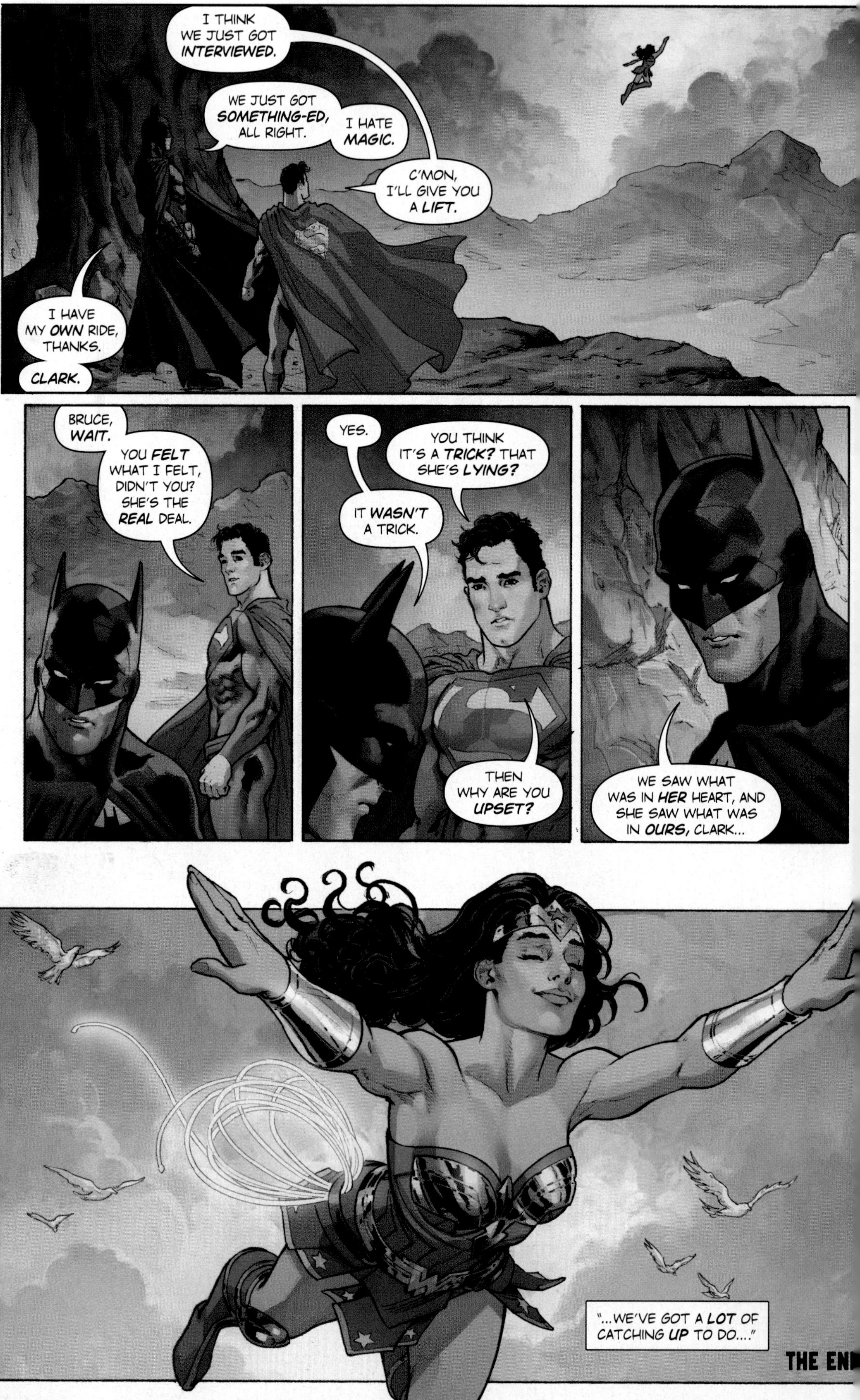

I THINK WE JUST GOT INTERVIEWED.
WE JUST GOT SOMETHING-ED, ALL RIGHT.
I HATE MAGIC.
C'MON, I'LL GIVE YOU A LIFT.
I HAVE MY OWN RIDE, THANKS.
CLARK.
BRUCE, WAIT.
YOU FELT WHAT I FELT, DIDN'T YOU? SHE'S THE REAL DEAL.
YES.
YOU THINK IT'S A TRICK? THAT SHE'S LYING?
IT WASN'T A TRICK.
THEN WHY ARE YOU UPSET?
WE SAW WHAT WAS IN HER HEART, AND SHE SAW WHAT WAS IN OURS, CLARK...
"...WE'VE GOT A LOT OF CATCHING UP TO DO...."

THE END

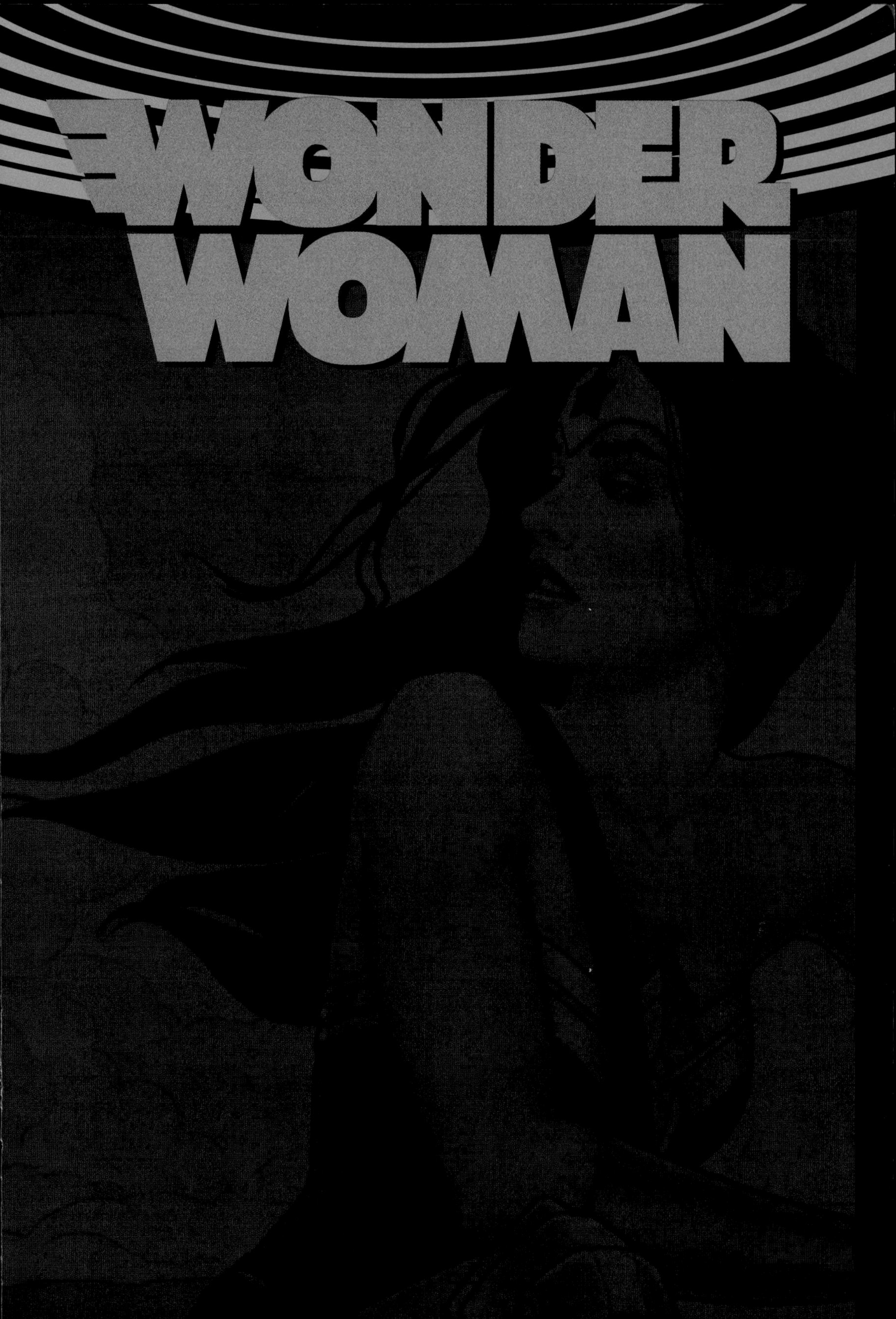
WONDER
WOMAN

VARIANT COVER GALLERY

WONDER WOMAN #16 variant cover by JENNY FRISON

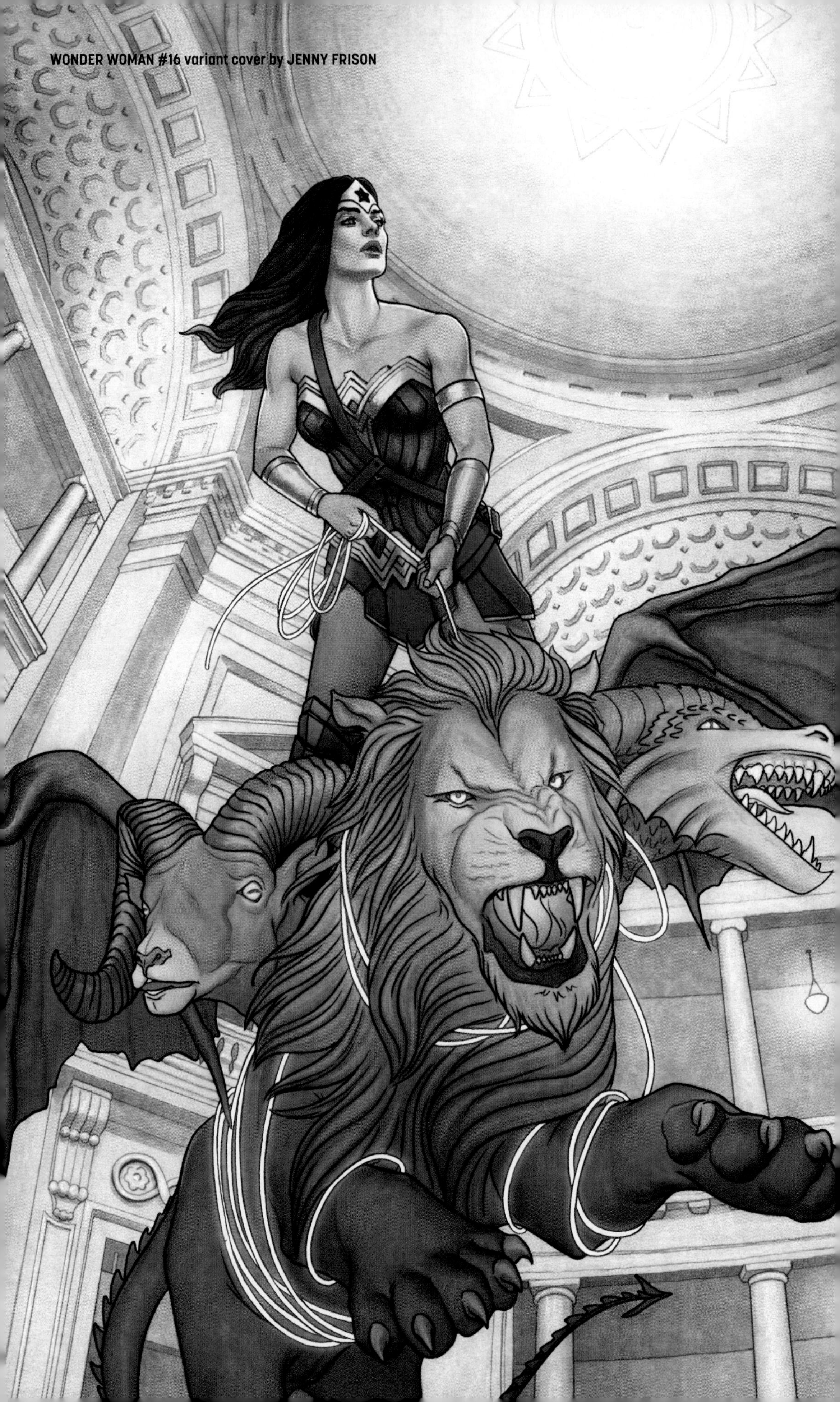

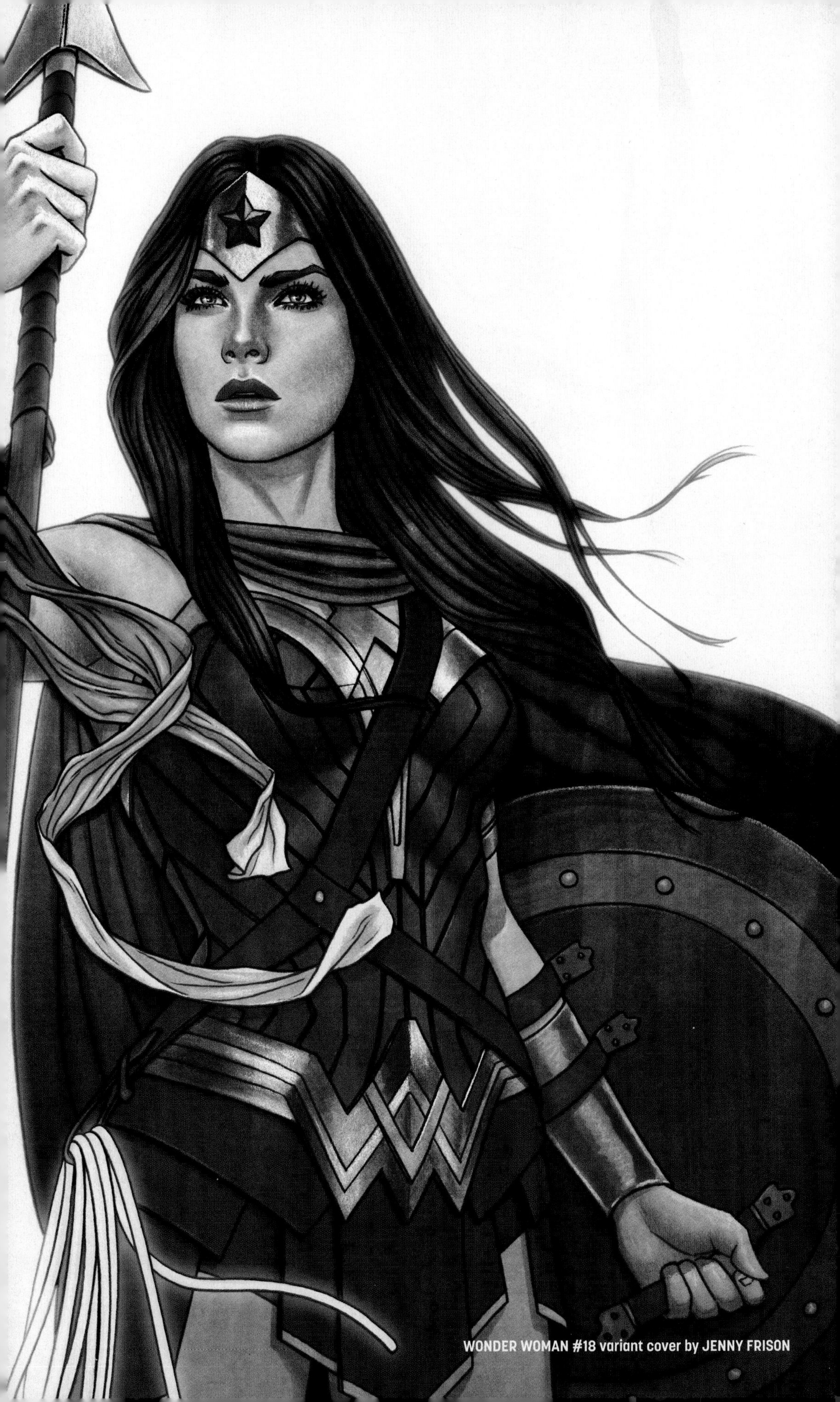

WONDER WOMAN #18 variant cover by JENNY FRISON

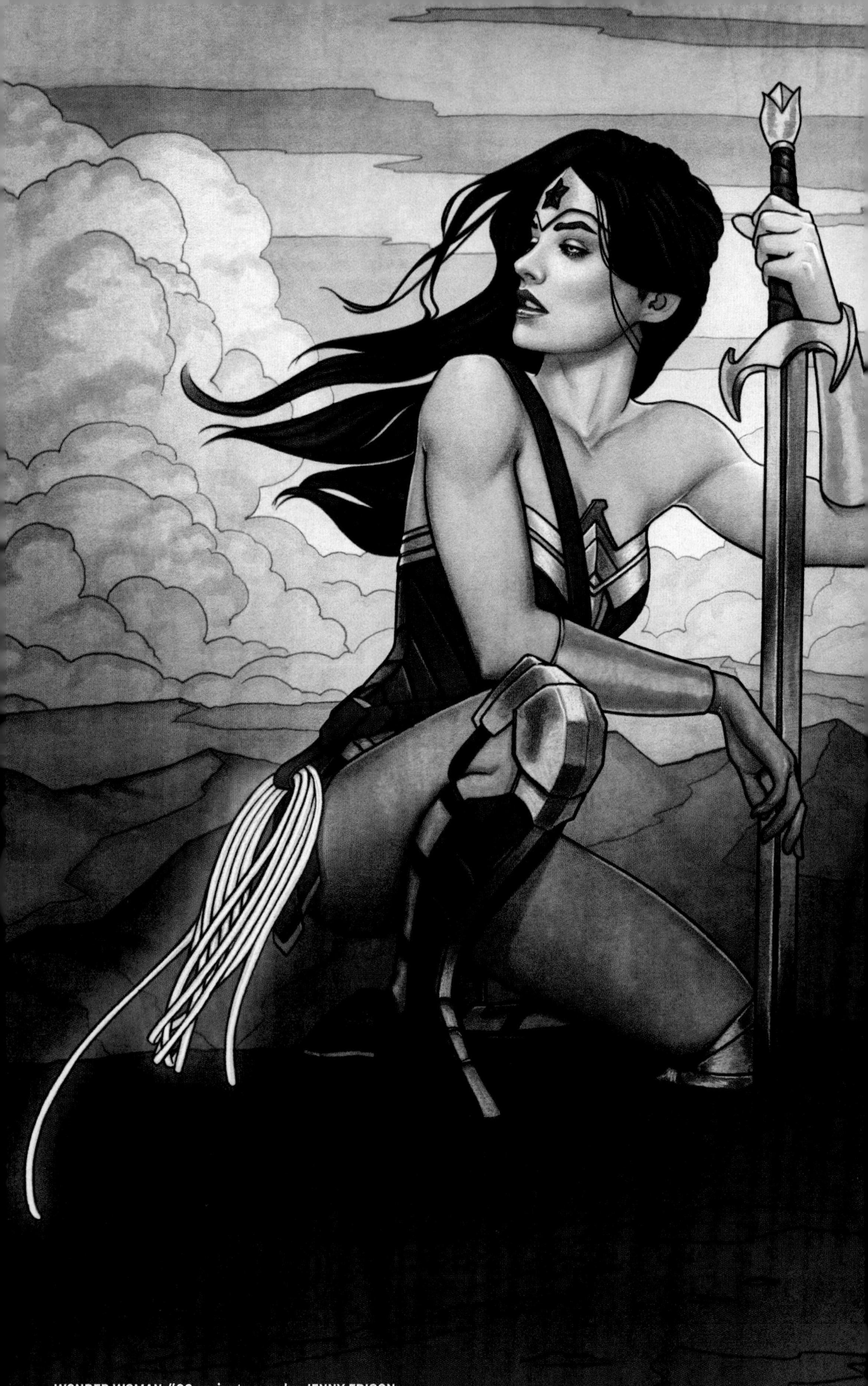

WONDER WOMAN #30 variant cover by JENNY FRISON

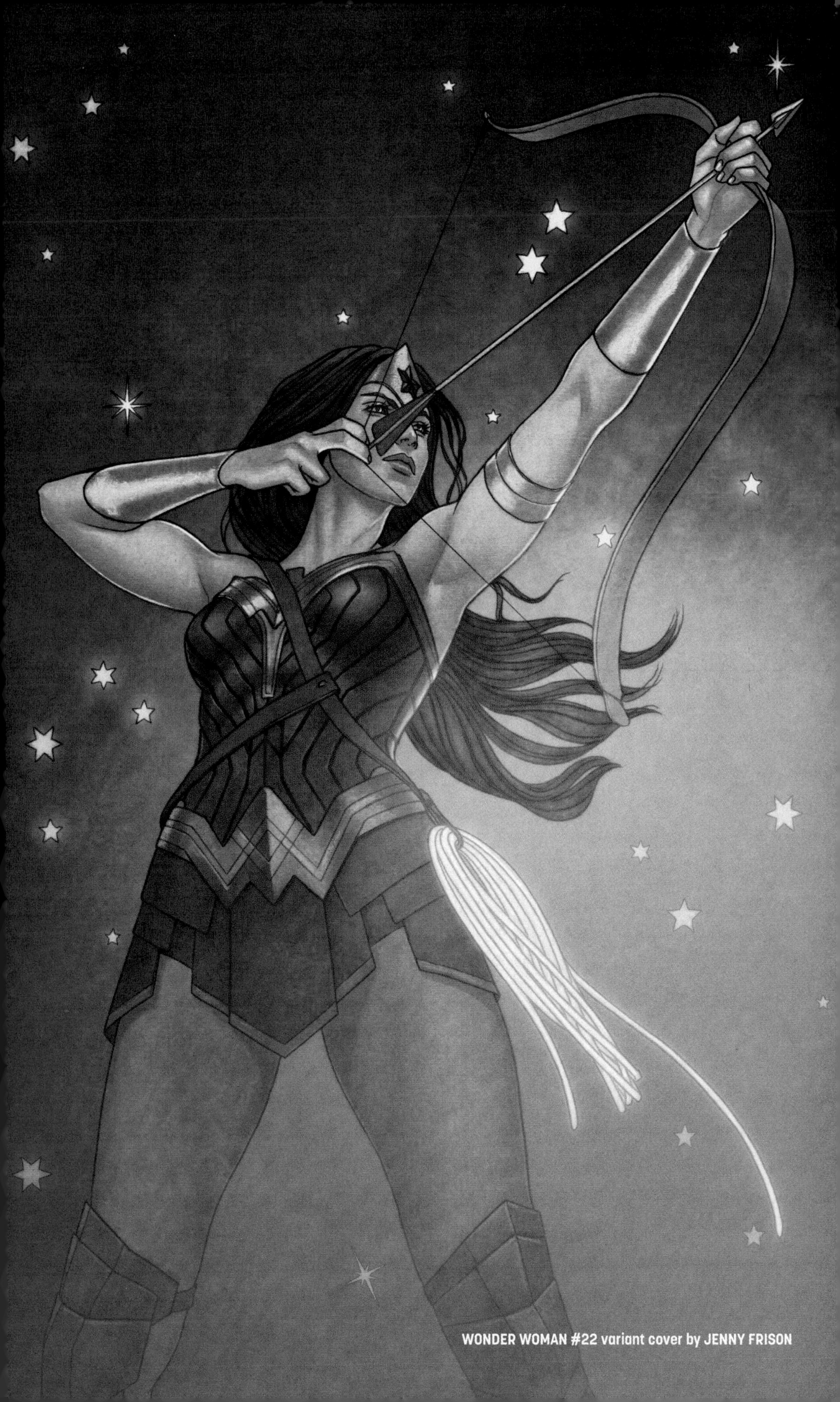

WONDER WOMAN #22 variant cover by JENNY FRISON

WONDER WOMAN #24 variant cover by JENNY FRISON

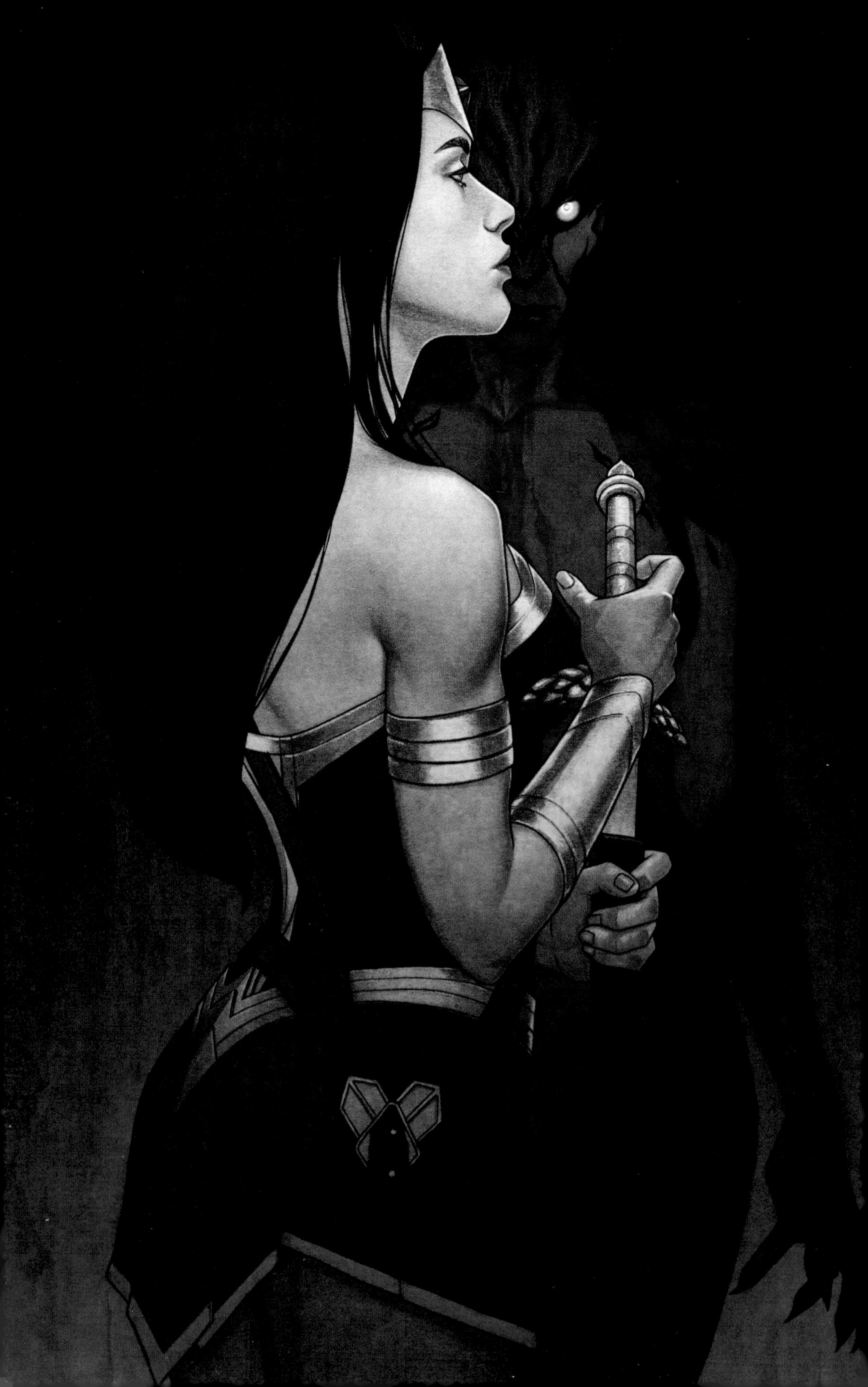

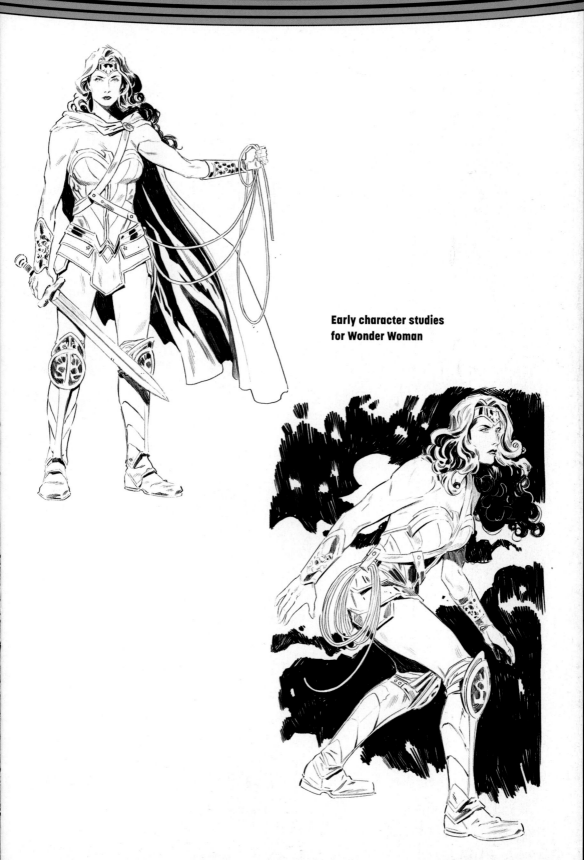

**Early character studies
for Wonder Woman**

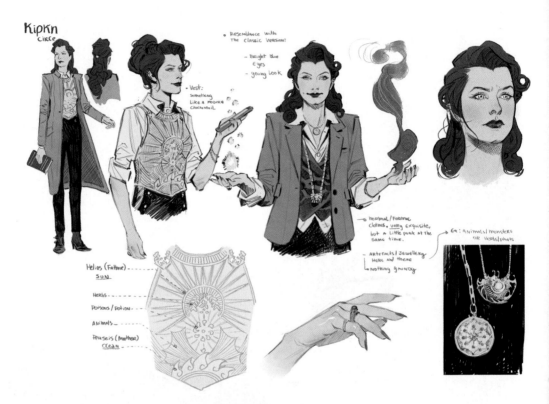

Kipkn
Circe

○ Resemblance with the classic version:
- Bright Blue Eyes
- Young Look

- Vest:
Something
Like a modern
Chainmail

→ normal / formal
clothes, very exquisite,
but a little punk at the
same time.

- Artefacts / jewellery
here and there
└ nothing gaudy

→ Ex: Animals/ Monsters
OR Herbs/plants

Helios (Father) ---- SUN

Herbs ----

Poisons / Potion ---

Animals ---

Perseis (Mother)
Ocean ---

**Concept art for the
Rebirth version of Circe**

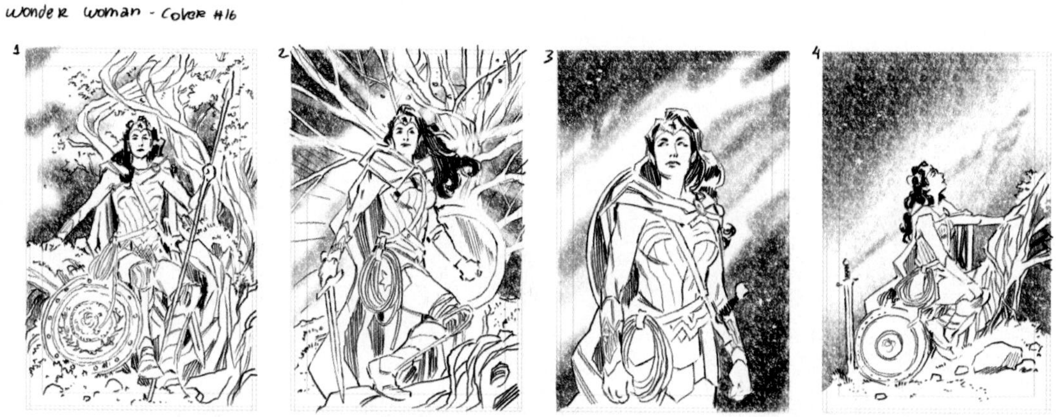
Wonder Woman - Cover #16
1
2
3
4

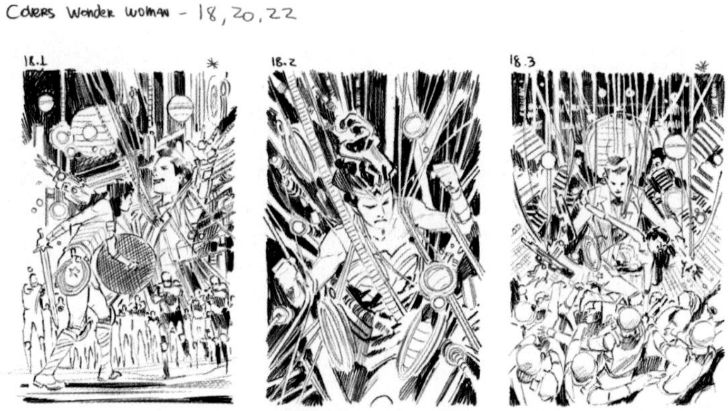
Covers Wonder Woman - 18, 20, 22
18.1
18.2
18.3

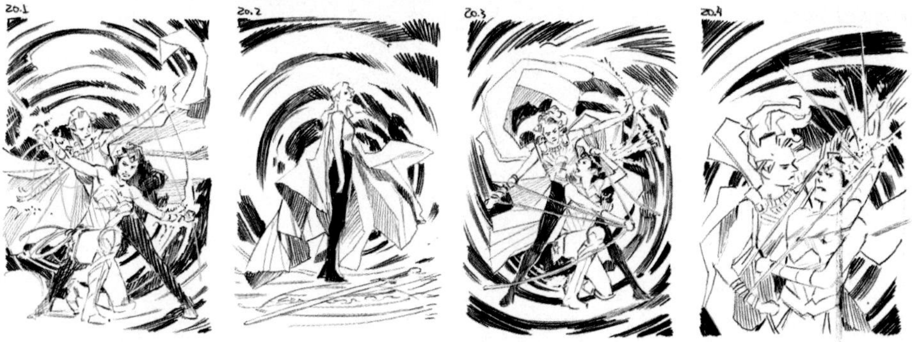
20.1
20.2
20.3
20.4

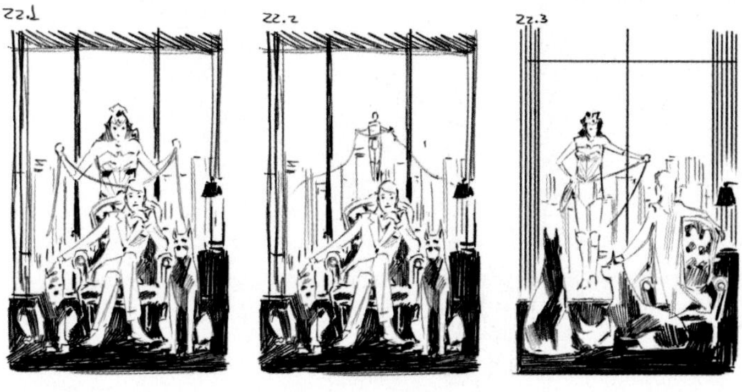
22.1
22.2
22.3

Thumbnail cover sketches for WONDER WOMAN #16, #18, #20 and #22

Thumbnail rough page layouts
for WONDER WOMAN #20

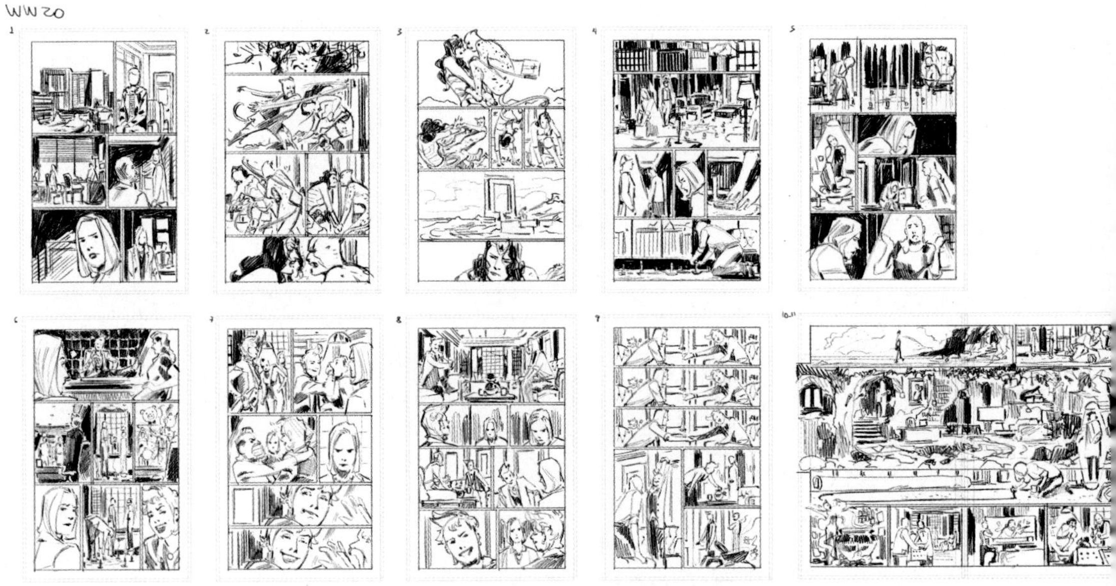
WW 20

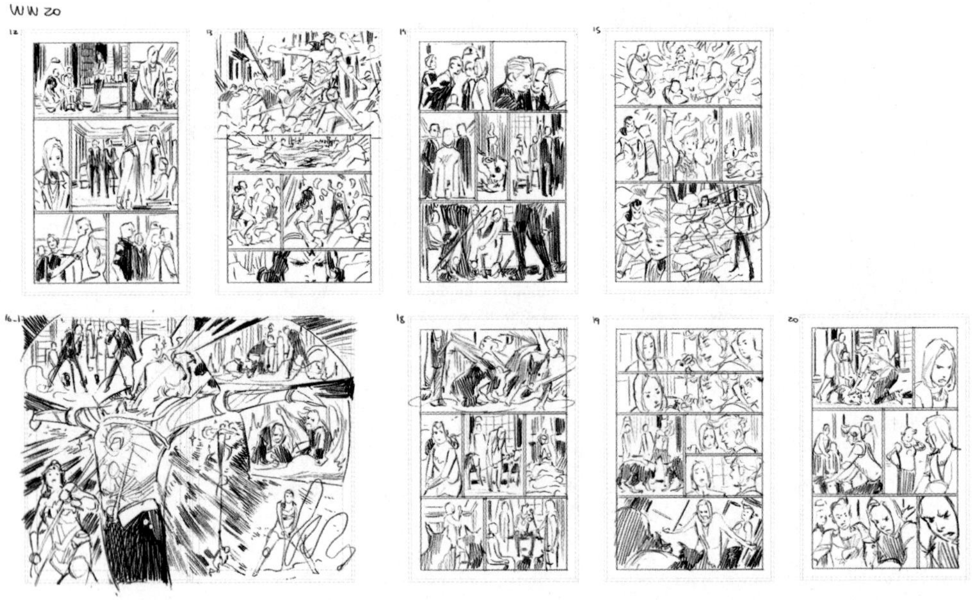
WW 20

Figure close-ups (shown with writing utensils for scale) showcasing the small-scale detail that goes into every panel of WONDER WOMAN

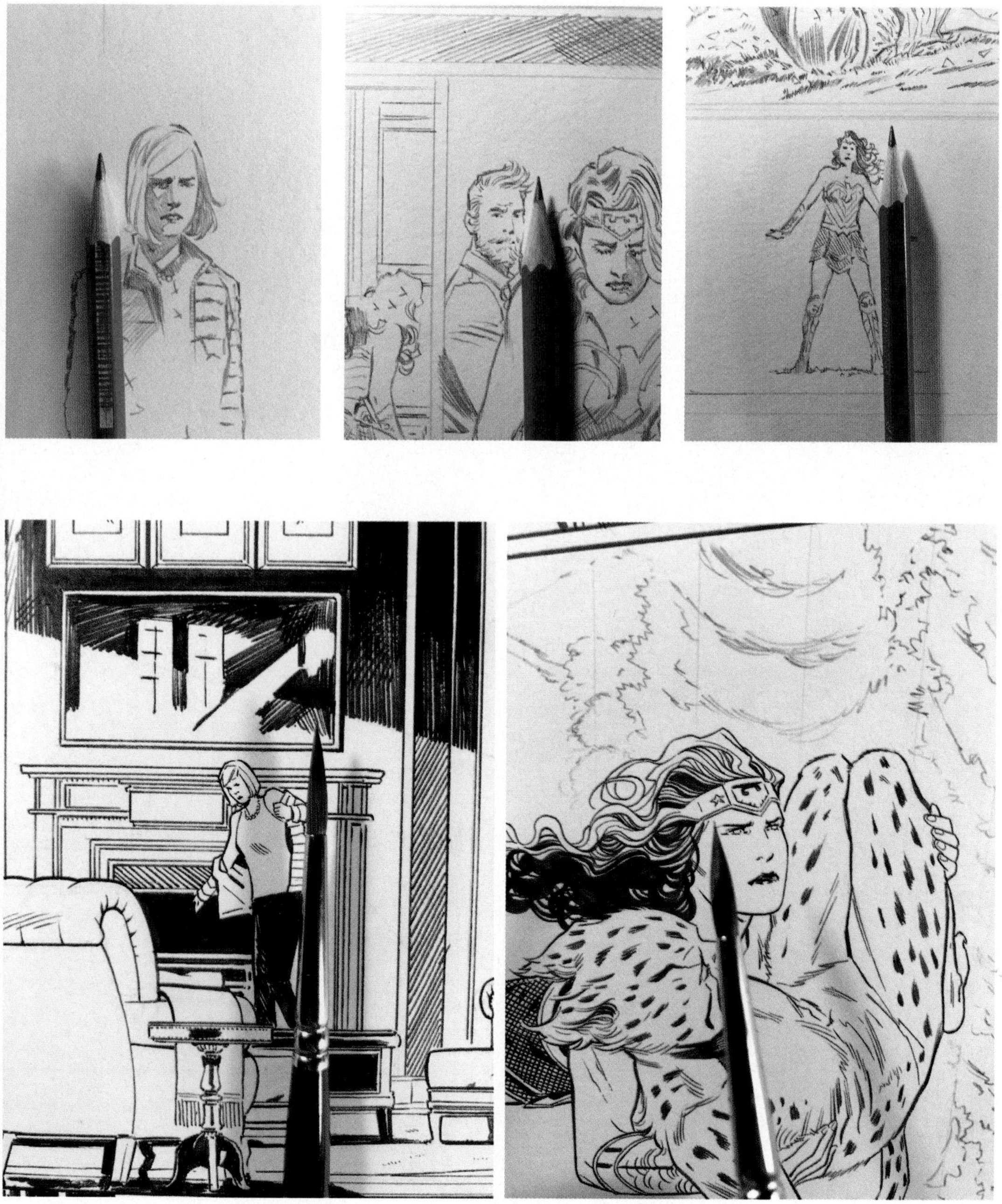

In-process rendering for WONDER WOMAN #20 pages 10-11

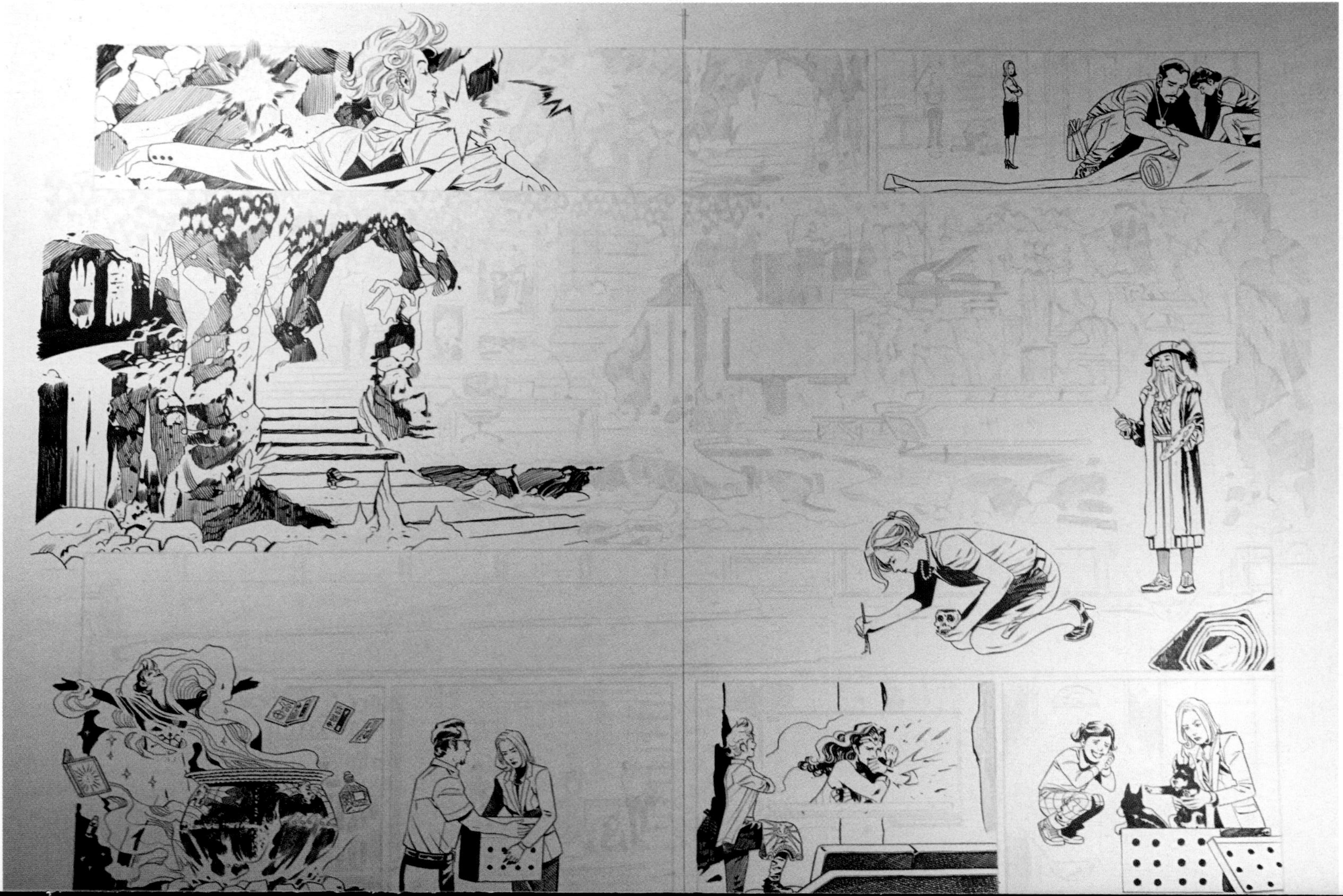

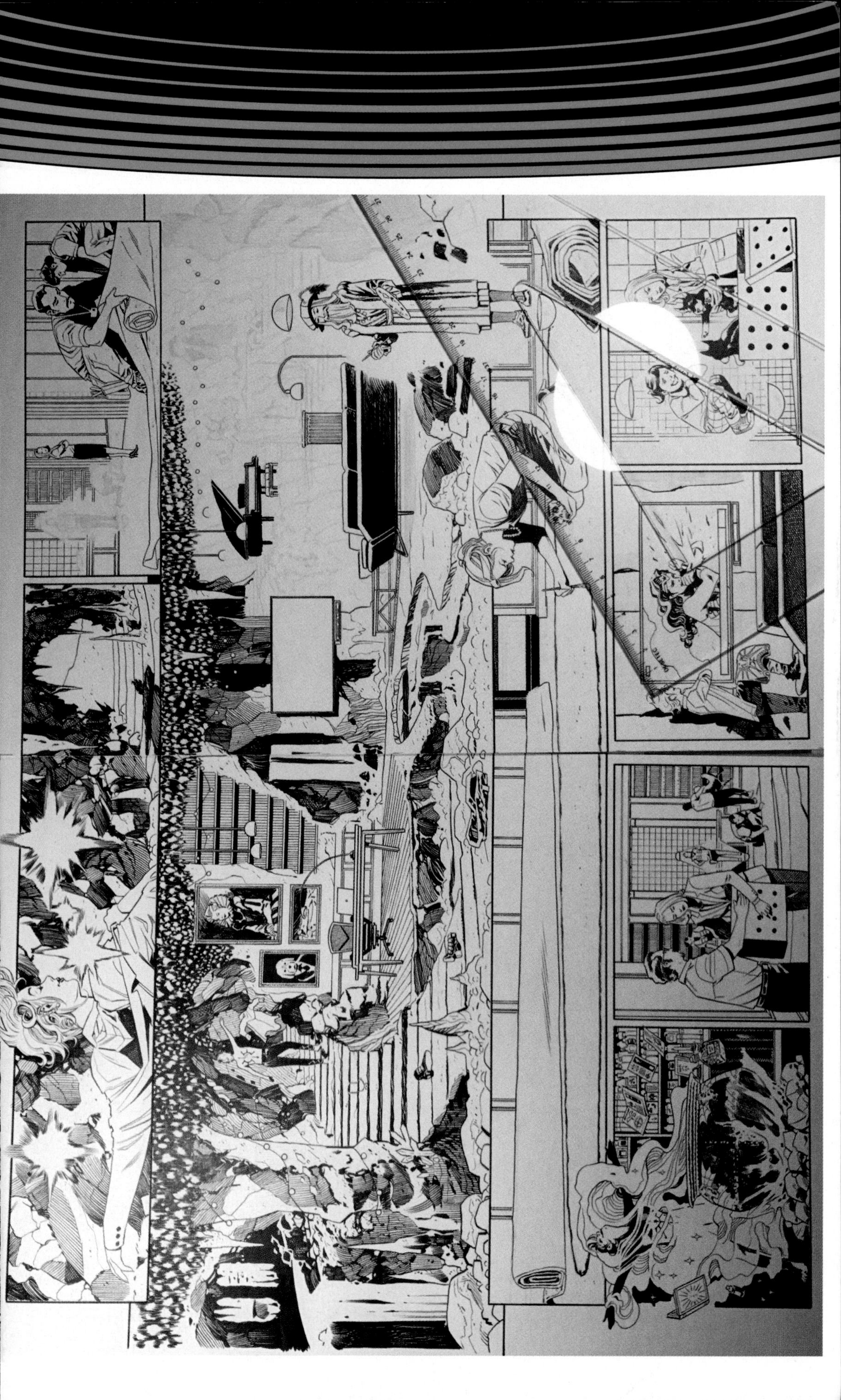

In-process rendering for WONDER WOMAN #24 pages 18-19 and page 1

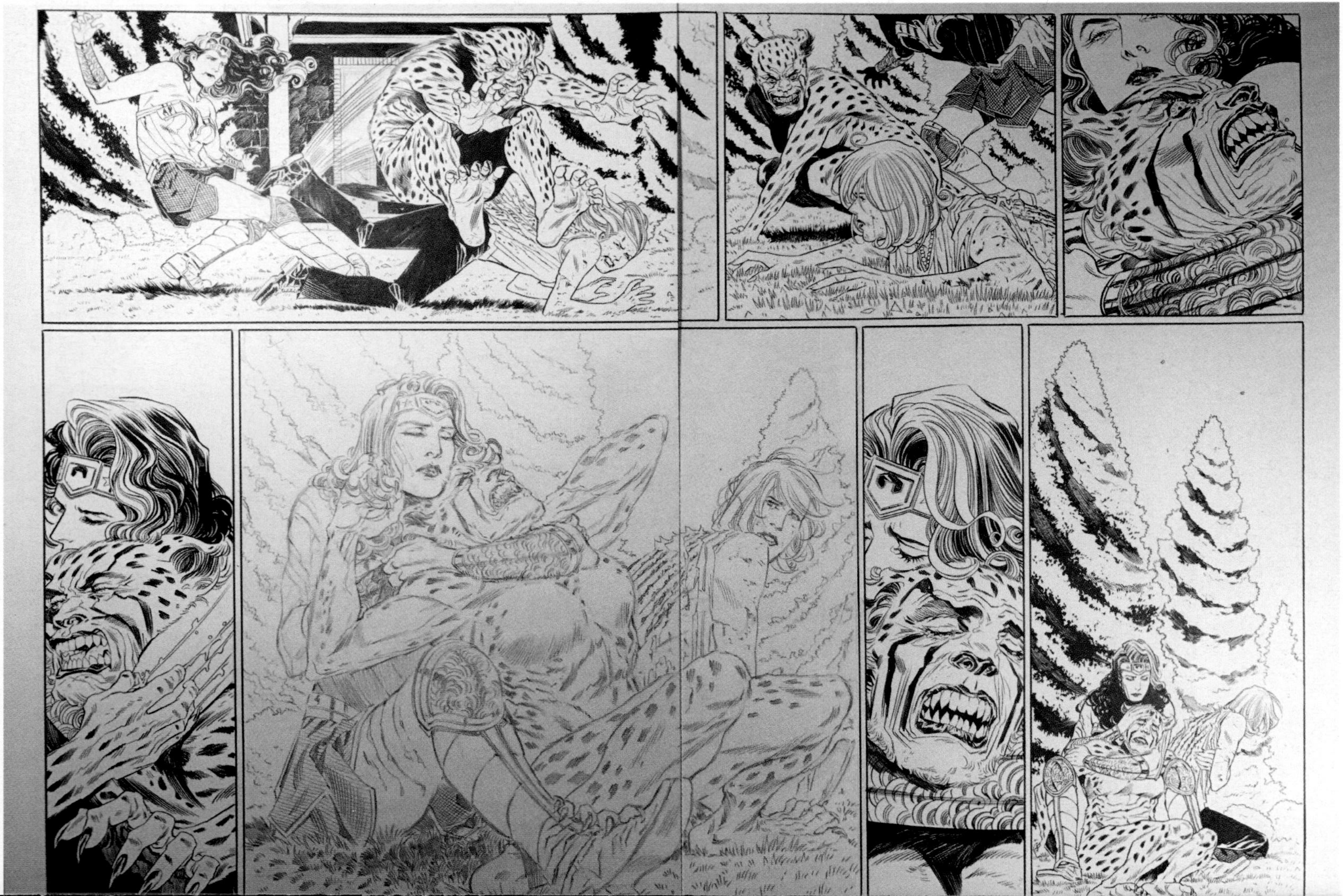

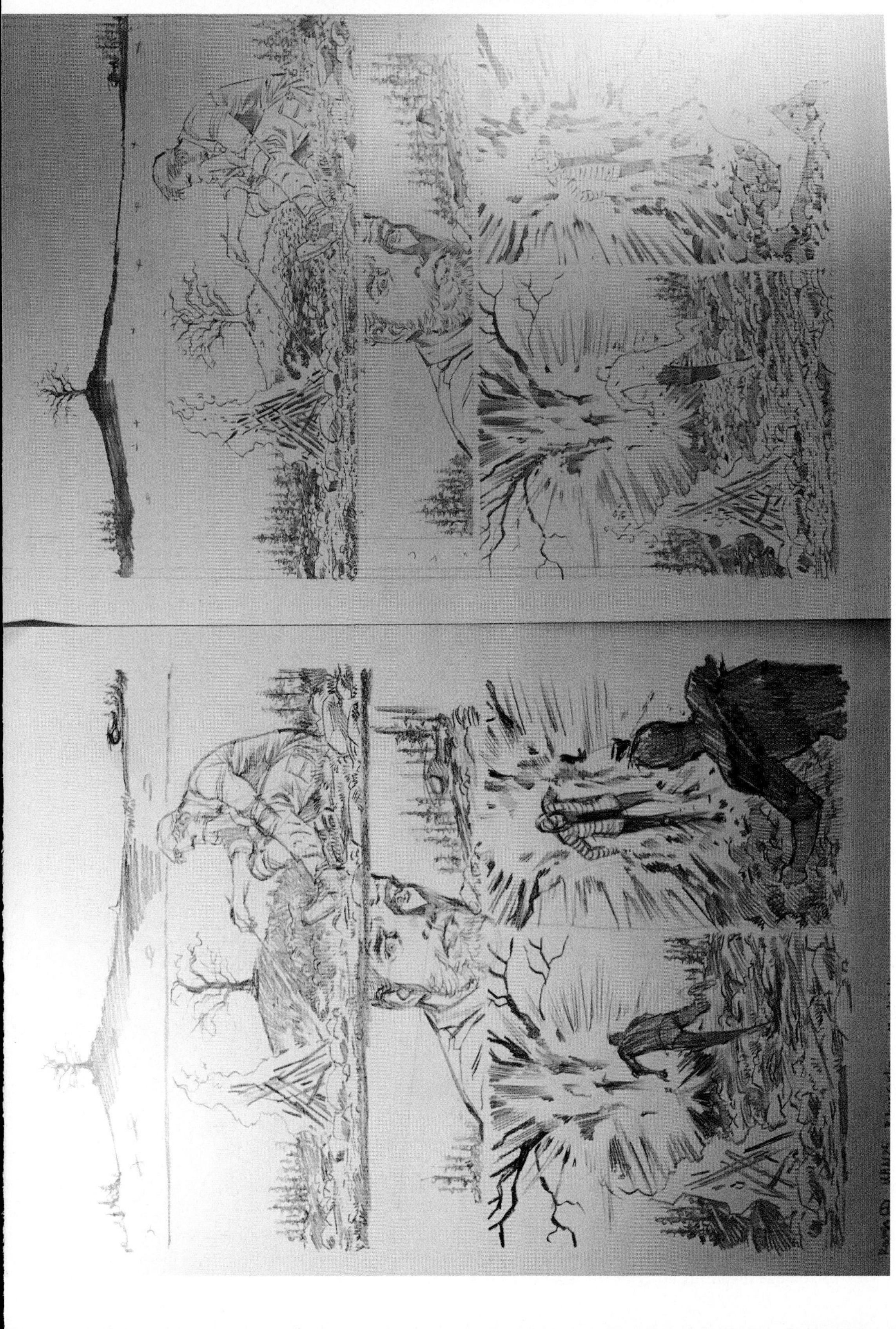

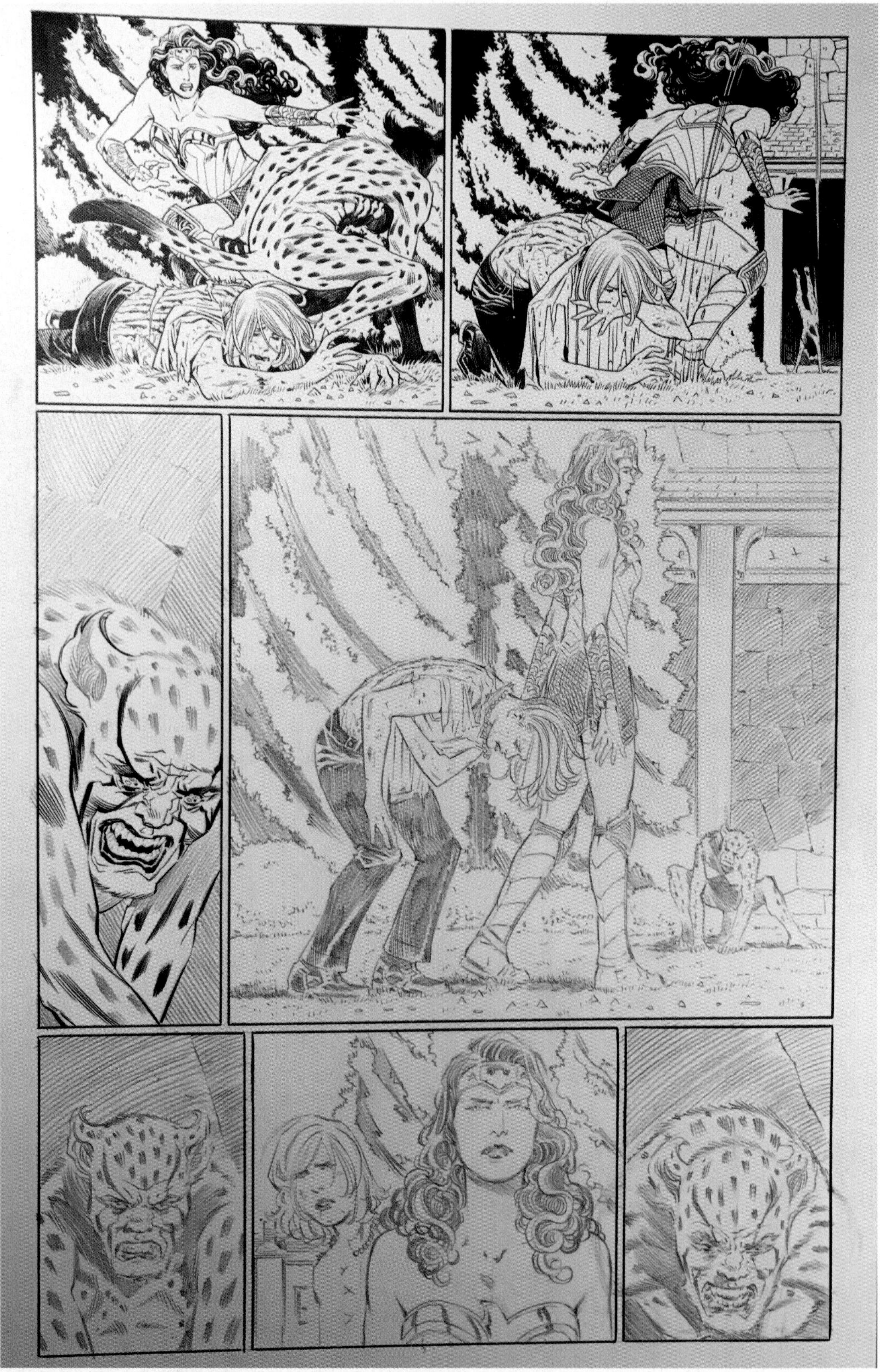

In-process rendering for WONDER WOMAN #24 page 17

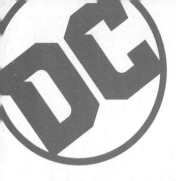

"Greg Rucka and company have created a compelling narrative for fans of the Amazing Amazon." **– NERDIST**

"(A) heartfelt and genuine take on Diana's origin." **– NEWSARAMA**

DC UNIVERSE REBIRTH

WONDER WOMAN

VOL. 1: THE LIES

GREG RUCKA
with LIAM SHARP

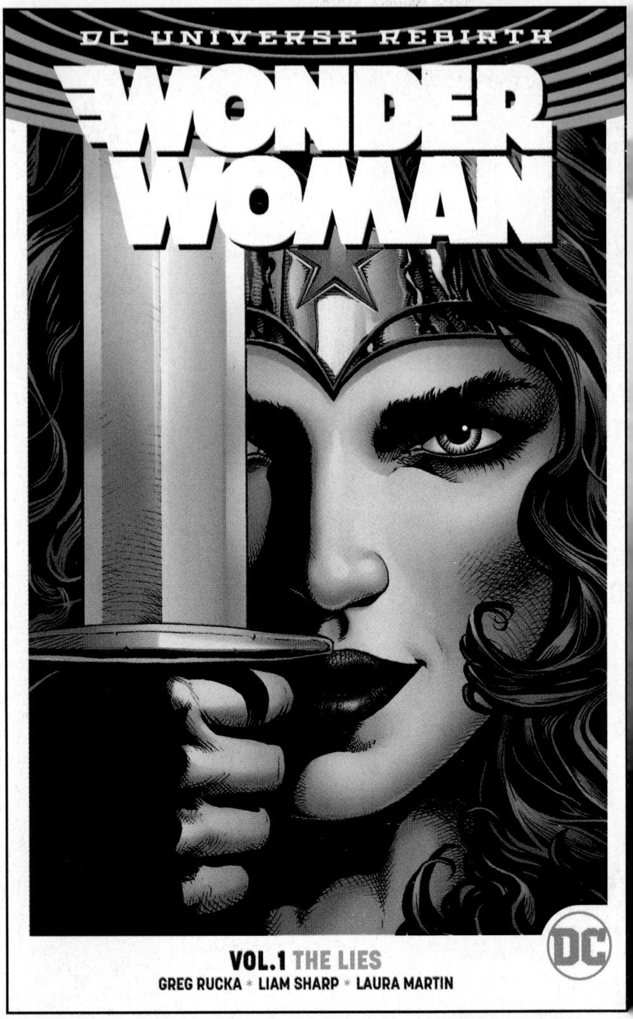
DC UNIVERSE REBIRTH
WONDER WOMAN
VOL.1 THE LIES
GREG RUCKA • LIAM SHARP • LAURA MARTIN

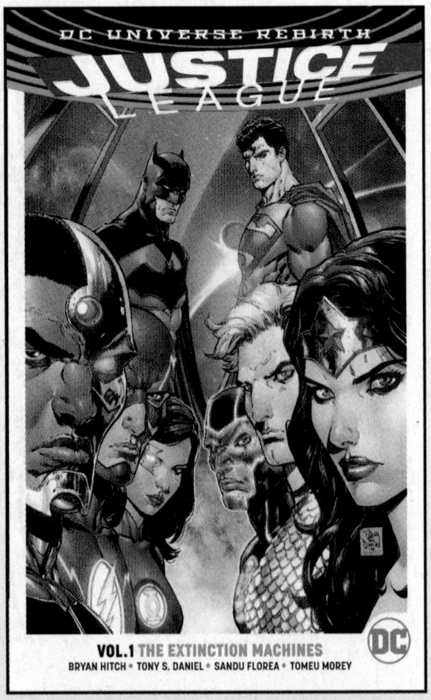
DC UNIVERSE REBIRTH
JUSTICE LEAGUE
VOL.1 THE EXTINCTION MACHINES
BRYAN HITCH • TONY S. DANIEL • SANDU FLOREA • TOMEU MOREY

JUSTICE LEAGUE VOL. 1: THE EXTINCTION MACHINES

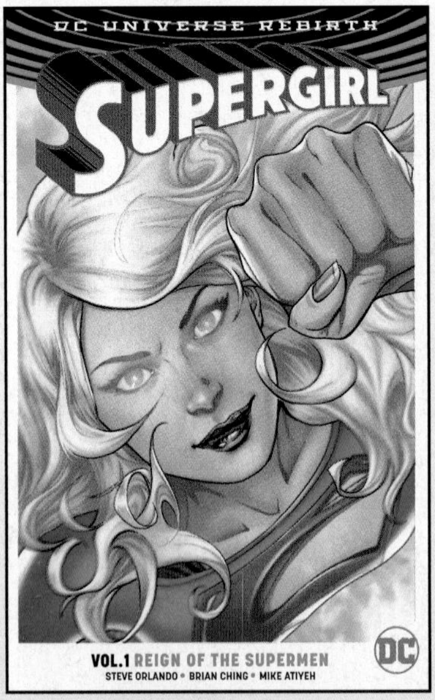
DC UNIVERSE REBIRTH
SUPERGIRL
VOL.1 REIGN OF THE SUPERMEN
STEVE ORLANDO • BRIAN CHING • MIKE ATIYEH

SUPERGIRL VOL. 1: REIGN OF THE SUPERMEN

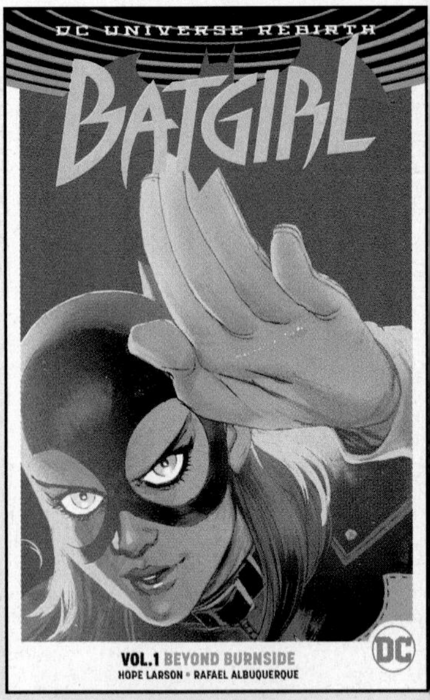
DC UNIVERSE REBIRTH
BATGIRL
VOL.1 BEYOND BURNSIDE
HOPE LARSON • RAFAEL ALBUQUERQUE

BATGIRL VOL. 1: BEYOND BURNSIDE

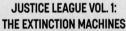

Get more DC graphic novels wherever comics and books are sold!